WITHDRAWN

The AMBIVALENCE of NATIONALISM

Modern Japan between East and West

Edited by
James W. White
University of North Carolina at Chapel Hill
Michio Umegaki
Keio University
Thomas R.H. Havens
Connecticut College

UNIVERSITY PRESS OF AMERICA

Lanham • New York • London

Copyright © 1990 by

University Press of America®, Inc.
4720 Boston Way
Lanham, Maryland 20706

3 Henrietta Street
London WC2E 8LU England

All rights reserved
Printed in the United States of America
British Cataloging in Publication Information Available

Library of Congress Cataloging-in-Publication Data

The Ambivalence of nationalism :
modern Japan between East and West /
edited by James W. White, Michio Umegaki, Thomas R.H. Havens.
    p. cm.
Includes bibliographical references.
1. Japan—Foreign relations—1868–1945.
2. Nationalism—Japan. 3. National characteristics, Japanese.
I. White, James W. (James Wilson), 1941–   .
II. Umegaki, Michio. III. Havens, Thomas R.H.
DS881.96.A46   1990   327.52—dc20   89–48833 CIP

ISBN 0–8191–7726–1 (alk. paper)

 The paper used in this publication meets the minimum requirements of American National Standard for Information Sciences—Permanence of Paper for Printed Library Materials, ANSI Z39.48–1984.

To

Marius B. Jansen

from his students and colleagues

with respect and affection

Acknowledgements

The editors would like to express their deep gratitude to the following individuals for the permission given to quote copyrighted material:

--to Mrs. Gregory Boyington, for permission to quote from Gregory Boyington's book, *Baa Baa Black Sheep*;

--to Martin Caidin, for permission to quote from his book, with Saburo Sakai, *Samurai*;

--to Mr. Kawashima Yutaka of Kojin-sha, Ltd., for permission to quote from Kuroe Yasuhiko's book, *Aa hayabusa sento tai: kaerazaru gekitsui-o*.

Contents

Introduction James W. White		1
1.	Rival States on a Loose Rein: The Neglected Tradition of Appeasement in Late Tokugawa Japan Bob Tadashi Wakabayashi	11
2.	Building the National Communications System: Adopting and Adapting Western Organizational Models in Meiji Japan D. Eleanor Westney	39
3.	Meiji Japan and the Educational and Language Reforms in Late Ch'ing China Yue-him Tam	61
4.	Shimazaki Toson's *Before the Dawn*: Historical Fiction as History and as Literature William E. Naff	79
5.	Forecasting a Pacific War, 1912-1933: The Idea of Conditional Japanese Victory Mark R. Peattie	115
6.	Japanese Policies and Concepts for a Regional Order in Asia, 1938-1940 Kimitada Miwa	133
7.	Prophet Without Honor: Kiyosawa Kiyoshi's View of Japanese-American Relations Shin'ichi Kitaoka (James W. White, trans.)	157
8.	Friend or Foe: The Ambivalent Images of the U.S. and China in Wartime Japan Ben-Ami Shillony	187
9.	A Matter of Transcendence: War Experiences and the Transformation of Japanese and American Fighter Pilots F. G. Notehelfer	213
Epilogue: National Identity, National Past, National Isms Michio Umegaki		251
Index		265

INTRODUCTION

James W. White[1]

Japan's relationships with the outside world over the last century have encompassed the creation of an internationally active nation-state, the growth of modern nationalism, a short-lived career as a major military power, and the construction and reconstruction of the predominant economy of East Asia. What it has never enjoyed, except perhaps for a brief interlude during the Meiji period, is certainty. Japan passed from a state of blissful ignorance of Western norms of international relations and behavior during the period of national isolation through periods of apprehension and fear, rapid defensive learning and borrowing, confident synthesis and adaptation, second thoughts about the optimal extent of foreign interchange and influence, and efforts at integrating foreign and indigenous elements in all areas of economy, polity, and culture. Such efforts gave way as the twentieth century wore on to an ascendant national consciousness--now proud at the exploits of Admiral Togo, now affronted by Versailles and by immigration restrictions, now anguished by a Great Depression, now defiant or aggressive at Mukden, Geneva, Nanking, and Pearl Harbor.

But as such widely varying expressions suggest, modern Japanese nationalism never achieved, either before or even amid World War II, a stable, certain perception of Japan's proper relationship with the world outside it. The purpose of the essays collected here is to portray this ambivalence: on the one hand, the juxtaposition of ever-increasing interactions, ever-growing knowledge of the world, ever-swelling national power, and determined official efforts to define Japan's international position and role; on the other, doubt, self-contradiction, wishful thinking, naivete, and dissent from official orthodoxy. The kaleidoscopic variety of responses to the outside world--especially to Japan's physical and increasingly cultural location between Asia and the West--can be seen on all levels of Japanese society, in macrocosm and microcosm, in policies and in personalities. Individuals and officials, and the idiosyncratic perceptions and public policies they set down, reflect the unresolved struggle to find an appropriate form and place for growing Japanese nationalism in the international arena: Was the world a place of "we" and "they" or of "all of us?" Did Japan's future lie in identification with Asia or the West or somewhere in between? Should Japan play an active or passive role in international affairs? Should this role be cultural or economic, diplomatic or military? Were Japan's neighbors on both sides of the Pacific partners, patrons, or clients, rivals or enemies?

As the multiplicity of questions indicates, the "nationalism" of our title is not simply nationalism of the political type, as expressed in either government policy or popular rhetoric--it importantly comprehends national identity, consciousness, image, and in particular self-confidence, as they derived individually and collectively both from indigenous experience and from unprecedented contacts with the outside world after the mid-19th century. Political nationalism is of course, as Michio Umegaki notes below, of crucial importance, and its relationship to national consciousness is complex and deserving of attention, but it is only one variant of the latter concept.

This volume is a record of the evolution of Japan's views of itself and the world, itself in the world, until the end of the Pacific War. Its focus is exemplary: Japan's relations with East and West are most frequently epitomized by its relations with the United States and China. It is also patterned: its authors trace a linear path leading from the particularism of the Tokugawa era through extroversion, attempts at integration, and ultimately overblown nationalism, a path superimposed upon another, a winding path from simplicity to complexity and then back to wartime simplification. But, as the essays show, neither path was followed to its end. The first path, toward introversion, remained half-trod--not all articulate witnesses of the war, even the warriors, were ultimately convinced of its propriety. And the second was a chimera--once experienced on both the official and private levels by the Japanese, the world could never again be reduced to the unidimensionality desired by some of their leaders. Even in wartime the ambivalence of Japanese national consciousness could not be resolved and, as both the epilogue to this volume and the front pages of our contemporary newspapers suggest, resolution remains an elusive goal today.

Bob Wakabayashi begins the consideration of our subject with a look at the late Tokugawa period, when Japan was searching for a coherent response to the West. His lens is the work of Aizawa Seishisai, who reflected and refracted the contradictory rays of the time. Aizawa recommended profiting from China's experiences with the Western nations and, like late Ch'ing statecraft thinkers, he wished to apply the diplomatic techniques of the traditional Chinese interstate system--such as using barbarians to control barbarians-- against the intrusive Westerners. But he also advocated learning from the West--in particular from the American Revolution. Internally weak China was for him a negative example of domestic political development. For Aizawa, as for many Japanese of his time, Chinese was a vital medium simply for learning about the West. Western books were imported on a large scale in the form of Chinese translations.[2] In fact, Western studies were largely mediated by the Chinese language until the 1860s. But aside from Aizawa, the substantive influence of traditional Chinese diplomatic practices was minor. Aizawa was as paradoxical as many of his time: a xenophobic but not nationalistic advocate of opening Japan, he wishfully imagined that Westerners, once admitted, could be controlled like the nomads of China's northern frontier.

The Westerners were indeed admitted and, although they were hardly controlled as Aizawa had hoped, Japan maintained its political integrity. It did so, however, at the price of wholesale introduction of things Western. At first, as Eleanor Westney describes in her essay on the development of Meiji Japan's postal, telegraph, and telephone systems, the policies that governed this process were inconsistent, unsystematic, and indiscriminate. The old system was now recognized as inadequate to the nation's new needs, and anything that promised to change the system was valued. Chinese models were of no interest, but almost anything Western was attractive.

This period of indiscriminate borrowing reflected national uncertainty and a lack of self-confidence, which gave way in the 1880s to a much more self-assured posture both domestic and international. Borrowings such as those analyzed by Westney became increasingly selective, calculated, and systematic. Indeed, as Westney points out, in the later period deviations from the adopted models were self-conscious adaptations to Japan's own (now accepted) distinctiveness, and in some cases the very fact of foreign emulation was denied. The process was transformed from one of relatively indiscriminate adoption to calculated adaptation, to the introduction of elements compatible with policies and institutions either indigenous or imported but already in place. The existing system was no longer something obsolete, to be replaced posthaste, but an ongoing, viable entity to be elaborated, enhanced, and strengthened. And those in control of it were now better informed, more sophisticated, more cosmopolitan, and certain--at least in the short run--of where Japan was going and how it should get there.

This was also the period when Japan made its greatest contributions to its neighbors, especially China. The mirror of the international relationship examined by Westney is that observed by Yue-him Tam: the provision by Japan of educational and linguistic models for a China trying, however inchoately, to modernize around the turn of the century. Now the tables were to some extent turned: many Chinese learned of the West through the medium of Japan, and they imported Japanese neologisms for the many Western terms they needed to make sense of a new multinational, modern world. But they also admired the Meiji synthesis examined in microcosm by Westney and took for themselves both the structure and curriculum of Japanese education. They were assisted in their efforts by the attitudes of Japanese officials and intellectuals of the time, who were receptive to the notions of an Asian community and to a Japanese contribution to the developing it. But the Japanese position was both overbearing--as exemplified in the assertion that China should adopt the Japanese *kana* writing system--and still ambivalent, foreshadowing the seesawing of identity between East and West whose conflictual implications are fully drawn out in the chapters by Kimitada Miwa and Ben-Ami Shillony below. It was also still not unilateral--even as they provided the Chinese with more modern institutions and examples, the Japanese were borrowing Chinese terms for certain new concepts they had themselves introduced from the West.

But China was no more able to incorporate all things foreign smoothly than was Japan. The fruits of educational and linguistic reform along Japanese lines were few, and negative national reactions ensued. In Japan, too, reaction had begun, and imperial rescripts and military adventures signaled the limits of openness to the outside world and its influences. But belligerent nationalism was not yet the order of the day; Japan was searching rather for integrity, for the ultimate, overarching adaptation which was achieved in such small niches as the communications system but which eluded the nation as a whole. It came nearly within the grasp of some, one of whom--the novelist Shimazaki Toson--is examined by William Naff. Shimazaki is a crucial figure in our study, bridging the Tokugawa (through his father) and the Showa eras. Perhaps "umbrella" is a better metaphor for his relationship to our study, as one can see from Naff's retracing of the almost *Rashomon*-like complexity of his role: his youth in the 19th century, his career pinnacle in the 20th, his 20th-century view (through his fiction) of the 19th century, and his 20th-century critics' evaluations of his perceptions of the 19th, a period about which the Japanese are ambivalent to this day.

Epitomizing the experience of so many educated Japanese of mid-Meiji, Shimazaki went through a youthful period of alienation from self and nation,[3] as Western education and Christianity and foreign travel pushed his horizons outward. Subsequently he "discovered" Japanese literature, and his work increasingly assimilated the disparate cultural elements, dealing with alienation and cultural stress. His *chef-d'oeuvre*, *Before the Dawn*, reflects his cosmopolitan background and suggests a cultural and historical integrity somewhere midway in time and cultural space between the determined (if decreasingly driven) and internationally acquisitive national *consciousness* of the Meiji period and the later (and increasingly determined and driven), internationally prickly, national*ism* of the Showa era. Did Japan find itself for a short period during the lifetime of Shimazaki?

Kenneth Pyle, in his study of intellectual conflict and cultural stress in Meiji Japan, suggests that it did, somewhere after the late 1880s. But despite such speculation, the subsequent course of events, policies, and individual experiences suggests no; Japan progressively lost a unified sense of national self. An open break with the West began in the realm of fantasy, as Mark Peattie makes clear in his essay on forecasts of war in early twentieth-century Japanese literature. The Japanese can hardly be exclusively blamed for making war thinkable--in large part the literature examined by Peattie emerged in response to the Yellow Peril and related genres of the West and, one must note, at the same time that the Japanese navy was beginning to hypothesize about U.S.-Japanese war, the U.S. government was doing precisely the same thing.[4] And the literature itself was widely varied--in some books the likelihood of war was small, in some, overwhelming; in some Japan won and in some it lost.

It is difficult to appraise the precise impact of such books on the thoughts of either the common people or public officials. Some were utter fantasy, but some were written by military men, and over time they became more and more serious and analytical about weapons, war production, tactics, and the national interests involved in war. Whether or not they made war more acceptable, their sales figures certainly suggest that they made it imaginable for a large number of people. And this literature foreshadowed not only concrete strategies but also--and here is perhaps its greatest cultural relevance--many of the national misconceptions, stereotypes, and biases that actually figured in Japan's decision to go to war with the U.S. and in the policies pursued during the war, as seen in the essays by Ben-Ami Shillony and F. G. Notehelfer. The ambivalence of a literature in which Japan sometimes won and sometimes lost prefigures reality: Pearl Harbor was greeted by the Japanese government with cries of patriotic resolve and victorious intent, and by Admiral Yamamoto Isoroku with foreboding that the sleeping American giant, now awakened, would prove a formidable adversary.[5]

Between the ambivalence of the pre-1930s war literature and that of 1941 intervened another reality, represented here by the essays of Kimitada Miwa and Shin'ichi Kitaoka. Miwa focuses on policy: the evolution of Japan's perceptions of its role in and relationship to East Asia just before the war. This evolution partook of many earlier currents, most importantly the debates over whether Japan was part of Asia and whether its relationship to Asia was one of brother, patron, or self-appointed savior and guardian. And it was characterized both by increasing romanticism and idealism and by increasing alienation from the West and from the international order it espoused.

Early Pan-Asianism was a vague concept, current primarily outside the pragmatic corridors of government; in its expression as the New Order in East Asia, announced in 1938, it still contained some uncritically romantic overtones of German geopolitical thought, married to indigenous notions of an Asian "community." And the depth and authenticity of "East Asianism" is open to question--as Miwa notes, some of Konoye Fumimaro's ideas on the subject were influenced by domestic political considerations (what the intellectuals would accept) or international ones (what foreign nations would accept).

But the New Order still presupposed the existing international system and its rules and structure--Japan was simply going to reshape one subsystem of an international system still generally accepted. The articulation of the Greater East Asia Co-Prosperity Sphere in 1940, however, signified a dramatic change. The area of the Sphere was larger than the area comprehended by the New Order, overlapping substantially with either possessions or spheres of influence of both the U.S. and Britain, among others. It was to involve much more than economic relationships--it was also a political concept, organized around the Way of the Emperor. And it essentially rejected the validity of the existing international system, its premises, and its rules. Its establishment had military implications that escaped some of its authors but were clear to others.

Some of these others--privileged contributors to the policy debate--recognized the ambiguities of the Co-Prosperity Sphere and its lack of content and tried to rectify these flaws, but they were eclipsed by the official rise of a fuzzy ultranationalism that had hitherto been successfully excluded from the policy-making arena. In Miwa's view this development reversed the previous policy posture: henceforth it was the government that represented romanticism and the outside observers who represented realism.

Overall, however, realism was on the decline in both official and private analyses of international policy. It had its advocates, and Miwa's essay deals with one such pro-government advocate, Royama Masamichi. Perhaps the most consistent and articulate antigovernment critic was the writer Kiyosawa Kiyoshi, the subject of Shin'ichi Kitaoka's chapter. This essay reveals the ambivalence of Japanese intellectuals amid the swirling international currents of the 1930s and the inability of the government to silence all dissenters, even though it was able to deny them a public hearing. Kiyosawa combined living experience in both China and the West, economic pragmatism, sympathy for Western liberal ideals, and a cold-eyed ability to appraise Japanese military and economic strength both at home and abroad. He attacked Japan's "special interests" in Manchuria, the New Order, and a whole string of jingoistic national leaders. He was tactfully silent about his fellow intellectuals, whose vacillation contrasted dramatically with his own consistency. "Internationalism" was a popular intellectual current until well into the 1930s. But it was often put into the service of rationalizing Japanese aims on the continent. When it ran up against the hard realities of the objective incompatibility of Japanese and League of Nations policy, such proponents as Nitobe Inazo resolved their own ambivalence by siding with the state.

Kiyosawa would have none of this, and the price he paid was obscurity. But he was not alone, in either the public or private realms, as the essays by Ben-Ami Shillony and F. G. Notehelfer that round out this volume make clear. Shillony takes for his subject official policy: the portrayal of China and America before and during the war years. This portrayal serves admirably to make the point of these essays overall: perceptions of the U.S. were before 1941 a mixture of amity, frustration, respect, solicitude, and dependence; friction was attributed largely to American misunderstanding. On 8 December 1941 America abruptly became a polyglot mob of racist barbarians, but this view too--as Peattie shows--had been part of the earlier, almost kaleidoscopic, image of America. And throughout the war hints of vacillation remained: at times the U.S. was portrayed not as inherently evil but rather as betraying its own praiseworthy values. And the evaporation of negative American images at the end of the war suggests the depth of ambivalence about them throughout. All this is not to say, of course, that the postwar period has seen a resolution of the tension. But even the nationally-energizing and unifying crisis of war was unable to resolve it, so one should not be surprised that more pacific times would see no better.

Images of China were no more consistent than those of America. Tokugawa admiration for the glories of Chinese culture had been superseded by Meiji feelings of superiority and condescension. By the twentieth century some Japanese were advocating *datsu-A*, or economic, political, and spiritual disengagement from an Asia that seemed to have little to offer a flourishing and modernizing Japanese

Empire. Chinese decay and backwardness were an embarrassment, and well-meaning Japanese efforts to show China the error of its ways and the wisdom of following Japan's course of development became patronizing and overbearing. The desire to help China--the source of so much of Japan's own culture--merged with frustration and annoyance: the Chinese, like the Americans, misunderstood Japan and were, to boot, too arrogant or dumb to know their own best interests. Japan, of course, could see these interests, and its blend of concern and disdain for China culminated in a paradoxically Sinophilic war against China, an attack on China in order to save it from its own folly. There was the good China of history and culture and the bad China of warlords and anti-Japanese boycotts; there were good Chinese (who cooperated with the Japanese) and bad ones (primarily the KMT). Throughout the war, according to Shillony, Japan was unable to sort out its perceptions of China or to locate Japan consistently in relation to China.

This confusion was not restricted to the dimension of official policy, as we see in F. G. Notehelfer's essay. His lens too is personal and private: the diaries and autobiographies of Japanese and American fighter pilots. Both sets of warriors entered the war with more than adequate supplies of stereotypes and disdain for their enemies. War proved a powerful solvent for both, however; combat brought stark realization of the shortcomings--often fatal--of cocky xenophobia and compelled reappraisal of the foe both as fighter and--given the close looks fighter pilots often got of each other--as human being. Official government perceptions and evaluations of the enemy could not easily survive combat, and many pilots ended up rejecting the received orthodoxy for a new esteem of the other and a new recognition of the self as well. Some of the transition, at least for the Japanese, may well have preexisted the combat experience. As Ivan Morris has shown, even the *kamikaze* pilots were hardly xenophobic fanatics; they were educated and sophisticated and evinced little hatred for their adversaries.[6]

Not all pilots, or other servicemen, came to a final stage of respect for their opponents as equals, but in Notehelfer's sources one can see the strain resulting from efforts at continued depersonalization and demonization of the enemy. Those who avoided reappraisal of their stereotypes seem to have worked hard to do so. Even amid the wartime apotheosis of national uniformity of message regarding the sworn enemies of the nation and its Emperor, Japan's national consciousness was unable to coalesce around a perceptually consistent point. It is instructive that Americans, like the Japanese, underwent change through combat. But the Japanese pilots appear less resistant to accepting the complexity, the ambivalence, the moral dilemmas, and the universalistic impulses occurring in modern air war.

Taken together, however, the evidence of Notehelfer, Shillony, Morris, and Peattie should serve to qualify more racist interpretations of wartime behavior and imagery.[7] They also suggest an alternative view of why the war-to-peace transition went so smoothly: perhaps it was not that racist images on both sides were simply and easily transformed, and demonological images imposed on Asian communists, but rather that the moral rupture between Japan and the West was never as total as wartime propaganda and rhetoric made it appear.

The end of the war did not, of course, mark the end of Japanese national consciousness or the contradictory threads inherent in it, of which racist images are of course one. Many of the subjects touched on in the essays that follow have run like *leitmotifs* through the postwar years, and many of these essays derive further significance from their foreshadowing of events of the more recent past. In his epilogue Michio Umegaki suggests a few of the ways these essays integrate the prewar history of modern Japanese nationalism with the postwar, as they illuminate the nature of national consciousness during Japan's modern century.

A note on usage: This book has adopted throughout Japanese and Chinese name order--surname first--except in bibliographic citations where the names are those of authors of English-language works (including the essays in this volume), in which case English name order is used. Macrons have not been used in Japanese words, nor diacritical marks in Chinese. The Hepburn form of romanization has been used in rendering Japanese words and the Wade-Giles form for Chinese, given the pre-1949 nature of the materials of interest here. The single exception to this rule is that Chinese place names have been rendered in the form current at the time of the reference thereto, e.g., a book published in the Chinese capital in 1950 was published in Beijing; if it had been published in 1945 the city's name would have been rendered Beiping; if in 1900, Peking.

NOTES

1. I am indebted to the comments of John Hall, Albert Craig, and Robert Ward in my organization of the themes expressed in this Introduction, and to Ronald Morse and the Woodrow Wilson Center of the Smithsonian Institution for providing the venue at which these themes were first presented. Responsibility for the ideas contained herein, however, is of course solely my own.
2. Osamu Oba, "The Role of Imported Chinese Books in the Tokugawa to Meiji Transition," unpublished ms., Kansai University, April 1982.
3. For a study of this phenomenon see Kennth Pyle, *The New Generation in Meiji Japan* (Stanford, 1969).
4. Dorothy Borg and Shumpei Okamoto, *Pearl Harbor as History* (New York, 1973); James Crowley, *Japan's Quest for Autonomy* (Princeton, 1966).
5. John Potter, *Yamamoto* (New York, 1965), pp. 128ff.
6. *The Nobility of Failure* (New York, 1975).
7. This position--that unequivocally racist images pervaded, preexisted, and powerfully survived the war period--is most forcefully argued by John Dower in *War Without Mercy* (New York, 1986).

1
RIVAL STATES ON A LOOSE REIN: THE NEGLECTED TRADITION OF APPEASEMENT IN LATE TOKUGAWA JAPAN

Bob Tadashi Wakabayashi

Five decades into the nineteenth century most Japanese knew little of the world beyond their shores. They were prohibited from setting foot outside their homeland, and so could not obtain first-hand information on contemporary events or world geography. Instead they had to rely on foreign writings to accumulate knowledge in those areas. Earlier in their history, the Japanese had gained some knowledge of Western affairs from contacts with Europeans during Japan's "Christian century," from roughly 1550 to 1650. Later, they had access to many seventeenth and eighteenth century Jesuit writings translated into Chinese. In addition, Dutch trading post officials periodically submitted written reports to the *bakufu* (the Tokugawa Shogunal government) in Edo on world conditions. And by the early nineteenth century, Japanese students of Dutch Learning had attained high levels of skill in translating Dutch materials and assimilating Western knowledge.

Even so, inquisitive late-Tokugawa Japanese were still gaining surprisingly large amounts of vital information on Western affairs from Chinese sources--Jesuit works translated into Chinese, Ch'ing studies of Western conditions, and written or oral reports tendered by Chinese merchants coming to trade at Nagasaki. Until 1860, when the bakufu formally renounced its policy of national isolation and sent modern Japan's first mission abroad, the Japanese probably learned more about Western affairs from China than from the West directly.[1]

Western knowledge gained from Chinese and Dutch sources was often outdated and incorrect. But this does not lessen its historical importance, for late Tokugawa thinkers applied that knowledge (accurate or not) to alter radically their strategic thinking and to discard long-cherished values and institutions. As we shall see, one important such thinker, Aizawa Seishisai (1781-1863) of the Later Mito School, learned of the American Revolution from *Kon'yo zushiki* (1845), a Japanese compilation of translated Dutch source materials, and from a Japanese edition of Wei Yuan's *Hai-kuo t'u-chih* (1847). This new knowledge led him to revise drastically his earlier view of the world and international relations.

Men such as Aizawa relied largely on traditional Chinese conceptions of the world order when they defined Japan's position *vis-a-vis* foreign states. But they had more than one "traditional" Chinese conception to draw on. In periods of strength, as under the Ch'ing dynasty, the Chinese deemed their empire the Middle Kingdom. According to this Middle Kingdom world view, well-known to us through the work of John Fairbank,[2] China was conscious of her superiority in wealth and strength to foreign barbarian peoples. In such eras, the Chinese treated foreign peoples as tributary subjects and forced them to accept indignities such as performing the kowtow. On the level of pure rhetoric or state ideology, many Tokugawa Japanese styled their *own* land the Middle Kingdom, and relegated Westerners to the role of barbarians. But when forced to deal realistically with Western nations who sought trade and diplomatic intercourse after 1853, many Japanese including Aizawa adopted a different set of diplomatic protocols derived from another school of Chinese statecraft: the "China among equals" world view which better suited Japan as a small, weak power.[3]

Too often we assume that East Asian states lacked rules for diplomatic intercourse.[4] But in China's Spring and Autumn period (722-481 B.C.), there was a multi-state system of alliances centered on the Chou house at first, and on hegemons such as Dukes Huan of Ch'i and Wen of Chin later on. In the Warring States period (403-221 B.C.), powerful autonomous kingdoms combined war with diplomacy to make or break interstate alliances. Even in later periods of centralized empire, China was not always strong enough to dominate foreigners in Middle Kingdom fashion, and often had to treat barbarian states as equal partners under treaties concluded to secure mutual concessions. In dealing with the Hsiung-nu in 51 B.C., for example, the Han emperor accorded the Hsiung-nu chieftain all the respect due to the head of a "rival state" (Ch. *ti kuo*, J. *tekkoku*), one of roughly equal power and status. Though nominally barbarians, the Hsiung-nu were not to be treated as inferiors or as a subject people. The Han emperor concluded a treaty of "peace and mutual conciliation" (Ch. *ho chin*, J. *washin*), and was careful that "the Han dynasty will not be the party to commit a fault first." The Han kept the Hsiung-nu on a "loose rein" (Ch. *chi mi*, J. *kimi*), "so that the blame of being crooked would always be on them."[5] According to the rules of this traditional diplomatic protocol, China was obliged to keep good faith and adhere scrupulously to treaty provisions. Aizawa drew on this "rival states" concept of diplomacy to formulate his policies of barbarian control.

In this chapter I will examine these two themes in late Tokugawa Japan between China and the West: 1) the rival states view of world order and loose rein diplomacy of appeasement that Aizawa adopted from early Chinese history to enable bakufu leaders to deal with the foreign threat in the years 1825 to 1863; and 2) how knowledge of the West, especially of American independence, gained from Dutch and Chinese sources forced him to promote a policy of opening Japan to the West within this tradition of Chinese diplomatic practices.

Pre-Opium War: A World of Rival States

The Edo bakufu first learned of America's independence in 1809, one year after the humiliating *Phaeton* Incident at Nagasaki Bay. For many years bakufu magistrates in Nagasaki had suspected that some Western ships calling there were not really Dutch. Their crews spoke a different language, and their logs revealed that they were registered in places like "Boston new [sic] England." In short, merchant ships from Britain's colony of "New England" and warships from the mother country were masquerading as Dutch vessels and coming to Japan in clear violation of bakufu law. In 1808, sailors from the *Phaeton*, a British man-of-war flying the Dutch flag, abducted a Dutchman in the custody of Japanese officials, one of whom haplessly fell overboard during the scuffle. To atone for this disgrace, a Nagasaki magistrate named Matsudaira Yasuhide committed suicide.[6]

This *Phaeton* Incident prompted the bakufu to gather information on "New England." It ordered two interpreters, Ishibashi Sukezaemon and Motoki Shozaemon, to interrogate the Dutch on Dejima. They did so for several weeks, and reported to Edo that the territory known as "North America" had fought Britain successfully from 1775 to 1781 and set itself up as an "independent land" (*jiritsu no tochi*). The "states" chose the government's leaders; and two of them, "Washington and Jefferson," had won renown. In fact, the nation's new capital was named after Washington. The report ended, "We have no recent books which tell the history of this event [America's independence]. So to substantiate it, we hereby submit silver coins minted of late in America."[7]

Only the highest of bakufu officials were privy to this

fascinating information--and they soon forgot it. When the Napoleonic Wars ended in 1815, European naval confrontations in East Asia ceased, and active bakufu interest in contemporary Western affairs lapsed. Until the 1840s, informed Japanese such as Otsuki Gentaku, Aizawa Seishisai, Watanabe Kazan, and Takano Choei continued to believe that North America was under English control. Aizawa wrote in his *New Theses* (*Shinron*) of 1825: "the country they call America is located at the rear end of the world, and so its inhabitants are stupid and incompetent." He clearly did not mar his invective with faint praise of America; nor did he believe America to be a land of any importance. But this disdain for America in 1825 stood in stark contrast to his admiration for other Western nations. Although he denigrated them as "barbarians," his rational analysis of objective world affairs discloses a healthy respect for the West.

In *New Theses*, Aizawa compared the Seven Great Empires he perceived in his day to the Seven Great Kingdoms in China's Warring States era (403-221 B.C.); that is, he likened Russia to Ch'in, Turkey (the Ottoman Empire) to Ch'i, the Mogul Empire to Han, Persia to Wei, the Ch'ing Empire to Ch'u, and Japan to Chou. The seventh power, Germany (the Holy Roman Empire), was no longer strong; and so he ranked her aside lesser powers such as France, Britain, and Spain. Through these comparisons Aizawa revealed his true assessment of Japan's international standing: she was analogous to Chou, an exalted but tiny kingdom whose precarious existence hinged on the tolerance of other, greater powers. He compared Russia to Ch'in, the ruthless unifier of ancient China. Russia, Turkey, and Ch'ing China were the world's greatest powers for him in 1825; they would decide the upcoming struggle for global supremacy. Aizawa also realized that even lesser powers such as Britain and Spain enjoyed a clear edge over Japan in precious metals and raw materials owing to their possession of overseas colonies.

Russia, though having suffered serious military setbacks on her Western front, remained the world's most powerful empire and was building up strength for a final drive to unify the world by subduing her long-standing nemesis, Turkey. But before doing that, Aizawa believed, she would try to dispose of the Ch'ing on her eastern front. To do this, she first would use Christianity to win over the Ezo territories north of Japan in concert with her British and Spanish allies, who were striving to capture Pacific islands to Japan's south. Russia and Britain then would subvert Japan proper by Christianizing her "stupid commoners" and suborn a new generation of Japanese pirates (*wako*) to attack and weaken China. With China so crippled, Russia could deliver the knock-out blow from the north. Aizawa's 1825 analysis reduced Japan to little more than a pawn in Russia's chess game of world conquest; indeed, Japan's national security depended on the Ch'ing and Ottoman Empires' allying to check Russia on the Eurasian continent.[8]

Aizawa's sources of information on world affairs in 1825 predated the Napoleonic era. For him the French Empire was unheard of, the United States still belonged to Britain, and the Mogul Empire (dead by 1757) was one of the world's seven great powers. In sum, his knowledge of current events was faulty. But he used that faulty knowledge in an innovative way, and contrasts with contemporary Ch'ing thinkers bear this out. Aizawa portrayed the world's nations, *including* Japan, as "rival states." Although he did not actually use this traditional Chinese term, *ti kuo*, he easily could have. Three foreign powers were stronger than Japan, and only balance of power alliances--"barbarians used to control other barbarians" in traditional Chinese strategic thinking--allowed Japan to remain independent. In 1825, Aizawa compared the world situation to that of China's Warring States era, a comparison that Hsu Chi-yu (1795-1873) only implied in 1848.[9] Aizawa likened Russia to Ch'in, an analogy that Wang T'ao (1828-1897) did not draw explicitly until the mid-1870s; and even then, Wang excluded China from the seven-power scenario.[10] This shows that Aizawa, from early on, realistically and keenly perceived Japan's weakness in a harsh world of competing states.

In his conception of national strength, too, Aizawa was ahead of his time. He knew that Western nations had been small and weak until they had begun to embark on extensive overseas expansion in the recent past. The true secret behind this sudden and massive expansion, he believed, was the ability of Russian, British, and Spanish sovereigns to instill active allegiance in their own and in foreign peoples by propagating their state cult of Christianity. Shrewd European rulers such as Peter the Great (r. 1682-1725) had won Aizawa's admiration as early as 1801:

> He devoted all his energies to stabilizing the people's livelihood and enriching the nation. He achieved great things indeed. He planted vineyards and orchards to secure enough food for his people. He established schools to propagate the official religion. He drilled Russia's army, and with it, struck terror in the hearts of her foes.[11]

Such European leaders exploited the potency of religious rituals as part of government. They were similar to the Sage Kings of antiquity, and Christianity was deceptively similar to the Confucian Way. Although Christianity was a wicked perversion of the Sages' Way, it was just as effective in winning popular submission, both at home and abroad. As such, it was a perfect instrument of expansion. Aizawa quoted a Ming anti-Christian polemicist, Su Chi-yu, to the effect that:

> The Western barbarians are adept at the ways of intrigue. Whenever they arrive in a country, it is doomed because they conquer it from within, by recruiting the local inhabitants into their ranks. Over thirty nations have fallen in this way.[12]

Through Christian subversion, Aizawa held, Western leaders practiced a key dictum from the *Sun Tzu*: to take over enemy states intact, so that the conquering forces suffered no casualties and the conquered peoples provided conscripts for still more foreign conquests. So Christianity permitted European rulers to annex territories and control populations far larger than their own. For Aizawa, the foreign threat Japan faced in 1825 was mainly ideological, not military. Russia, England, and Spain were scheming to beguile Japanese subjects into subverting the bakufu and the feudal lords' (*daimyo*) domains; then they could recruit Japanese forces to help subdue China. To combat this danger from abroad, Japan had to strengthen itself by adopting Western ships and weapons. But more importantly, it first had to win the hearts and minds of its own people, so that they would remain devoted to their feudal rulers rather than join the enemy's ranks.

Before the 1840s, enlightened Japanese thinkers including Aizawa, Watanabe Kazan, and Takano Choei, subscribed generally to this world view of "rival states."[13] They believed Japan to be a third-rate power--a pawn to help knock over the Westerners' real target, Ch'ing China. Even so, Aizawa was convinced that they would not attempt a direct, massive invasion of Japan as the Mongols once had; instead they would try to win Japan over through Christianity and the lure of trade. They would alienate Japanese commoners from their rulers and foment rebellions similar to the Buddhist-inspired *Ikko ikki* earlier in Japan's history. Aizawa's xenophobia was class-bound and resembled that of the contemporary Ch'ing ruling elite: he feared foreign-inspired insurrections within Japan more than direct foreign invasions. He did not fear a Western military presence--or even the granting of privileges to foreigners--in Japan as such. What he feared was that aggrieved Japanese commoners and low-ranking warriors (*samurai*) or hostile vassals of the Shogun (Outside Lords or *tozama daimyo*) would take advantage of the foreign presence to rebel and overthrow the bakufu.

Given this type of indirect foreign threat, the bakufu's best long-range policy for national defense was to emulate astute Western leaders who used Christianity as a state religion. Edo leaders should have the Emperor in Kyoto perform Shinto rituals as part of a state cult designed to create national unity and integration, or *kokutai*. In 1825 Aizawa assumed that the Western powers would not attack Japan in force; and during the 1820s and 1830s objective conditions in East Asia bore him out. The *Phaeton* Incident was a repercussion of the Napoleonic Wars in far-off Europe. After 1808, the main violators of Japan's territorial waters were unarmed Western whalers and merchant ships, not warships. Moreover, in 1825 when Aizawa wrote *New Theses*, the Industrial Revolution had yet to tip the technological scales decisively in Europe's favor. So Westerners brandished no overwhelmingly superior weapons in East Asia. The armed expulsion of Westerners was fully within Japan's power; it made perfect sense in the first third of the nineteenth century. Not until the decade and a half between the outbreak of the Opium War and Perry's visits to Edo Bay did world conditions force Japanese strategists either to revise their traditional view of international relations or to alter their policies of armed expulsion and national isolation.

From the Opium War to Perry and Harris

Japanese strategists tended to interpret the Opium War (1839-42) in two ways. A few men such as Takashima Shuhan (1798-1866) were willing to believe Dutch reports about the conflict which stressed that England's superior weapons accounted for its overwhelming victories. But many more men, such as Torii Yozo (1804-74), dismissed Takashima's uncritical acceptance of Britain's reputed victories. The Dutch reports were wildly exaggerated, Torii believed. Preferring to trust Chinese accounts, he came away with quite a different picture. One account out of Chapu dated the twelfth lunar month of 1841, for example, glossed over Chinese defeats and hinted that the real fight had just begun:

> although they have fire-wheel boats [steamships], these cannot navigate our inland rivers and run aground on mud flats. If we work up a rage and dispatch Heavenly Warriors, how can we fail to annihilate them?[14]

When we consider how Japanese strategists had tended to assess world affairs up to then, the Chinese reports doubtless seemed the more plausible. Many saw England as a second-class power--strong, but still weaker than Russia, Turkey, and Ch'ing China. Even if England had won a few hit-and-run coastal skirmishes, so what? And since bakufu law still forbade foreign travel, no Japanese might actually witness the conflict in China first-hand to confirm or disprove either version of its outcome. When similarly distorted and confusing hearsay accounts of the Taiping Rebellion reached Japan in the early 1850s, many clear-thinking Japanese concluded (rightly or not) that Christianity and trafficking in opium had produced China's woes. Had not these two evils, both brought by Westerners, undermined China's national unity and strength by creating treachery, piracy, and rebellion within? Such internal weakness, not inferior weapons, had stymied Ch'ing efforts to control the foreign barbarians and preserve China's territorial integrity.

Such news out of China during the 1840s and early 1850s, before the coming of Perry, provided a stern warning to politically-active Japanese. In response to it, most of them reaffirmed the bakufu's policies of national isolation (*sakoku*) and armed expulsion (*joi*). One Western observer in Japan during the 1860s explained why xenophobia had been so popular and compelling in the 1850s:

> Nor can it be wondered that Japan ... which had seen the humiliation of China consequent upon disputes with a Western Power arising out of trade questions at the very moment when she was being torn by a civil war which owed its origin to the introduction of new religious beliefs from the West, should have believed that the best means of maintaining peace at home and avoiding an unequal contest with Europe, was to adhere strictly to the traditions of the past two centuries [*sakoku* and *joi*].[15]

Like many Japanese of the 1840s and early 1850s, Aizawa welcomed the crisis next door. For him it was a long-hoped-for stimulus to provoke reform and reinvigoration among complacent bakufu and domain officials. In *Kagaku jigen* (1847), his opus written after having learned of events on the Asian mainland, Aizawa observed:

> As Mencius said, "A nation facing no rival states or danger from abroad (*tekkoku gaikan*) will perish." Thus the sages used [the pretext of] rival states and foreign danger to boost military strength, subdue barbarians, and consolidate rule at home. Here is our chance to turn foreign danger into good fortune.[16]

After the Opium War Aizawa obtained new, more up-to-date information on world affairs from two important sources. One was *Kon'yo zushiki*, translated and compiled by Mitsukuri Gempo

(1799-1863) and Mitsukuri Shogo (1821-46).[17] The other was "Amerika soki," a section from Wei Yuan's *Hai-kuo t'u-chih*, translated and edited by Hirose Tatsutaro, a samurai from Yodo domain.[18] Wei Yuan (1794-1856), noted late Ch'ing statecraft reformer, was the compiler of *Sheng-wu chi* (*Records of Imperial Achievements*) and *Hai-kuo t'u-chih* (*Illustrated Treatise on the Maritime Kingdoms*).[19] Aizawa was one of many late Tokugawa thinkers and leaders who read these two Chinese works in the original or in Japanese editions.

New knowledge gained from *Kon'yo zushiki* and *Hai-kuo t'u-chih* did much to reshape Aizawa's picture of world power alignments in *Kagaku jigen*. Out went the Mogul Empire and Persia; now the first-class world powers were Russia, the Ch'ing, England, and Turkey, followed by Germany, France, Spain, and Prussia.[20] But Aizawa noted that the Ch'ing had been on a long decline, Germany remained an empire in name only, and Turkey and Prussia did not engage in overseas expansion. So he concluded that "Britain, Russia, and to a lesser degree, France, are the powers seeking to conquer foreign lands."[21] These were the powers Japan would have to contend with thereafter. Unlike Ch'ing thinkers and leaders, the Japanese worried little about continental foes. The Japanese readily perceived the threat posed by maritime European powers because no steppe nomadic tribes had attacked Japan after the thirteenth century.

But Aizawa also learned of European maritime weaknesses. He was heartened to find that Western empire-builders had lost their magic touch: they could no longer "cherish men from afar," a stock Confucian phrase usually used to describe how the Chinese Son of Heaven won control over foreign peoples and territories.[22] Aizawa discovered much evidence of popular rebellion in colonial areas throughout the world, and he assumed this to mean that oppressed native peoples everywhere aspired to cast off the yoke of European domination:

> finally, rebellions have occurred in the states of India. In North America, Washington has risen to expel the English, and in South America, Bolivar has risen to expel the Spanish. Chile and other states have followed suit; all have become independent nations.[23]

The emergence of these free independent states, known to Aizawa as "republics" (*kyowaseijishu*) through Mitsukuri's translation, altered his strategic thinking drastically.[24] And from his class-bound, pro-bakufu standpoint, this brought new hope. A close analysis of how Aizawa construed the American Revolution and its world-wide political ramifications will show his grounds for optimism on the eve of Perry's visits.25

By the Gembun and Kampo eras (1736-44), according to Aizawa, Britain's North American colonies had begun to achieve prosperity in trade and agriculture. This prompted the rapacious English king to raise taxes levied in the colonies so that he could better finance his wars. He was then buying tea from China, transporting it to North America in royal English ships, and selling it to the colonists. He decided that taxing the tea sellers alone did not raise enough revenue, so he tried to tax buyers as well; the Americans refused to pay. His measure met boycotts and armed opposition in South Carolina, Virginia, and New York. The colonists excluded English tea ships from colonial ports, and one night a group of aborigines who had sided with the colonists stormed an English ship and threw its tea cargo overboard. Angered, the English king sent more warships, and he imposed a new tax twice as high. The Americans, hating his greed and violence, vowed to resist to the death.

In 1774, the elders of each colony met in Virginia. Both the aborigines and immigrant peoples agreed to make peace (end the French and Indian Wars?). They petitioned the English king for redress of grievances: to withdraw his armed forces and to restore the old order under which only tea sellers, not buyers, paid taxes. But quite to the contrary, the king sent still more troopships to invade the colonies. His forces burned city walls and looted. Such greed and violence enraged the Americans. Their elders secretly met and agreed that each colony should recruit men and build ships to be placed under the command of General Washington. Finally, on 4 July 1776 they composed a "Call to Arms" that justified their actions, and they circulated this document to all the world's nations:

> The Lord-on-High (*shang t'i*) created the people, and though countless families of men exist, all are as brothers. He granted life to each and made sure that each would find peace in its proper place in the world. He was greatly worried that the mighty would overpower the weak, the many would oppress the few, and stupid commoners would come to live like the birds and beasts unless properly edified. That is why he established sovereigns to protect the peoples. The Lord-on-High did not establish sovereigns so that they might work violence against their peoples or make their peoples into servitors. Our land, America, had never had a ruler. But when the English king came here, he made himself king, and our people, his subjects. Our people were delighted because they believed he meant to love and protect us, not harm us. Had the king's

administration been without grave evils, we would remain subject to him even now. But he has not been content to oppress us once; he has oppressed us repeatedly.... This we can tolerate no longer....

When the king realized that the thirteen colonies were united against him, he sent a huge fleet of troopships to invade them. The two sides fought to a standoff for over a year. France sent forces to aid the colonists, but the war dragged on for six or seven years, involving 160 to 170 warships and 600,000 to 700,000 men.

In 1784, the English king finally realized that victory was not to be had, and he sent his minister to seek peace. But the colonists were distrustful. They knew that France would withdraw her forces, American soldiers would return to their farms, and Washington would retire to his estate. The British might violate the peace and try to retake the colonies by force during this period of weakness. The American elders also knew that their land had no ruler, so no one would settle disputes or handle litigation. They decided to establish a leader and laws, so that their country would be forever at peace and in order. They had the foresight to realize that, although this leader might rule well during his own lifetime, his descendants might be inept or derelict, or they might become tyrants; then the country would fall to disorder. The leaders met in Virginia in the spring of 1788 to devise some solution to this problem. They elected Washington to be President and decided that after he died, a worthy successor should be chosen every four years based on popular opinion. Each elder went home to deliberate with his people, and returned the next year to ratify these resolutions.

So America, which Aizawa in 1825 had derided as a land of foolish barbarians, had become a power to be reckoned with. He discovered that this resolute colonial people, led by the heroic Washington, had fought England to a standoff for eight long years and forced that world power to sue for peace. What is more, he discovered that other colonies in North America had joined the original thirteen: California and Mexico had revolted from Spain and joined the United States.[26] America's population stood at 28 million; it surpassed Japan's 25 million.[27]

The conclusions from all this were clear to Aizawa and many like-minded Japanese. Granted, the English had inflicted defeats on Ch'ing China in a series of lightning-fast raids against a disunited, apathetic rabble. But China's humiliations stemmed in truth from domestic weaknesses. The American Revolutionary War seemed to show that the English could not win a protracted land war in countries where the entire people resolutely supported and fought for their leaders. The mighty Europeans were vulnerable to popular revolutions in their colonies all over the globe. Since the Westerners' strength supposedly came from their ability to enlist such native colonial peoples in foreign campaigns, Aizawa could logically conclude that world-wide independence movements were seriously undermining European imperial powers such as England. The Opium War showed that the bakufu had to cultivate domestic strength and national integration by forging bonds of loyalty between itself and the daimyo, samurai, and commoner classes. Aizawa believed that it could accomplish this by exploiting the Emperor as a potent, unifying religious symbol. The popular unity so created at home, coupled with the rising power of newly liberated republics such as America, Bolivia, Peru, Chile, and others, would forestall Western incursions in Japan. In this sense, his understanding of current events reinforced his traditional rival states world view, and he had high hopes that the newly independent barbarian peoples would offset and curb old established barbarian nations. But this optimism was shattered when Commodore Matthew C. Perry forced his way into Edo Bay in the summer of 1853.

Perry, Harris, and the Opening of Japan

On this first visit, Perry forced the bakufu to accept letters from President Millard Fillmore and himself which called for an end to Japan's seclusion. He threatened to return the next year for a favorable reply, and made good his threat seven months later commanding one-quarter of the United States Navy. Edo was indecisive about how to deal with the Americans. Tokugawa Nariaki, the daimyo of Mito, served the bakufu as a special advisor on coastal defense. As a collateral house of the Shogun, Mito enjoyed great prestige; and Nariaki, a vigorous and able reformer, was a popular opinion-leader among daimyo and samurai. On his order, Aizawa composed replies to Perry and Fillmore in classical Chinese.[28] Although never delivered, these two letters are historically significant. They tell us how Aizawa the xenophobe tried to convince foreign states that Edo's policy of seclusion was just, and failing in that, why he eventually came to advocate opening Japan to the West. Aizawa consistently formulated his ideas within the traditional Chinese rival states framework and argued for a loose rein policy of mollifying Westerners through peace treaties and bilateral concessions.

Aizawa sought to refute the two key points Perry made in his letter to the bakufu.[29] First, Perry claimed that Japanese officials and commoners treated shipwrecked Americans as if they were enemies, in contrast to the humane treatment given shipwrecked Japanese in America; and he insisted that a treaty of peace and amity (*washin*) would rectify this problem. Second, he argued that present-day world conditions made the bakufu's policy of seclusion anachronistic and unworkable; so the United States and Japan could avert an unfriendly collision only by concluding such a treaty. The redoubtable Aizawa countered by asserting that Japan was *not* in seclusion: at Nagasaki Japan had an official reception point for representatives of foreign nations seeking to relay messages to the bakufu.[30] Most foreign vessels coming to Japan in recent years were not shipwrecked at all; they came to ports *other than* Nagasaki under their own power. Nagasaki was like the gate to a private home: it was there for anyone with legitimate business to enter, and anyone intruding elsewhere deserved to be treated as an enemy.

Aizawa came up with a more involved argument to rebut Perry's second point. The times may have changed, he granted, but the Will of Heaven--that every ruler bring peace and stability to his people--was immutable. Quoting from the *Book of Rites*, he declared: "Good faith needs no covenants," and went on to state that concluding a treaty of peace and amity with America would bring disorder and suffering to Japan's people--the very opposite of what Perry claimed to be seeking. A genuine desire to preserve peace and amity, not the treaty itself, was what mattered:

> If you really come in peace, you will not wish to cause death and destruction; that is what you would do to those you hate. To bring death to our people would be to lack benevolence; to transform our orderly rule into chaos would be to lack righteousness. Because you too cherish your people, you would not start a war rashly disregarding benevolence and righteousness.[31]

Aizawa did not say why Perry would not wish to harm the Japanese people by forcing bakufu leaders to sign his treaty. To understand why, we must examine Aizawa's reply to Fillmore's demand for setting up regulations to govern trade and the exchange of ministers between Japan and the United States:[32]

> Heaven has created every land with a distinctive character. [As Mencius said,] "diversity is the proper condition of things." The Way of Heaven and Earth decrees this. Hence, some peoples traverse the seas, and some devote themselves to agriculture. These differences stem from their folkways. Alter those folkways and the people in question will lose their livelihood. And that, of course, would cause great hardship. The Japanese people have

engaged in agriculture from time immemorial. They produce only enough to meet their own needs and have nothing left over to sell to others. This is the condition Heaven has granted us; it cannot be changed.[33]

Fillmore was mistaken, he continued, in assuming that southern Japan produced large amounts of coal. Japan produced just enough to meet its own needs, so there was no surplus for American ships. Fillmore's call for friendship was fine, but his proposed exchange of ministers was not. Because Heaven had forbidden the Japanese to traverse the seas, the bakufu could not send a minister to America; and that would violate proper protocol. On the other hand, if America broke bakufu laws by dispatching a minister to reside in Japan, that would stir up large-scale popular unrest and contradict Fillmore's expressed aim: not to "disturb the tranquility of the Shogun's dominions."

But most important, Aizawa argued, Westerners in centuries past had brought Christianity to Japan and fomented massive rebellions that had not been easy to quell. The Christian scourge became so deep-rooted that generations had been required to eradicate it. Should the bakufu make an exception for Fillmore and allow American consuls to reside in Japan, it would have to grant similar dispensation to other foreign nations. And those other foreigners, unlike Americans, might flout sacred bakufu laws against disseminating subversive Christian teachings.

From 1853 until his death in 1863, Aizawa would strive to bolster bakufu authority in Japan and counter foreign demands for trade and diplomacy by appealing to a Confucian-inspired theory of Heavenly Providence. Heaven, he claimed, had the best interests of all peoples in the world at heart, and it desired that they all find happiness and prosperity, each in its own distinctive way. To this end, Heaven had decreed specific cultural and economic patterns, institutions, and values "appropriate for each land."[34] Furthermore, Heaven had assigned rulers, "from supremely majestic emperors to lowly tribal chieftains," to all countries. Each was charged with the onerous duty of upholding the "character" peculiar to his land and ridding it of violence and disorder. Only then would every people enjoy peace and contentment; only then would everything remain in its proper condition. Heaven was impartial:

> Since Heaven seeks to uphold tranquility, no one thing among its creation receives special favor to the detriment of any other. Instead, Heaven has endowed each thing with its own particular character. Things rooted in the soil, it

makes grow; things that lean to one side, it topples over. Heaven does not force creatures with hoofs to fly; it does not prompt those with wings to gallop. Heaven allows each to do what it does best, and does not force any to do what it cannot.... Likewise, some peoples live solely by the plow; others trade what they have in excess to obtain what they lack. Those too poor to supply their own needs depend on other nations; those who can, live off the produce of their lands. Either way, the ruler's task is to ensure his people's livelihood by making do with what his land has been endowed with.... No ruler tries to change his nation's character; he does not make his people accept anything they are averse to.[35]

If Westerners would but honor this providential intent of Heaven, Aizawa claimed, there would be no wars and no need of treaties. But instead, Westerners flouted Heavenly Providence. They "judged all peoples in the world according to Western ways." They sought to force their own customs of navigation and trade on other peoples, reasoning that: "to exchange the special products of one area for those of another is to uphold Heaven's Will because different parts of the world grow different crops and produce different goods." This Western reasoning was not lost on Aizawa; nor did he deny that the Westerners had certain grounds for it: "in out-of-the-way, poorly endowed countries, the land's produce does not meet the people's needs, so they must procure goods from abroad to make up for the deficiency." But this Western claim lacked validity because it falsely assumed that uniformity, rather than diversity, was "the proper condition of things."

Aizawa seems to echo Kaempfer's *History of Japan* when he asserts that Japan enjoyed unique material blessings due to Heavenly Dispensation:[36] "our soil is rich, our climate fair, and our products plentiful; so we have no need to import any goods."[37] Heaven had made Japan perfectly self-sufficient. Levels of production and consumption matched perfectly; nothing was lacking and nothing went to waste. But Westerners, Aizawa went on, risked "upsetting this delicate balance in nature's creation." Japanese folkways were "to live off the land and drink from the well," just as Western folkways were to sail the seas and trade. "How would Westerners like it if we forced our folkways on them?" he asked.[38]

This Confucian-inspired theory of Heavenly Providence satisfied Aizawa's two categorical imperatives. It reinforced bakufu authority at home: because Heaven had appointed the Shogun ruler of Japan, any opposition to him violated Heaven's Will. Even more importantly, the theory gave the bakufu a clever and face-saving route of diplomatic manuvering: because Fillmore also was a Heavenly-appointed ruler, the bakufu might properly treat him as an equal when sending or receiving diplomatic messages. Aizawa could so skirt the thorny issue of having to treat Westerners as inferior barbarians in face-to-face negotiating sessions, while continuing to denigrate them as "barbarians" in correspondence to fellow Japanese.[39] Aizawa derived this two-faced approach to barbarian control from the Chinese tradition of keeping rival foreign states on a loose rein by binding them to treaties of peace and mutual concession. Ch'i Ying and I-li-pu, for example, used this technique in negotiating with the British after the end of the Opium War.[40]

But the tactic was poorly received in Japan. Nariaki chose not to deliver Aizawa's missives, and even if he had, they probably would not have swayed the Americans. In March of 1854, Perry forced the bakufu headed by Abe Masahiro to sign a treaty of "peace and amity" (*washin joyaku*) granting all American demands. In Mito, Aizawa was certainly displeased by this turn of events. But he never argued to abrogate the treaty once signed. Though bakufu authorities labeled it "provisional" to soften criticism at home, Aizawa saw positive value in Perry's treaty. Not only did classical traditions of statecraft sanction it, even more importantly, using the treaty was the only way to control these foreign "barbarians" given Japan's clear military inferiority to them. That is why, in the years after 1854, he would be so insistent about the reciprocity of benefits and concessions that such treaties always had been designed to guarantee.

Perry's treaty of 1854 opened two ports, Shimoda and Hakodate, to supply coal and provisions to American ships, and it ensured humane treatment for shipwrecked Americans in Japan. But true to Aizawa's fears, once the bakufu had signed a treaty with the United States granting special privileges to Americans, other Western nations demanded similar treaties and privileges--and Edo was powerless to refuse. Bakufu leaders now had no choice but to control *all* the foreign barbarians by binding them to treaty provisions. As Aizawa and the Japanese understood it, Perry's 1854 treaty was not a commercial pact and did not permit trade on a regular basis. What is more, it explicitly provided that bakufu approval be gotten before any foreign consular official might reside in Japan.

Japanese interpretations notwithstanding, however, Townsend Harris took up his post as American Consul-General at Shimoda in the summer of 1856. Among other things, Harris sought to open four ports to American trade and to secure residence for American commercial agents in Edo, Osaka, and the ports to be opened. Moreover, he insisted on presenting his demands in person to bakufu leaders at Edo, and in the fall of 1857 an American man-of-war transported him there for that purpose despite vigorous Japanese objections. In Edo, Harris had an audience with the Shogun and delivered a personal message from President Pierce. Toward the end of 1857 he visited the home of Hotta Masayoshi, the new bakufu head who had replaced Abe in 1855. Harris lectured Hotta for two hours through Dutch and Japanese interpreters.[41] He underscored the evils that British opium trafficking had produced in China and stated that the English schemed to set up an opium trade with Japan as well. Opening Japan to Western trade was inescapable, he contested. So the bakufu had better sign its first commercial treaty with the United States, a friendly nation which had refused to sell opium or wage war in China, and which would protect Japan by restraining more malevolent powers such as Britain, France, and Russia.

By early 1858, negotiations with Harris in Edo had produced a draft treaty that included all his demands. Hotta, however, would not sign it on bakufu authority alone. He feared he could not guarantee popular compliance with it unless he first gained approval from the imperial court in Kyoto. This he went to get early in March. But his task was complicated by political intrigues in Edo at the time. The heir-less Shogun Iesada was sickly and near death, and Nariaki got his son, Yoshinobu, named as one of the two candidates for succession. Nariaki schemed to achieve two related goals. First he knew that upholding seclusion was out of the question, but he wished to postpone opening the ports as long as possible so that Japan could somehow strengthen itself in the interim. Second, he sought more power for himself and Mito in bakufu councils. This he hoped to gain by playing on the court's xenophobia and forcing Hotta to support his son's candidacy. Nariaki had his followers in Kyoto goad the court into withholding approval for the Harris treaty and telling Hotta that, because this matter was vital to the nation's interests, he should consult further with the heads of the three Tokugawa collateral houses (Mito was one) and with the Outer Lords. After four vexing months in Kyoto, Hotta came to believe he could get imperial sanction for the treaty only by supporting Yoshinobu's candidacy and opening bakufu decision-making to collateral house participation.

Unable to win court approval, Hotta retired in disgrace. His willingness to accommodate the collaterals and Outside Lords had created a backlash in the bakufu that brought Ii Naosuke to power. Ii championed the cause of Tokugawa direct retainers--the *fudai* and *hatamoto*. They jealously guarded their monopoly on power in bakufu councils and refused to share it with the court or collaterals.

Ii moved to boost the bakufu's sovereign power in foreign and domestic affairs. Armed with the nativist theory of imperial investiture--that the court had granted Tokugawa Ieyasu and his shogunal descendants full authority to govern Japan as they saw fit--Ii decided to settle the treaty issue. It was pressing. Harris was fast losing patience, and he made that clear whenever he felt the bakufu needed a little prodding. Back in January he had begun to growl that:

> the President had sent me to Yedo on a most friendly mission, having solely the benefit of Japan in view; that the United States asked nothing for themselves; ... their [the bakufu's] treatment of me showed that no negotiations could be carried on with them unless the plenipotentiary was backed by a fleet, and offered them cannon balls for arguments.[42]

Only because of this angry outburst did the bakufu start negotiating with Harris in earnest.[43] Harris shrewdly used this tactic throughout the following months "to bring about a crisis," as he put it.[44]

His threats did not ring hollow. They gained frightful cogency when he reported that Britain and France had just defeated China in yet another war and had forced the humiliating Tientsin Treaty on the Ch'ing. With this in mind, Ii discreetly ordered that Harris' treaty be signed, and it was, on 29 July 1858. Similar treaties with Holland, Russia, Britain, and France followed; and foreign traders and officials such as British Consul-General Rutherford Alcock arrived in Japan even before the ports were to open officially. Ii also moved to silence domestic opposition. He rejected the candidacy of Nariaki's son, Yoshinobu, and declared a young boy, Yoshitomi of the Kii House, shogunal successor. For good measure, Ii also sentenced Nariaki, Matsudaira Yoshinaga, and other prominent supporters of Yoshinobu to house confinement. Because Hotta had already raised the issue of imperial sanction, Ii had felt it best to obtain court and daimyo approval for the treaty. But Harris' threats and news of the Tientsin Treaty made Ii sign before that was possible.

Harris' demands and threats, then, had forced Ii to open the nation without imperial approval; and Ii silenced the opposition through punitive measures that soon set off a bloody internecine feud in Mito.[45] One faction, the radicals, pursued Aizawa's rhetoric to "revere the emperor and expel the barbarians" literally and fanatically; another, the conservatives, discarded that rhetoric in favor of realpolitik. This cleavage largely followed age and class lines. In general, young low-ranking samurai and wealthy peasants sought to rouse bakufu leaders into executing imperial commands for the expulsion of foreigners. But contrary to their intentions, their assassinations, coups, and insurrections ended up impairing Edo's ability to govern Japan and inviting Western armed reprisals and demands for indemnity payments. For these men, the bakufu existed to carry out the Emperor's orders; should it expire in the attempt, its glory would be all the greater.

The Mito conservatives looked on this reckless abandon with horror and repugnance. The daimyo, domain elders, and their advisors--men in positions of political responsibility--strove to uphold and strengthen the bakufu, not ruin it. Such men, Aizawa included, wanted the bakufu to retain its hegemony over the court and over potentially hostile Outside Lords. Their idea of reforming the existing national power structure was to broaden its base to include Mito, Echizen, and other collaterals plus a few Outside Lords traditionally loyal to the bakufu.

The crisis in Mito came to a head in September of 1858 when Nariaki's supporters prodded Emperor Komei and the court to issue an imperial edict that criticized the bakufu for signing the commercial treaty with Harris and for punishing Nariaki and the collaterals. It urged Ii to consult with the daimyo of the land in order to formulate effective measures to uphold domestic order and end humiliations at the hands of foreigners. The court issued this edict not only to the bakufu. It delivered the same message directly to Mito domain authorities and told them to circulate copies among the daimyo. Ii quite rightly viewed this Mito-instigated court meddling as an act of defiance to bakufu supremacy, and he purged ruthlessly all who had been opposing him. Over one hundred persons would suffer punishment--court nobles, daimyo, and activist samurai and commoners. Ii clamped down on Mito severely: Nariaki, his sons Yoshinobu and Yoshiatsu, domain elders, and several Mito samurai suffered punishments ranging from house arrest to torture and death. Ii also ordered Mito domain officials to disobey the Emperor by withholding the edict, and he demanded that Mito turn over its copy to bakufu authorities in Edo.

Aizawa and the conservatives argued to comply with bakufu orders, at least in the main, by returning the edict to the court in Kyoto, even though this meant countermanding the Emperor's will. The protesting radicals--samurai and commoners alike--encamped *en masse* at Nagaoka and Kogane on the Mito *kaido*, the main highway linking Edo and Mito. There they forcibly blocked any attempt by domain officials either to surrender the edict to Edo or return it to Kyoto. Repeated appeals to disperse resulted in bloodshed. Some of the protesters committed suicide, to resolve their dilemma of remaining loyal to both the court and bakufu while demonstrating their hostility to Ii and their own domain superiors. The radicals would not simply obstruct Mito officials from obeying Ii's orders; they murdered Ii in late March of 1860. This act kicked off a five-year period of terror, assassination, and insurrection that ultimately proved fatal to bakufu hegemony.

Only against this background of lawlessness and unrest can we understand why Aizawa, late in life, disowned his earlier views on bakufu foreign policy and agreed to open Japan to Western trade and diplomatic intercourse. One month before his own students, admiring readers of *New Theses*, would kill Ii, Aizawa was livid in his denunciation of them:

> I understand [the rebels] at Nagaoka proclaim that their actions are to "revere the emperor and expel the barbarians." But in truth they twist the meaning of those words to suit their own purposes.[46]

Aizawa's memorials and letters, from 1858 to his death in 1863, show that his prime concern was to preserve bakufu and daimyo supremacy in Japan, not Japanese territorial integrity against foreign encroachment. He harped on the need for bilateral concessions under any treaty of "peace and amity" such as that signed with Perry. In 1858, for example, he proposed that this message be sent to Harris:

> Treaties of peace and amity permit the states involved to remain well-ordered, and their peoples, in tranquility: only then are treaties worthwhile. Should you force upon us a [new] treaty, whose provisions totally ignore our hallowed folkways, popular opinion here would reject it. We would fall to chaos and our people would suffer the horrors of war. Then what good would the treaty of peace and amity be? Thus we should devise treaties carefully suited to each other's spiritual make-up, so that both sides benefit.[47]

So far the bakufu had bent over backward to accommodate Harris. It had yielded on numerous crucial points: relaxing ancestral laws to open ports other than Nagasaki, letting Harris reside in Japan and have a shogunal audience in Edo, and allowing trade and residence to foreigners in other ports. Harris was endangering the bases of political order in Japan by forcing such concessions on the bakufu--all of which violated hallowed Japanese laws and ran counter to Japan's immutable Heavenly endowed folkways. "To achieve the purpose behind the [first] treaty (*washin*)," Aizawa held, "both sides must make concessions."[48]

It was now time for Harris to yield on a few points, including his demands for the freedom to propagate Christianity and for the opening of sensitive areas like Hyogo and the Kinai to foreign trade and settlement:

> To open these without [court] approval would invite insurrection and civil war. If the American barbarians insist on this point, they would only be provoking civil war in Japan; and there would have been no purpose in signing a treaty of peace and amity in the first place.[49]

Bakufu negotiators should explain Edo's predicament in these terms, Aizawa argued; then the dictates of reason (*jori*) would be crystal clear to Harris. Should he persist in trying to extract unreasonable concessions, "all the world's nations could tell without a doubt which side was right, and which, crooked."[50]

Given Harris' persistence, and in view of how other Western powers were behaving in China, this statement of principle would mean little unless the bakufu was willing to risk an immediate military showdown. But it wished to avoid precisely that. Hotta, for example, had been painfully aware that "because America is the world's strongest nation, ... any lame effort to expel them by force would lead to defeat and national humiliation."[51] Nariaki too felt constrained to support Hotta's plan "to dilly-dally and be evasive" (*burakashi*).[52] By this he meant to grant the foreigners' demands for opening Japan until the strength to expel them, it was hoped, somehow could be cultivated. Edo leaders would have to promise the court that, although the bakufu had let foreigners into Japan, it was preparing earnestly to drive them back out. Nariaki died in 1860, before this double-dealing had discredited the bakufu in both foreign and Japanese eyes. Aizawa was not so lucky.

In 1862, one year before he would die, Aizawa was a frustrated old man fretting over the bakufu's future. Fifteen years earlier he had been much more of an optimist. He had welcomed news of America's liberation, a victory won by Washington after seven years of resolute fighting against the colonial power, Britain. The emergence of America and other independent republics, Aizawa had hoped, signaled the decline of Western territorial expansion around the globe. These former colonial peoples might aid the bakufu by haltering their old European masters. But Perry dispelled all these hopes in 1853 and 1854. Aizawa realized that the United States was no different from other Western barbarian states making incursions in East Asia. By appealing to reason and to the Confucian-inspired theory of Heavenly Providence, Aizawa hoped that he could persuade the Americans to go away, so that Japan's natural economy of perfect self-sufficiency and her natural condition of political seclusion would not be impaired. After all, Heaven had had a reason for denying foreign trade and diplomacy to the Japanese. But this hope too proved delusive, for Harris and his countrymen would not be dissuaded in 1858.

Aizawa then tried to apply the traditional Chinese diplomatic technique of controlling powerful barbarian states by binding them to treaty provisions that guaranteed mutual benefits and bilateral concessions. Such a loose rein policy would blunt the more dangerous foreign demands by placing foreign heads of state under legal restraints as spelled out in treaties. But this tactic failed too. By 1862, Westerners were in Japan to stay, and they were demanding even more privileges. The bakufu's legitimacy rested on its pledge to expel these foreigners--a pledge it could not keep. By 1862 Edo leaders had to convince a xenophobic court and bellicose samurai activists that the bakufu's opening of Japan was actually beneficial, not just unavoidable. Aizawa tried to provide such a rationale in his "Policy for Affairs of the Day" ("*Jimusaku*"). He wrote this tract to enlighten young Mito extremists in 1862, and he might possibly have intended to submit it Tokugawa Yoshinobu, then shogunal regent.[53]

In this tract, Aizawa asserted that important national policies such as banning or permitting foreign trade and diplomacy had to be based on a realistic assessment of the times and of the strength of foreign nations. In Ieyasu's day, foreign nations were weak and Christianity posed no grave peril. So "he did not cut diplomatic ties with all nations; he kept them with some." Only because of the Shimabara Rebellion in 1637--after Ieyasu's death--did the bakufu end diplomatic relations with all nations and institute its seclusion policy. This stern measure was "appropriate for those times," because bakufu leaders in the 1630s judged that the danger of Christianity was life threatening and that Westerners were too weak to challenge Japan militarily. In other words, having failed to rationalize bakufu policy-making through metaphysical principles like Heavenly Providence, Aizawa turned to arguments of political expedience and historical relativism. Seclusion and the expulsion of Westerners were not immutable "hallowed laws" established by the all-wise Ieyasu at the very outset of Tokugawa rule. A latter-day bakufu had adopted those measures, and only because they met the needs of its time; so the present-day bakufu should not cling blindly to them. Policies adopted out of expedience in one era could be dropped without qualms in another, when changed historical conditions made them inappropriate.[54]

But most important about Aizawa's "Policy for Affairs of the Day"--and this sets him apart from Nariaki and other Mito ideologues--is the assertion that Japan must openly admit military inferiority to Westerners and act discreetly toward them. Aizawa explicitly repudiated the jingoistic rhetoric of his 1825 *New Theses*, which was now a bible for fanatic expulsionists. Edo leaders should not imitate Yueh Fei (1103-41), the rashly resolute Sung general and war-party leader who insisted on resisting Jurchen invaders to the bitter end. Japan's fighting men should not just battle to the death without caring whether the nation survived or perished. "Defeat would be a national disgrace," he declared. "We would have to sue for peace. The Westerners customarily demand indemnities to cover their war costs, and these would be more than we could pay." His explanation went on:

> The foreign nations are immensely powerful, and all states in the world submit to a confederation. This is like when Duke Huan of Ch'i [r. 685-643 B.C.] and Duke Wen of Chin [r. 636-628 B.C.] were confederation masters in the Spring and Autumn period. All lords of the realm entered into relations of friendship. If any refused to submit, all the rest would attack him, and he would be unable to maintain his state's independence for a single day. The situation now is similar. If we refuse to enter into friendly relations, we will make all foreign states our enemies and will not be able to maintain independence among them.[55]

Aizawa sought to rationalize Japan's submission to superior Western military might through this clever distortion of early Chinese history. Membership in the Chou confederation he cites was not coerced. And under the hegemons Huan and Wen, the confederation's chief purpose was not to suppress fighting among its members. Instead, the small states of the north China plain, then fearful of stronger barbarian neighbors such as Ch'u to the south, approached Ch'i and Duke Huan for protection. So it was due to their appeals that this league of Chinese states under nominal Chou rule came into being.[56] A more correct historical analogy would have been to compare the United States and other Western powers to Ch'u, and to liken Japan's daimyo domains under bakufu hegemony to the Chinese feudal lords who allied to defend themselves against barbarian encroachment. Aizawa resorted to this historical ruse in order to gloss over the bakufu's military impotence and inability to preserve Japan's territorial integrity. This is a far cry from his earlier views of controlling the barbarians: now they are controlling Japan. Though insisting that treaty concessions be bilateral and benefits be mutual, Aizawa would not risk war to make the West keep its half of the bargain.

Conclusion

In the 1840s and 1850s, before overseas travel enabled the Japanese to study world affairs and Western conditions first-hand, many Tokugawa thinkers relied on Chinese sources of information to learn about the barbarian menace facing them, and some employed traditional Chinese diplomatic practices to forestall it. Most rallied to the clarion call, "revere the Emperor and expel the barbarians." Most have been hailed as national heroes by prewar Japanese historians, and most have been denounced as early proponents of Emperor-state nationalism by postwar Japanese historians. Aizawa would seem to qualify on both counts. But few postwar scholarly books and articles have been devoted to his thought in the period 1826 to 1863--after he wrote *New Theses*.[57] And strangest of all, no prewar multi-volume *Complete Works* exists for him. In the ultra-nationalistic 1930s and 1940s, Japanese publishers eagerly printed and sold the collected works of far less eminent late Tokugawa xenophobes. Why has Aizawa suffered such cruel neglect?

This chapter indicates that the strategic thinking which emerges from Aizawa's post-1825 unpublished writings would have sullied forever his reputation as the Japanese Spirit incarnate. His views on late Tokugawa foreign policy resemble those of late Ch'ing officials such as Ch'i Ying and I-li-pu: open the country to Western semi-colonial domination in return for concessions to help bolster a tottering regime against domestic opposition. The resemblance lies in Aizawa's loose rein tactic for mollifying barbarian states: bind them to treaty provisions designed to benefit both signatories. Whether based on genuine naivete or (more likely) crass opportunism, this credulous faith in treaties signed with Westerners reveals the limits of Aizawa's xenophobia and sets him apart from other contemporary advocates of Japanese nationalism. Aizawa could not conceive of Japan's sovereignty and national autonomy apart from bakufu rule. He at first welcomed news of America's independence. But he did so in the hope, shared with late Ch'ing strategists such as Wei Yuan and Hsu Chi-yu, that America and other newly liberated peoples would help check the European imperialist advance in East Asia, and so reduce dangerous foreign pressures on the Edo regime. When he discovered that Perry and Harris were in the vanguard of that advance and would not be put off by sophistry, he ended up advocating little more than appeasement.

NOTES

1. One of the first to stress this point was Osatake Takeki, *Kinsei Nihon no kokusai kannen no hattatsu* (Tokyo, 1932), pp. 51-52.
2. John K. Fairbank, ed., *The Chinese World Order* (Cambridge, 1968).
3. Morris Rossabi, ed., *China Among Equals* (Berkeley, 1983). For a recent study which interprets the transformation of nineteenth century Ch'ing China and Tokugawa Japan within Wallerstein's comparative framework of "modern world systems," see Nagai Kazu, "Higashi Ajia ni okeru kokusai kankei no hen'yo to Nihon no kindai," in *Nihon shi kenkyu*, no. 289 (September 1986), pp. 102-129.
4. For a seminal revisionist thesis on Tokugawa foreign policy within the East Asian context see Ronald P. Toby, *State and Diplomacy in Early Modern Japan* (Princeton, 1984).
5. Quoted in Lien-sheng Yang, "Historical Notes on the Chinese World Order," in Fairbank, ed., *Chinese World Order*, pp. 23. Also, Gungwu Wang, "The Rhetoric of Lesser Empire," in Rossabi, *China Among Equals*, pp. 46-65.
6. On the *Phaeton* Incident, see Tabohashi Kiyoshi, *Zotei kindai Nihon gaikoku kankei shi* (Tokyo, 1937), pp. 275-281; Tokutomi Iichiro, *Kinsei Nihon kokumin shi 25, bakufu sekkin jidai* (Tokyo, 1936), pp. 362-376.
7. Numata Jiro et al., ed., *Nihon shiso taikei 64, yogaku, jo* (Tokyo, 1976), p. 560. (Hereafter cited "*NST*".)
8. For a more detailed analysis of Aizawa's strategic thinking in *New Theses*, see B. T. Wakabayashi, *Anti-Foreignism and Western Learning in Early-Modern Japan* (Cambridge, 1986), pp. 58-134.
9. See Fred W. Drake, *China Charts the World: Hsu Chi-yu and His Geography of 1848* (Cambridge, 1975), p. 4.
10. See Paul A. Cohen, *Between Tradition and Modernity: Wang T'ao and Reform in Late Ch'ing China* (Cambridge, 1974), pp. 93-96.
11. Aizawa Seishisai, *Chishima ibun*, manuscript held by Mukyukai bunko (Machida-shi, Tokyo).
12. Imai Usaburo et al., eds., *NST 53, mitogaku* (Tokyo, 1973), pp. 103-104. This is Aizawa's amplification of Su's original statement quoted in Kenneth Ch'en, "Matteo Ricci's Contribution to, and Influence on, Geographical Knowledge in China," in *Journal of the American Oriental Society*, vol. 59, no. 3 (September 1939), p. 349.
13. However, Watanabe and Takano estimated English power to be much greater than did Aizawa. See Sato Shosuke et al., eds., *NST 55, Watanabe Kazan, Takano Choei, Sakuma Shozan, Yokoi Shonan, Hashimoto Sanai* (Tokyo, 1971), p. 24 and pp. 167-168.
14. Quoted in Sato Shosuke, *Yogaku shi kenkyu josetsu* (Tokyo, 1964), pp. 315-316.
15. Sir Ernest Satow, *A Diplomat in Japan* (Rutland, Vermont, 1983), p. 44.
16. Aizawa Seishisai, *Kagaku jigen* (Mito, 1892), p. 82.
17. In his *Kagaku jigen* of 1847, Aizawa cites "A Dutch book translated by Mitsukuri Shogo" ("Mitsukuri Shogo yaku ransho"): Aizawa, *Kagaku jigen*, p. 90. *Kon'yo zushiki* was published under the name of Mitsukuri Shogo, but according to Kure Shuzo, it was largely a product of Shogo's adoptive father, Mitsukuri Gempo. See Rangaku shiryo kenkyu kai, ed., *Mitsukuri Gempo no kenkyu* (Kyoto, 1978), pp. 186-187. I have used the 1845 woodblock edition of *Kon'yo zushiki* held by the Harvard Yenching Library.
18. Aizawa's hand-copied manuscript, "Amerika soki," is held by the Kodokan in Mito. I wish to express my deepest gratitude to Yoshida Toshizumi of the Ibaraki-ken rekishi kan in Mito for his assistance in allowing me to gain access to this key document and for helping me photograph it.
19. Studies on Wei Yuan which I found helpful are Peter M. Mitchell, "The Limits of Reformism: Wei Yuan's Reaction to Western Intrusion," and Susan Barnett, "Protestant Expansion and Chinese Views of the West," both in *Modern Asian Studies*, vol. 6, no. 2 (April 1972); also Jane Kate Leonard, *Wei Yuan and China's Rediscovery of the Maritime World* (Cambridge, 1984), and Peter M. Mitchell, "Wei Yuan (1794-1857) and the Early Modernization Movement in China and Japan," (Ph.D.

dissertation, Indiana University, 1970).
20. Aizawa, *Kagaku jigen*, p. 97.
21. *Loc. cit.*
22. *Loc. cit.* Aizawa's Chinese phrase is "*huai-jou yuan-jen.*"
23. Aizawa, *Kagaku jigen*, p. 96.
24. *Loc. cit.*, for the term "*kyowaseijishu.*" However, Mitsukuri designated the United States nation as a "*kyowaseijishu,*" his translation of the Dutch term "free new states." See *Kon'yo zushiki, maki no yon, ge*. Aizawa uses the term generically, to designate all the newly established republics.
25. Information and quotations in the following paragraphs derive from Aizawa's hand-copied manuscript, "Amerika soki."
26. Aizawa, *Kagaku jigen*, p. 96.
27. For the U.S. population figure, Aizawa, *Kagaku jigen*, p. 96; for the Japanese, p. 83.
28. "Gasshukoku suishi teitoku ni fukusuru no sho" to Perry, and "Gasshukoku daitoryo ni kotauru no sho" to Fillmore. Both are manuscripts in *Seishisai bunko*, held by Mukyukai bunko (Machida-shi, Tokyo).
29. Found in W. G. Beasley, *Select Documents on Japanese Foreign Policy: 1853-1868* (London, 1955), pp. 101-102.
30. Aizawa, "Gasshukoku suishi teitoku ni fukusuru no sho."
31. *Loc. cit.*
32. The text of Fillmore's message is in Beasley, *Select Documents*, pp. 99-101.
33. This and the following paragraphs derive from Aizawa, "Gasshukoku daitoryo ni kotauru no sho."
34. "Arai Chikushu Romajin o satosu sho ni gisu," a manuscript in *Seishisai bunko*, held by Mukyukai bunko (Machida-shi, Tokyo).
35. *Loc. cit.*
36. On how Kaempfer's *History of Japan* strengthened the argument in late Tokugawa to keep Japan closed, see Kobori Keiichiro, *Sakoku no shiso* (Tokyo, 1974).
37. Aizawa, "Arai Chikushu Romajin o satosu sho ni gisu."
38. *Loc. cit.*
39. Copies of Aizawa's letters from 1856 to 1862 are held by the Tokyo University Historiographical Institute (Tokyo, Japan).
40. See the classic study by John K. Fairbank, *Trade and Diplomacy on the China Coast* (Stanford, 1969), pp. 84-113.
41. An English translation of the Japanese text of Harris' speech is in Beasley, *Select Documents*, pp. 159-165.
42. Mario Emilio Cosenza, ed., *The Complete Journal of Townsend Harris* (Rutland, Vermont, 1959), pp. 495-496.
43. Ishii Takashi, *Nihon kaikoku shi* (Tokyo, 1972), p. 256.
44. Cosenza, *Journal of Townsend Harris*, p. 495.
45. For a recent account, see Yoshida Masahiko, "Bogo mitchoku mondai to shimpanteki koki mitogaku," in *Nihon rekishi*, no. 404 (January 1985), pp. 86-103. For an older, less satisfactory account, see Tanaka Mitsuaki, ed., *Mito bakumatsu fuunroku* (Mito, 1976), pp. 233-252.
46. *Mito han shiryo johen ken* (Tokyo, 1970), p. 690.
47. *Aizawa Yasushi fujiko*, manuscript held by the Tokyo University Historiographical Institute (Tokyo, Japan).
48. *Loc. cit.*
49. *Loc. cit.*
50. *Loc. cit.*
51. *Mito han shiryo johen ken* (Tokyo, 1970), p. 19. These are the words of Tsutsui Masanori and Kawaji Toshiakira. But as Ishii Takashi notes, because they were aides to Hotta Masayoshi, it is valid to assume that Hotta shared these sentiments and also advocated the same *burakashi* policy (see the following note) to deal with the foreign crisis; see Ishii, *Nihon kaikoku shi*, p. 7.
52. *Mito han shiryo johen ken*, pp. 19-20. The slang term "*burakashi*" means "to stall," but as Toyama Shigeki interpolates, the connotation is clearly "to be evasive and to deceive"; see Toyama Shigeki, *Meiji ishin to gendai* (Tokyo, 1968), p. 65.

53. The text is included in Imai *et al.*, eds., *NST 53, mitogaku*, pp. 362-367. See also Seya Yoshihiko's "Kaidai" in the same volume, pp. 504-506.
54. *Loc. cit.*
55. Imai *et al.*, eds., *NST 53, mitogaku*, pp. 362-362.
56. See, for example, Charles O. Hucker, *China's Imperial Past* (Stanford, 1975), pp. 35-37.
57. The only study I know of dealing with Aizawa's thought after *New Theses* is Yamaguchi Muneyuki, "Bannen no Aizawa Seishisai," in Yamaguchi, *Bakumatsu seiji shiso shi kenkyu* (Tokyo, 1967).

2
BUILDING THE NATIONAL COMMUNICATIONS SYSTEM: ADOPTING AND ADAPTING WESTERN ORGANIZATIONAL MODELS IN MEIJI JAPAN

D. Eleanor Westney

Since the early 1970s, the continuing economic success of Japan and the competitive strength of Japanese firms have led to major debates over whether organizational patterns that are effective in Japan can be transplanted into Western social environments. These debates have produced a renewed interest in the Meiji application and adaptation of Western organizational models.[1] The cross-societal "transplanting" of organizational patterns is by no means unique to Japan, but in the Meiji period it seemed uniquely salient: it was particularly deliberate and wide-ranging; it took place in a relatively short space of time; and it drew on a number of Western countries for models, rather than on one. The exploration of the processes by which certain organizational forms were adopted and adapted in the Meiji environment can be seen not only as an important element of understanding the institutional development of Meiji Japan but also as a case in which to develop insights into the more general patterns of cross-societal organizational emulation.

In his discussion of the adoption of the Prussian model in Japanese municipal government in 1888, George Oakley Totten has portrayed the emulation of European governmental systems in Japan in the 1880s as follows:

The first step was to understand them in general terms, making some preliminary choices on the basis of the apparent success of certain countries. The next step was to examine the history of Japan's own institutions so that choice would correspond with both conditions and needs in Japan. The next step was a more detailed study of Western countries, involving longer stays abroad and the hiring of foreign advisers to come to Japan for detailed technical advice in the drawing up of new codes.[2]

Totten makes clear that this is not a general model of Meiji organization-building but a model of the reorganizations of the legal and administrative systems of the 1880s. It also applies to the framing of the Constitution along German lines--probably the most studied of the many cases of Meiji organizational emulation and the one that fits most closely Totten's model. But it is this image of Japanese institutional development that has long been dominant among Western scholars of social change.[3]

However, the emulation processes of the mid-1880s reflect the experience of over a decade and a half of building and rebuilding organizations on Western models. The early processes of emulation, which began in the military and the administrative structures of the bakufu[4] and which accelerated and broadened in early Meiji to include also the educational system, banking, the police, the postal system, the telegraph, publishing, commerce and industry were considerably less systematic. They exhibit enormous variation in the range of alternatives considered, the level of organizational information gathered, the extent to which foreign advisers were used, and the degree to which the adoption and adaptation processes were consciously influenced by "conditions and needs in Japan." Indeed, the "conditions and needs in Japan" that Totten cites as an important influence on the emulation processes of the mid-1880s were more profoundly shaped by the institutional development of the 1870s than by the "traditional" legacy of the previous regime. And in the early 1870s, Meiji organization-builders were preoccupied not with fitting organizational models to the "conditions and needs of Japan" but with using organizational models to transform those conditions. Much has been written about "late developer effects" on Japan's modernization, but Japan was later in developing certain institutions than others, and the variations across those institutions can be important in illuminating the processes of social and organizational change. Some of the key differences between the organizational emulation of the 1870s and that of the 1880s can be seen in the development of the three great communications technologies of the nineteenth century:

the postal system, the telegraph, and the telephone.

Selecting a Model

Great Britain was the world leader in developing both the telegraph[5] and the postal system, and it was Great Britain that provided the model for both Japanese systems. The adoption of the British model, however, differed considerably from the careful selection processes of the 1880s described by George Oakley Totten.

Telegraph equipment was first introduced into Japan by Commodore Perry, who presented a telegraph set to the Shogunate as part of his effort to impress the Japanese with the technological superiority of the West.[6] It remained something of a plaything for more than a decade: Satsuma's Shimazu Nariakira, for example, had a telegraph line strung between his castle's central keep (*honmaru*) and his tea house as early as 1856. The Shogunate made the first effort to build a telegraph system, when in 1867 it granted permission to a French entrepreneur to set up a telegraph in Japan.[7] The fall of the Shogunate nipped this effort in the bud: the new regime repudiated the telegraph contract, although it took delivery of a considerable amount of telegraph equipment that the Shogunate had ordered and used it in its own development of a telegraph system.

The Meiji system was begun in 1869. Terajima Munenori, an official in the administration of Kanagawa prefecture who had been involved in Shimazu's early experiments with the telegraph, was entrusted with the construction of a telegraph line, first within Yokohama, and then linking Yokohama and Tokyo. He asked the British foreign adviser who was working with him on building the system of navigation facilities and lighthouses, William Brunton, to recommend advisers for the construction of the telegraph system. Brunton of course recommended British engineers, who brought to Japan not only the physical technology of the telegraph but also the organizational system that supported it: they had the operators' manuals of the British system translated into Japanese to guide the operation of the system.[8] Once the British were ensconced as advisers, their role continued: the Telegraph Bureau employed fifty-nine foreign advisers between 1869 and 1878, fifty-four of them British. They served in all aspects of the telegraph system, from construction supervisors to telegraph operators.[9]

The adoption of the British model of the postal system was no more the product of careful consideration of alternatives than it was in the telegraph. In 1870, Maejima Hisoka, whose department, the Bureau of Posts, had inherited the old system of relays of runners and horses from the Shogunate, persuaded the government to experiment along the coastal *Tokaido* highway with a "Western-style" post. It was

"Western-style" in that it used postage stamps, set rates (although the cost varied by distance instead of using the "flat rate" of the penny post), and was accessible to everyone (in contrast to the dual system of the official posts and the commercial messengers' guilds of the Edo period), but it did not have a monopoly even on the one main route it served. No sooner had the system been set up, however, than Maejima was sent to England to try to negotiate a railway loan, a task for which he was chosen by virtue of his background in English language study. While in England, he took as much time as he could--unofficially--to investigate the workings of the British General Post Office: copying regulations, visiting postal stations, opening a postal savings account, and even buying a large photograph of Sir Rowland Hill.[10] On his return, he vigorously pushed for a national post on the British model. His observation of the British postal system provided not only the inspiration for the general structure and functions of the post, but the materials on which the procedures and rules of the new system were based.[11]

The adoption of an organizational system for the telephone took much more time, and involved a much more systematic search for information before a commitment to a particular system was made. The first step identified in Totten's model, "to understand [foreign models] in general terms," was taken in 1883. The head of the Telegraph Bureau, Ishii Tadaakira, returned from a trip to Shanghai much impressed with the development of that city's telephone system, and concerned that Japan was falling behind in the development of this new communications technology. Based on information he gathered there and on other materials assembled in Tokyo, Ishii prepared a document for the Council of State urging the development of a telephone system in Japan and outlining the three possible strategies of development: a state-owned system (like that of Germany); a mixed system where entrepreneurs built and operated some exchanges and the government assumed responsibility for areas where private initiatives were inadequate (like that adopted in France in 1882); and a private enterprise system (like that of the United States).[12] The decision in 1890 to adopt a system of state ownership based very much on the German model was preceded by no fewer than four study trips to Europe and the United States, one paid for by a group of Tokyo businessmen with aspirations of developing the telephone system themselves.[13] In addition to the various reports from these on-site investigations, the Ministry of Communications used the materials accumulating in Tokyo to produce in 1886 a two-volume report on the telephone systems of Europe and the United States.[14]

The contrast between the hasty, almost accidental resort to the British model in the post and the telegraph and the lengthy and deliberate accumulation of information in the case of the telephone system raises two sets of questions: what were in the similarities and differences in what was driving the search and selection processes in the three cases? and once the commitment to the model was made, what departures from it proved necessary to adapt it to its new environment?

The Search for a Model
The key factor behind the resort to the British model in the post and the telegraph was access to information. Compared to other industrializing nations of the nineteenth century, Japan in the early Meiji period faced formidable problems in obtaining detailed information about organizational models. Neither the contiguity of European countries, which allowed relatively easy passage of information and personnel, nor the waves of immigration which carried information and skills across the oceans to the United States and the British dominions provided Japan with access to organizational information. In the early 1870s, Japan confronted not only the geographical separation from the centers of organizational development but also a formidable language barrier: among the industrializing nations of the nineteenth century, Japan alone possessed a non-Indo-European language. Information was therefore a key factor in the emulation of Western organizational forms during the first and most far-ranging period of such emulation, the 1870s, and it was recognized as such by Japanese leaders. They put enormous effort and considerable financial resources into obtaining information, by hiring foreign advisers in a wide range of roles; by sending students abroad; by dispatching upper and middle level officials on observation missions abroad; and by bringing in published materials and organizational regulations and descriptions. But information continued to be one of the most problematic resources, especially in the first decade of the Meiji period.

The selection of models tended therefore to be a cumulative process: that is, the selection of a model from one society increased the likelihood that the same society would serve as a source for further models, especially in related areas. Language was a key factor in this: Western language facility was a rare commodity in Japan during the first decade of the Meiji period. It was not Maejima's interest in the postal system that provided him with the opportunity to study the British system, but his language training, which made him a valuable aid in the loan negotiations. Moreover, the selection of one model opened channels of communication with officials in the foreign country and provided networks of personal contact which facilitated the utilization of that country's institutions as models in other fields, especially related fields--as the contact with Brunton in the lighthouse system opened a channel for hiring British engineers for the telegraph system.

Over time, Japan's stock of people who were educated in the language, technology, and culture of the Western nations expanded, and communications linkages with the major western powers routinized and deepened. By the mid-1880s, Japanese resources for gathering information on and assessing various telephone systems were considerable. The Telegraph Bureau had been training engineers and administrators since 1869, employing British instructors for the early years. This school, the Kobu Daigakko, also with a complement of British instructors, had by 1885 (when it was absorbed into Tokyo Imperial University) enrolled 478 students and graduated 211 engineers, all of whom had significant foreign language training as well as a technical education.[15] There was a network of Japanese students in most countries of Europe and in the United States. Indeed, a Japanese student was enrolled in Alexander Graham Bell's speech classes in Boston, and early in 1877 he brought some of his Japanese friends to Bell's laboratory to find out whether the telephone could speak Japanese.[16] Finally, Japan's extensive, multi-level international contacts in communications-related areas further eased the information-gathering process: two of the four study missions mentioned earlier were coupled with attendance at international communications gatherings, that of the Vice-Minister of Communications at an international Postal Conference, and that of a senior engineer at an international exhibition of communications equipment.

Yet despite the wider accessibility of information, the Japanese were slower to adopt an organizational system for the telephone than they had been for either the telegraph or the post. The lag cannot be attributed to a lack of demand: as the delay in developing a system continued, those who recognized the potential of the telephone went ahead and built their own lines. In 1885, there were 350 kilometers of telephone lines built and operated by the Home Ministry for the use of the police; 230 kilometers built by the railways; and 39 kilometers used by private companies, for a total of 624 kilometers. By 1888, this had tripled, to 1,850.[17] In 1887, the Ministry of Communications constructed Japan's first long-distance line, between Tokyo and Atami; it was used for government business.[18] And private entrepreneurs recognized the demand: several petitions had been submitted to the government for a license to set up telephone companies.

How, then, can one explain the delay? Did the very availability of information and the wider range of perceived alternatives itself slow the process? The answer would seem to be no. Had the Vice-Minister of the Communications Ministry and the head of the Telegraph Bureau enjoyed in the mid-1880s the same level of autonomy that Maejima Hisoka had in the early 1870s, a German-modeled state telephone system would in all probability have been adopted in 1886 instead of 1890. Late in 1885, Vice-Minister Nomura had returned from a visit to Germany a strong advocate of a state telephone system administered through the same government Ministry that supervised posts and telegraphs. The head of the Telegraph Bureau, Ishii Tadaakira returned early in 1886 from a trip to Europe with a similar, though less strongly expressed, inclination. And had the Council of State (and later the Cabinet, including the Minister of Communications) been able to enforce its will in communications policy over the resistance of the Communications Ministry bureaucracy, a privately-owned system would have been opened in the mid-1880s.[19] The problem was therefore demonstrably not uncertainty caused by too wide a range of perceived choice, but an increasingly complex decision-making environment, in which a wider number and range of actors influenced the selection process than was the case in the early 1870s. This in turn was complicated by the fact that the object of the selection process was a system that was relatively new and still in flux in most of the Western countries that were potential providers of models.

One factor which complicated the decision-making environment was a lower level of perceived urgency in adopting new organizational systems. The organizational emulation of early Meiji was driven by two major concerns: national security, both external and internal, and the elimination of the various institutional symbols of Japanese inferiority to the West embodied most gallingly in the unequal treaties. The case for the early and rapid development of the telegraph and the post involved both factors. The role of rapid and accurate communications in coordinating and controlling the administration of the country and providing rapid warning of unrest among the citizenry or unreliability on the part of local officials was clearly recognized by the Meiji government.[20] The early adoption of the telegraph system was driven in part by this perception, and in part by the threat of foreign control of a key part of the Japanese communications system. By the late 1860s, with the completion of the overland Britain-India telegraph link (1865), the laying of the first successful trans-Atlantic cable (1866), and the completion of the trans-Siberian line to Vladivostok (1867), the global telegraph network was virtually complete. Japan remained the last link in the chain. In 1870, Denmark's Great Northern Telegraph Company applied to the Japanese government for permission to construct an undersea telegraph cable between Nagasaki and Yokohama, and under considerable pressure from the foreign embassies in Tokyo, the government acceded.[21] When one of the government's foreign policy advisers, Du Bousquet, examined the signed agreement, however, he pointed out that its assignment of all the profits from the line to the Company was unfair to Japan, and he agreed with the reservations of several members of the government that it was hardly desirable to have a key trunk line in the hands of a foreign company. The Japanese government therefore made the construction of an overland Nagasaki-Yokohama line a major priority, in order to pre-empt the Danish firm, and accelerated their hiring of British telegraph experts in every aspect of the system, from construction of the line to operations and training.[22] The rapid building of the system was of greater importance than the careful consideration of organizational alternatives.

The sense of urgency that characterized the government's approach to the telegraph did not extend to the post. The rapid adoption of the British model was largely the result of Maejima's own determination, although his arguments that a modern post was both a critical element in building the order and prosperity of the nation and a potential source of revenue won him the tolerance of the government leaders for his efforts, if not their enthusiastic support. But nationalism also reinforced his case: the post was one of the many cases in which the foreign powers exercised their privileges of extraterritoriality. Great Britain, France, and the United States each opened post offices in the treaty ports in the late Tokugawa period. These processed mail between Japan and their respective home countries, and delivered mail within the treaty ports, using their own stamps and postal regulations. Moreover, when the Japanese postal service began in 1870, any mail destined for overseas had to use the stamps of the country to which it was sent, in the absence of postal treaties with other countries. Maejima's strenuous efforts to win international recognition for the Japanese post began as early as 1873, when he sent Samuel M. Bryan to negotiate Japan's first postal treaty with the United States, and culminated with Japan's entry in 1877 into the Universal Postal Union.[23] These early successes did much to establish the credibility of the postal system with the central government and indeed with the populace at large.

The government priorities of the early 1870s--national security and the restoration of full sovereignty to Japan through the elimination of all aspects of extraterritoriality--were still important policy drivers in the mid-1880s. However, it was not clear that the telephone system had any contribution to make to either. Indeed the role of the telephone in society was a matter of considerable debate in the West during the 1880s. In the United States, it was seen as providing a means of rapid urban communication--a replacement for city messenger services. In Germany, it was seized upon by the state telegraph authorities as a medium that, because it required a much lower level of skill to operate, could substitute for the telegraph in linking small rural communities with the national communications system. In several societies, there were experiments that used the telephone as an entertainment and communications medium, transmitting music and news--a role that would be played with much more success in the twentieth century by radio and television.[24] As the rapid development of the technology of the long-distance telephone made it a potential competitor to the telegraph, those societies like Japan where the telegraph was a state monopoly faced a serious dilemma: what, if any, advantages of the telephone over the telegraph justified the enormous investment involved in developing a new system to replace one that seemed to be working quite satisfactorily.

While communications historians have concurred with nineteenth century observers in blaming governments' desires to protect their state-owned telegraphs for the relatively slow development of the telephone system in Europe, in fact telegraph officials were frequently among those who supported telephone development most strongly. The most serious--and effective--resistance in most countries, particularly Great Britain and France, came from state financial officials, who opposed the investment in telephone systems as a burden on the treasury.[25] Japan followed the European pattern: while the Telegraph Bureau was a vocal advocate of telephone development, the Finance Ministry throughout the 1880s opposed any financial outlay by the government on a telephone system.[26]

In the early 1870s, by contrast, the rudimentary state of budgeting and financial controls had meant a high level of autonomy for organization-builders like Maejima Hisoka, an autonomy that was hard on government finances but a boon to organizational development. By the mid-1880s, however, the budgeting process had increased in sophistication and influence, and the Finance Ministry was formally consulted on each of the proposals for a telephone system. Its refusal to budget the necessary expenditures prolonged the period in which information on various systems was gathered, proposals were generated, and individual organizations took the initiative into their own hands and built small-scale private systems.

In France and England, the finance-driven solution took the form of the state's granting to private telephone companies the right to build a telephone system, on condition that they paid a proportion of their profits to the state and that at the end of a fixed time, the telephone lines and equipment would become the property of the government. This solution had the natural effect of focusing the efforts of the companies on the largest cities, where they could charge very high rates and develop a volume of business that would quickly repay their investment and provide substantial and immediate profits. The resulting high cost and restricted service brought increasing criticism in both countries. In Japan, the Telegraph Bureau proposed a reverse compromise, modeled not on the French or British pattern but on Japan's own experience with infant industries in the 1870s: the government would build the system, and then sell it to private enterprises.[27] Not surprisingly, the idea was vetoed by the Finance Ministry.

The resistance of the Finance Ministry to an investment in a state-owned telephone system was abated somewhat by the financial recovery of the late 1880s, and also by growing convergence in the European patterns. In contrast to the telegraph, which by the time it was adopted in Japan had been solidly established throughout Europe as a state system, there was enormous variation during the 1880s in telephone system ownership patterns. Only in Germany and Switzerland did the state undertake from the first to develop the telephone system directly; elsewhere it was undertaken by private companies that were closely regulated by the state. By the late 1880s, however, there was growing evidence in Great Britain and France, two countries which Japan monitored closely, that reliance on private entrepreneurship was not working well. France moved to nationalize the telephone system in 1889, against such determined opposition from company owners that the state was compelled to use force.[28] In Great Britain, as Colin Cherry has noted, "between 1885 and 1887 a mounting tide of public opinion called for the nationalization of the telephone under the aegis of the Post Office,"[29] and several proposals for nationalization were put forward, all vetoed by the Treasury on the grounds of their cost. But even in Britain, it was becoming clear that eventual state ownership was inevitable; the main issue in dispute was the timing.[30] One of the arguments for nationalization in both France and Great Britain was that they were falling behind Germany in the development of a communications medium whose importance for commerce and the modern business enterprise was becoming increasingly obvious.[31] Just as France and Great Britain worried about falling behind Germany and the United States in the application of the telephone, so Japan began to worry about falling behind the West. One more source of pressure towards a state system was generated by the growing use of the telephone by the police, who had proceeded to build their own lines. This created an important constituency within the government whose opposition to private ownership of the telephone system grew as their use of the technology expanded: the police were reluctant to trust the confidentiality or the priorities of private entrepreneurs.

In 1890, therefore, the telephone system joined the telegraph and the post in the state-managed communications system of Japan.

Adapting the Model

When organizational forms are transferred from one society to another, change and innovation are virtually inevitable, however strong the aspirations to reproduce the original as faithfully as possible. Imperfect information about the model, changes to adjust to a context where the resources and the surrounding organizations differ from those in which the original model developed, the bringing into the new organization of people whose previous experience has involved different patterns, the opportunity to "leapfrog" the model and adopt immediately changes that are still being resisted in the original[32]--all these will produce departures from the original model. Over time, the new organization may become more like its original model, either because many of the initial adaptations are regarded as temporary concessions to an "underdeveloped" environment, or because the new organization anticipates changes that later occur in the original organization. On the other hand, the initial adaptations to the very different social context may set the organization on a pattern of development that diverges substantially from that of the original.

We would expect to see more departures from the model in the postal system than in either the telegraph or the telephone systems, for several reasons. Both the telegraph system, which employed more than fifty British experts in its first decade, and the telephone system, whose adoption was preceded by extensive investigation of foreign systems, would seem to have left less room for initial departures from the model because of inadequate information. Moreover, although the telegraph and the telephone systems were centered on more complex physical technologies, the postal system entailed a much larger and more complex organizational system and depended on a more extensive set of external supporting structures, especially in terms of transport. Finally, both the telegraph and the telephone involved radically new technologies and organizations; the postal system built, in its earliest years, on an existing network of posts that differed substantially from the infrastructure of the modern post.

Surprisingly enough, even in the postal system there were remarkably few departures from the model that can be attributed to imperfect information. In part this is due to the difficulty of tracing such departures in a historical context. They are most likely to occur in the lower reaches of the organization, since information-gathering is directed by those at the top of the new organization and is therefore focused on upper level tasks. However, it is the activities at the lower levels of the organization that are least likely to be documented for posterity. More important is the fact that the postal system was heavily bureaucratized and rule-bound. In order to standardize services throughout Britain, the General Post Office had drawn up extremely detailed regulations routinizing virtually all aspects of the postal system. Maejima, by bringing back and translating these regulations, could provide fairly complete information on the workings of the British model.

Turning information into reality, however, was far from easy. When Sir Rowland Hill introduced the changes that created the modern postal service in Great Britain, he could build on a national postal system that was already handling over a million pieces of mail a year and that was supported by a network of railways that could move large volumes of mail rapidly and cheaply. When Maejima returned to Japan determined to develop a national post on the British model, he had as a base only a single government-operated postal route (along the Tokaido) that competed for business with messengers' guilds (*ton'ya*) and, in the absence of railways, used a combination of runners and carriages. Indeed, it was not until the 1890s that Japan had as many kilometers of railway as Great Britain had at the time of the introduction of the modern postal system in 1840.

Maejima's initial challenge was therefore to obtain the monopoly necessary to the modern post and to build mail volume. The British model provided a way of overcoming resistance to the first: mail delivery was subcontracted to private transport companies off the main postal routes. Maejima aggressively encouraged the ton'ya to become transport companies by publishing detailed guidelines for the formation and organization of companies (*kaisha*), and postal officials encouraged the creation of networks and amalgamations among companies to produce firms with the necessary geographic and organizational scope. In consequence the postal system became an important influence on the development of the land transport industry in early Meiji.[33] Another departure from the model was in rates: for the first decade, the volume of mail remained too low for the British single-rate system to be economically feasible, so rates were based on a system of regional categories until 1883.[34]

The challenge of building the postal business would seem to have been formidable enough, but Maejima was also eager to introduce all aspects of the activities of the British model, including money orders, postal savings, and life insurance. Despite some initial resistance from the Finance Ministry, which doubted that postal employees could be trusted to handle money transactions, Maejima introduced both money orders and postal savings in 1875, following in virtually every detail the British regulations and routines--with the exception that the local post offices at first relied on the local tax offices to supply the necessary currency. The slow development of the banking system made both services of especial importance during the first two decades of the Meiji period. Maejima's 1875 proposal to begin postal life insurance, however, was opposed by his own ministry on the grounds that there was neither the popular demand nor the financial and administrative capacity in the postal system to support it. It was not until 1916 that postal insurance was finally introduced.[35]

All these departures from the British model were--and were seen as--temporary concessions to the less developed Japanese environment. On all these features, the Japanese system moved closer to its model over time, as the organizational capacity of the system expanded and as the environment became more like that of Britain. Indeed the postal officials actively pushed changes in the environment as well as in their own organization. The active role in the formation of transport companies is only one example. Unlike its British model, which disdained advertising as beneath its dignity, the Japanese postal system used a variety of techniques to bring its services to the attention of the public, from advertising in newspapers and handbills to the use of large postal flags on all its equipment and buildings. But they continued to expand their base of information not only on the British system, but on Western postal systems generally. From early 1873 until 1881, the Postal Bureau maintained a Translation Section (*Hon'yaku-ka*) to collect and translate materials from foreign postal systems.

A small number of departures from the British model were not viewed as temporary, but as adjustments to aspects of the environment that were not "less-developed" but different. One such change was the addition of another administrative layer to the control system of the post. In the British postal system, the central General Post Office governed directly the activities of post offices in all categories throughout the country. In Japan, with its greater distances and less rapid communications, it was necessary to create an intermediate level to act as the control surrogate for the center. However, because the British system did not provide a model for this kind of structure, the Meiji period witnessed a series of changes and adjustments in the postal administrative structures too complex and numerous to detail here.[36]

There were also departures that were introduced to maintain traditional patterns. One was the use of the "free post." In Great Britain, members of Parliament could use the postal system free of charge for official correspondence. In Japan, Maejima first used the free post in reverse: to allow citizens to send petitions to the government without charge, a system which lasted until 1882. A second change was the decision not to employ women in the postal system. In Great Britain, the local postmistress was a familiar figure. In Japan, however, it was not seen as appropriate to confer this status on women. Not until the introduction of the telephone system in 1890, in which women were hired as operators on the Western model, did women enter the communications system. Once the precedent was set, resistance to their further employment weakened, and women employees were introduced into both the telegraph and the postal savings systems in 1900.[37] Finally, when the rules were being drawn up for the adoption of the postal savings system, Justice Ministry officials protested that allowing anyone, regardless of age or sex, to open a postal account would undermine the control of the household head over the family's resources, and they insisted that the permission of the household head be required for anyone opening a postal account. In all three of these cases, although the departures were not viewed as temporary at the time they were made, they proved to be so.

One major departure from the model was beyond the control of the postal system: its linkage into the administrative structures of the state. While Maejima could adopt the British system internally and could encourage the development of the structures in the environment that were needed to support the post, he could not shape the overall administrative structures of the state, which were modeled not on those of Great Britain but on those of France. In contrast to the status of the General Post Office in Great Britain, where it was an independent department whose top official, the Postmaster-General, was a member of the Cabinet, in France the postal system was supervised by a bureau within the Interior Ministry. The Japanese system followed the French pattern rather than the British until 1885, when a new Ministry of Communications was created that merged the telegraph and the post and incorporated other communication and transport activities under a single authority. One consequence of the earlier system was that during its first decade and a half the Post Office, instead of offering a permanent career ladder, lost many of its most able senior administrators to other departments of the ministry of which it was a part.

Another departure that was beyond the control of the postal officials was the separation from the telegraph. In Britain, the telegraphs were taken over by the Post Office in 1870. In Japan, in part because of the hastiness of the adoption of the British model and the focus on the internal workings of the system rather than its linkage into the government, the telegraphs developed independently of the postal system until 1885, although both were state systems. The telegraphs remained under the Ministry of Industry; the postal bureau migrated around among several ministries (Finance, Home, Agriculture and Commerce). The separation made for the relatively slow development of the synergies between the two systems, synergies that were being cultivated in Great Britain and in Europe.

The departures from the British model in the postal system fall into three general categories: adaptations to maintain highly valued traditional patterns (such as the use of the free post for petitions); adjustments to different geographic or social scale (such as the addition of an intermediate administrative layer); and adaptations to a different social context. Departures in this third category were clearly the most numerous. Especially important were the adjustments made because of the absence of external organizations that in the original model provide important inputs to the organization and those that disseminate or consume the products or services. Those adjustments took three forms:

1. The organization turned to another type of structure or organization that already existed within its environment to serve as a functional equivalent (for example, in the absence of the railways and the transport companies that provided the infrastructure of the British post, the Japanese system turned to the traditional mode of using relays of runners as carriers for the first long-distance postal routes).
2. The organization eliminated that particular activity (for example, the elimination of insurance from the portfolio of post office activities).
3. The organization undertook to act as what Arthur Stinchcombe has called "an organization-creating organization," and mobilized resources to establish new organizations to perform the required activities (the best example being the fostering of transport companies).

The telegraph is a case which provides an example of a fourth strategy:

4. The organization can be adapted to internalize the performance of a task or set of tasks performed outside the organization in the original setting.

The two most critical inputs for the telegraph system were equipment and technical experts, and for both, the telegraph system developed its own internal structures for providing the resources it needed. The telegraph began by importing its equipment, but it quickly sought domestic alternatives. The first move was to adopt the "organization-creation" alternative: in 1873, it invited a seventy-five year-old craftsman, Tanaka Kucho, who had long had an interest in Western technology to set up a factory in Tokyo to manufacture transmitting equipment. The factory was owned by Tanaka, but the telegraph system was the adviser and major customer. In 1878, however, the government purchased the manufacturing equipment from Tanaka's factory, whose capacity and technology had not kept pace with the evolving needs of the system, and set up its own manufacturing center. Tanaka turned to the production of general machinery, and his firm evolved into the forerunner of today's electrical equipment giant, Toshiba.[38] The direct government involvement in equipment manufacture was a departure from the British model, which had facilities for repairing equipment but only a very limited capacity for original manufacture.

For personnel as well, the telegraph system took the initiative in filling its own needs: in 1869, telegraph officials set up a training institute, and even when the College of Engineering was established in 1873, with specialty courses in telegraphy and electrical engineering, the telegraph system maintained its own training facilities, with both technical and administrative courses of instruction. When the post and telegraph facilities were amalgamated in 1885, the telegraph provided a model for the postal system, and the training institute, renamed in 1890 the Tokyo Postal and Telegraph School (Tokyo Yubin Denshin Gakko), incorporated courses in postal as well as telegraph administration. Again, these activities had no direct counterpart in Britain; instead, they followed a pattern common in other Meiji organizational systems for rapidly developing the cadre of skilled personnel needed to operate the new systems. And in the application of the telegraph model of formal training to the post, the Japanese communications system presented an advance over its British model.

By the time the telephone system was set up in 1890, both the knowledge base within Japan's technical community and the general social and administrative context into which it was introduced were very similar to those in the European countries that provided the model for the system. The extended investigation of the alternatives and the increasing study of telephony in the engineering school at Tokyo Imperial University meant that in terms of personnel, the government could find enough experts within its own Ministry of Communications and its recent recruits to staff the new system. It continued to send a number of students abroad to study telephony, and in 1900 a formal structure for selecting and supporting such students was introduced.[39] Equipment manufacture had begun in Japan even before the system was formally adopted: over 300 telephone receivers were manufactured in Japan within the Ministry of Communications, many for its own use, and by 1891 this had reached 926, at a time when there were barely 1,000 subscribers to the public system.[40] In contrast to the telegraph system, however, the telephone system was able to turn very quickly to private industry to meet its equipment needs. Japanese entrepreneurs sought out technical linkages with the leading Western firms, and two reached formal agreements with key Western suppliers (Oki Electric with Siemens, and Nippon Electric with Western Electric).[41] As in several European countries, including Germany, close linkages developed between the private firms that supplied equipment and the technical arm of the telephone system that tested and repaired that equipment. Therefore even in the technical aspects of telephone development, where the system placed the greatest demands on its external environment, the telephone system required fewer major adjustments to the organizational model derived from Europe.

In one further respect the Japanese environment for the adoption of the telephone more closely resembled the Western environment than had the society of the early 1870s: the willingness to accept women into the government communications system. In the early postal regulations, the British practice of subcontracting the operation of local post offices to women was deliberately avoided, on the grounds that employing women would lower the status of the post. By 1890, however, the Western practice of employing young women as telephone operators encountered very little resistance in Japan. Women had been recognized as obedient and comparatively cheap labor in certain industries, such as textiles, and the government systems were too strongly entrenched to have their legitimacy threatened by the admission of female employees. Once admitted to the ranks of government workers in the telephone system, women employees were admitted to the telegraph and postal savings offices (in 1900).[42]

Although one could make the case that the accumulation of detail on foreign telephone systems that took place in the 1880s did not, after all, have a major impact on the selection process, it certainly eased the tasks of organization-building once the model had been selected. So did the fact that unlike the post and the telegraph, the telephone was adopted into an existing national communications system that after two decades of development and of close monitoring of Western developments closely resembled that of the major western societies--whose own systems, it should be noted, had developed through close interaction and extensive cross-societal emulation.

The similarities of the development of the Japanese telephone system with those in Europe extended to its major organizational problem: the reluctance of the government to invest substantial amounts in extending the system and pressure from the state treasury not only to cover its own costs, but to make a profit and contribute to state finances. As a result, rates remained high, and in Japan as in Europe (and in contrast to the United States), the telephone through the first decade and a half of the twentieth century remained primarily an instrument of official and business communication.

Conclusion

The foregoing discussion has focused on the relationship between the emerging organizations of the communications systems of Meiji Japan and their western organizational models. Of course this is only part of the story of their development, but it is an important and often neglected part. By the end of the Meiji period, Japanese themselves were engaged in downplaying the importance of their country's emulation of specific organizations.[43] In large part this was a justifiable reaction against the assertions by many foreigners, both those who had been employed in building the new systems and those who had merely observed their similarities to their Western counterparts, that Japan was a nation of copiers that owed its institutions to Western organization-builders. The assertion of Hugh Byas in 1942 that

> Englishmen organized the navy. Americans created a modern educational system. A Frenchman codified Japanese law. Germans directed the whole of the higher medical education. An Englishman reformed the mint and gave Japan a uniform currency. Posts, telegraphs, the army, the land survey, sanitary reform, prison reform, cotton and paper mills, improved mining methods, harbor works, modern shipping and navigation--all were the creation of foreign advisers.[44]

is far from being an isolated example of an attribution of Japanese "success" to the benevolence of Western teachers and a facility for copying. Even today, there are many who argue that Japan's modern success is "made in America"--built on the teaching of Western quality control experts and the insights of American management.[45] Such assertions downplay the role of Japanese organization-builders in the emulation processes and ignore the changes made in foreign models as the patterns took root in Japan. A focus on where a particular set of organizational patterns came from may gratify Western sensibilities, but it obscures two important factors. One is the complexity of the selection process--in which Western pressures that had very little to do with any form of "benevolence" played a major role. The other is the generalizability of the adaptation processes, which can illuminate processes that are common to organization-building in all societies, and provide the basis for more general frameworks with which to approach the role of institutional and organizational development in the study of social change.

NOTES

1. See for example the chapter on the origins of the Japanese industrial relations system in Ronald Dore, *British Factory Japanese Factory: The Origins of National Diversity in Industrial Relations* (Berkeley, 1973), and the ensuing debate between Dore and Robert Cole over the nature of "late development" or "period effects": Robert Cole, "The Late-Developer Hypothesis: An Evaluation of its Relevance for Japanese Employment Practices," *Journal of Japanese Studies*, vol. 4, no. 2 (1983); and Ronald Dore, "More about Late Development," *Journal of Japanese Studies*, vol. 5, no. 1 (1984). See also vol. 15, no. 4 (December 1977) of *Developing Economies*, devoted to "The Adaptation and Transformation of Western Institutions in Meiji Japan."
2. George Oakley Totten III, "Adoption of the Prussian Model for Municipal Government in Meiji Japan: Principles and Compromises," *Developing Economies*, vol. 4 (December 1977), p. 487.
3. William Foote Whyte's description captures this interpretation very succinctly: "Japanese imitation was really highly selective. Japanese change agents examined models from various more 'advanced' countries and selected in terms of their judgment of what would best fit into Japan." From "Imitation and Innovation: Reflections on the Institutional Development of Peru," *Administrative Science Quarterly*, vol. 13 (1968), pp. 372-3.
4. See Conrad Totman, *The Collapse of the Tokugawa Bakufu 1862-1868* (Honolulu, 1980).
5. The first public telegraph line was opened in 1839 between Paddington and West Drayton.
6. Perry set up a telegraph line about a mile in length. He recorded in his diary his astonishment at the curiosity of Japanese officials, their diligence in learning how to use it, and their rapid mastery of the basic skills. Yuseisho, *Yusei hyakunen shi* (Tokyo, 1971), p. 21.
7. Teishinsho, *Teishin jigyo shi, dai-san sho. Denshin* (Tokyo, 1944), p. 79.
8. Takahashi Zenshichi, *Oyatoi gaikokujin. Tsushin* (Tokyo, 1969), pp. 26-31.
9. Yuseisho, *Yusei hyakunen shi*, p. 115.
10. Oda Takeo, *Maejima Hisoka* (Tokyo, 1958), pp. 108-110.
11. D. Eleanor Westney, "The Postal System" in *The Transfer of Social Technologies in Meiji Japan* (Cambridge, 1987).
12. Yuseisho, *Yusei hyakunen shi*, pp. 226-27.
13. In 1885-86, a senior engineer in the Telegraph Bureau took advantage of his attendance at an international exhibition in London to travel to France and Germany to study their telegraph and telephone systems; in 1886 the Vice-Minister of the newly created Teishinsho visited Germany and brought back 230 pages of notes on conversations with German officials, including the head of the German postal and telegraph systems, Ernst Heinrich Stephen; in 1887 Sawai Yasushi, an engineering graduate of Tokyo University, was sent by a group of Tokyo businessmen to the United States and Europe to study their telephone systems and prepare proposals for a private enterprise-based system in Japan; and in 1887, the Teishinsho dispatched an engineer, Oi Saitaro, to Germany for more detailed technical study. Teishinsho, *Teishin jigyo shi, dai-yon sho. Denwa* (Tokyo, 1944), pp. 69-75.
14. Teishinsho, *Denwa*, p. 71.
15. Asakura Haruhiko, *Meiji kansei jiten* (Tokyo, 1969), p. 217.
16. One of those friends was Kaneko Kentaro. Marion May Dilts, *The Telephone in a Changing World* (New York, 1941), pp. 4-5.
17. Yuseisho, *Yusei hyakunen shi*, p. 226.
18. Yuseisho, *Yusei hyakunen shi*, p. 230.
19. Teishinsho, *Denwa*, pp. 68-69.
20. Howard Payne, describing the centralized administration of the Second Empire of Louis Napoleon, asserts that, "The Paris bureaucracy of the Interior would have withered on the vine without speedy and regular communication with the prefects. Technology played an important role." He refers both to the telegraph and "routine

informational and instructional correspondence up and down administrative chains of command from the ministries to the smallest commune" carried by the post. *The Police State of Louis Napoleon Bonaparte* (Seattle, 1966), pp. 38-39.
21. Takahashi, *Oyatoi gaikokujin*, pp. 38-39.
22. Takahashi, *Oyatoi gaikokujin*, pp. 74-75.
23. Great Britain, advised as usual by the choleric Sir Harry Parkes that Japan was not ready for the equality conferred by a postal treaty, refused to ratify such a treaty until after Japan's entry into the Union. Yuseisho, *Yusei hyakunen shi*, p. 123.
24. Asa Briggs, "The Pleasure Telephone: A Chapter in the Prehistory of the Media" in Ithiel Pool, ed., *The Social Impact of the Telephone* (Cambridge, 1977), pp. 40-65.
25. Colin Cherry, "The British Experience," in Pool, *Social Impact*, pp. 77, 84-5; Arthur Holcombe, *Public Ownership of Telephones on the Continent of Europe* (Boston, 1911), pp. 285-88.
26. The Matsukata deflationary policy of the early and mid-1880s involved strenuous efforts to reduce government expenditures, even to the extent of the consideration of a proposal to sell off the telegraphs.
27. Yuseisho, *Yusei hyakunen shi*, pp. 227-28.
28. Holcombe, *Public Ownership*, p. 280.
29. Cherry, "The British Experience," p. 87.
30. A major consideration was that the government would have to assume a much greater financial burden if it nationalized before the Bell patents ran out in the 1890s.
31. Cherry, "The British Experience," p. 80.
32. The best-known example of this in the Meiji period is the adoption by the Japanese army of the General Staff structure, before it was adopted by the Germans from whom the inspiration came; the step had long been advocated by army reformers in Germany but opposed by the military conservatives.
33. Yabuuchi Yoshihiko, *Nihon no yubin sogyo shi - hikyaku kara yubin e* (Tokyo, 1975), pp. 67-70.
34. The system involved three categories of rates: within the urban areas in which the letter was posted; other urban areas; and rural areas outside the system of established routes.
35. Asakura, *Meiji kansei jiten*, p. 639.
36. Details can be found in Westney, *Transfer of Social Technologies*, pp. 100-145.
37. Yuseisho, *Yusei hyakunen shi*, p. 317.
38. Tokyo shibaura denki kabushiki kaisha, *Toshiba hyakunen shi* (Tokyo, 1977), pp. 2-3.
39. Teishinsho, *Denwa*, pp. 93-94.
40. Teishinsho, *Denwa*, p. 411.
41. In the latter case, Western Electric purchased a majority interest in the company, and introduced U.S.-style bookkeeping, billing, and other control systems. Kigyo kenkyu sogo kiko, *Nihon denki* (Tokyo, 1970), pp. 27-29.
42. Yuseisho, *Yusei hyakunen shi*, p. 317.
43. See for example, the accounts of various organizational systems given in Shigenobu Okuma, ed., *Fifty Years of New Japan* (London, 1910).
44. Hugh Byas, *Government by Assassination* (New York, 1942), pp. v-vi.
45. See for example Leonard Nadler, "What Japan Learned from the U.S.--That We Forgot to Remember," *California Management Review*, vol. XXVI, no. 4 (1984), pp. 46-61.

3
MEIJI JAPAN AND THE EDUCATIONAL AND LANGUAGE REFORMS IN LATE CH'ING CHINA

Yue-him Tam

Introduction

China's defeat in the Sino-Japanese War of 1894-95 conclusively convinced the Chinese that China needed fundamental reforms along Western lines within the shortest possible time. Thus, the years from 1895 to 1911 saw a series of reforms in many fields, including government, industry, the military, education and language. Among these, educational and language reforms were particularly fundamental and fruitful, since they were partly intended to cultivate a new kind of citizen to implement nation-building, and they enjoyed greater support by both the liberals and conservatives than the other reforms. Even the failure of the Hundred Days in 1898 and the Boxer Uprising in 1900 did not cause more than a temporary delay in most of these reforms.

Beginning in 1901 the government took steps to transform the old educational system into a general system of public schools on modern lines. A modern school system was established in 1904, the time-honored civil service examination was abolished in 1905, students were sent abroad to study, foreign books were translated, modern newspapers and magazines were published, and the Chinese language and its writing system were reformed to facilitate learning for the masses. For the first time, the importance of educational and language reforms became a national concern.

The forces behind the educational reforms in this particular period came not only from the Chinese themselves, but also from foreigners, particularly the Japanese, who served directly or indirectly as mentors or stimuli in many of the reform projects. China looked to the West for the quickest way to modernize, but it was Japan's example of learning from the West that China chose to imitate. Japanese books were indiscriminately translated into Chinese, and many Japanese teachers went to China to teach. Tens of thousands of Chinese students and military personnel went across the Eastern China Sea to study in Tokyo and returned with secure jobs as civil and military officials and teachers in modern schools. Before the First World War the Japanese who went to China did not seem to have labored under the difficulty which usually plagued the Westerners in China, who were considered by the Chinese as completely alien to the Oriental environment. Also, the relatively fresh experience of the Meiji Japanese in educational and language reforms was treasured by many Chinese as more relevant and practical than learning directly from the West. Ts'ai Yuan-p'ei, the great educator in modern China, for instance, was among the outspoken advocates of the Japan-first school.[1] The most direct outside force promoting educational reforms in late Ch'ing and early Republican China (1895-1918) came from Japan rather than the West.

Meiji Japan's contribution to the educational and language reforms in late Ch'ing China, however, remains largely a neglected subject of scholarly study.[2] It is this aspect of the cultural relationship between Japan and China that this chapter tries to explore.

Educational Reforms and Japan
Meiji Japan had obvious advantages as a model for Chinese reforms. As the renowned scholar-official Chang Chih-tung observed:

> Japan is nearby and inexpensive for travel, so many can go; it is close to China, and students will not forget their country. Japanese writing is similar to Chinese, and it can be translated easily. Moreover Western learning is extremely varied, and the Japanese have already selected its essentials.[3]

Economic reasons and convenience aside, the Meiji synthesis of the old and new, which became apparent in the 1880s as the Japanese restlessly searched for their cultural identity,[4] was treasured as invaluable experience by such Chinese leaders as K'ang Yu-wei and Chang Chih-tung. They hoped to synthesize Chinese and Western ways, and maintained that while Chinese learning should continue as fundamental, Western learning should be taught for pragmatic use. A government report had succinctly summarized the reformers' views of Meiji Japan in 1901:

> Japan is of the same continent with ourselves; her change of methods is quite recent, and she has attained to strength and prosperity. Her experience has been so nearly like our own that we may derive instructions from it.[5]

On the Japanese side, too, as pointed out by Saneto Keishu and Marius B. Jansen, many Japanese leaders had developed a strong sense of an Asian community, which made China and Japan appear natural allies. They had also established personal relations and cultivated mutual trust and co-operation with their Chinese counterparts, including Chang Chih-tung, Liu K'un-i, Yuan Shih-k'ai, and Liang Ch'i-ch'ao.[6]

Among the various educational reforms, the adoption of the Japanese school system in 1904 was the most important. Resulting from the laborious work of the Imperial Educational Commission established in 1903, which consisted of Chang Chih-tung, Chang Po-hsi, and Yung Ching, this set of school laws created a modern school system in China for the first time, outlining in great detail the course of study from kindergarten to the Imperial University.[7]

According to the School Laws of 1904, in the national and provincial capitals there should be universities, in the circuits and provinces middle schools, and in the counties and below primary schools. The whole period of schooling was to be over twenty years. In addition to regular schooling, there were technical schools to provide vocational training in government, agriculture, commerce, industry, and the like. There was also a separate track devoted to teacher training. There was no provision for the education of women, but the five-year course of lower primary school was compulsory for boys aged 7 to 11. Free of tuition fees, the lower primary school was to be financed by local people. The School Laws of 1904 required that in the first five years, a lower primary school had to be established in every community of 400 households, and in the next five to ten years, the number of schools ought to be doubled in that community. Graduates of the national schools received degrees, and became eligible for public offices. Those who graduated from the missionary schools or private, unrecognized political institutions would not be given the same security or job opportunities.

TABLE 1

Chinese and Japanese Education:
Institutional Structure, 1880s

Chinese System	Japanese System
Research Institute 5 years	Post-Graduate School 1 or more years
University 3-4 years	University 3-4 years
Higher School 3 years	Higher School 3 years
Middle School 5 years	Middle School 5 years
Higher Primary 4 years	Higher Primary 2 or more years
Lower Primary 5 years	Ordinary Primary 6 years
Kindergarten	Kindergarten

When this system is compared with the Japanese school system in the 1880s, the similarity is strikingly obvious. As shown in Table 1, with the exception of the research institute and the higher primary school, the two schemes are almost identical. In Japan the higher primary school was an extension for graduates of the ordinary primary school who would not go on to middle school. In China the higher primary school was intended to serve as an intermediate educational stage between the elementary and middle schools, so as to provide a longer period of schooling to teach both the Chinese classics and new subjects. Similarly, to allow time for the study of both the old and the new, the research institute in the Chinese system encompassed a longer time. Other than these, the differences were so few that one would think of the Chinese scheme as no more than a copy of the Japanese system.

The Japanese influence is found not only in the organization of the school system, but also in many details of the curriculum and method of instruction. For instance, like their Japanese peers in the

1880s, Chinese pupils in primary school were required to study ethics (*hsiu-shen*, Japanese *shushin*), in addition to the following basic courses: Chinese Classics, Chinese language, history, geography, arithmetic, natural science, and physical training. And they might be offered drawing, handicraft, and elementary commerce as optional courses. Chinese and Japanese pupils alike now studied arithmetic, geography and natural science, for which the texts were based on translations from American and European sources. At the same time they studied the Confucian classics in the original. They also received physical education and military training. The new schools to be established as a result of the education reform were designed to replace teaching in the teacher's home or the pupils' ancestral clan halls. Classrooms were to be modernized, equipped with blackboards and maps. Pupils were required to wear uniforms in school, and to speak in the national tongue--Mandarin Chinese. As the curriculum was broadened, the school schedule was relatively tight; pupils were required to study 30 hours per week for about 240 school days a year.[8]

The School Laws of 1904 appear to be a synthesis of Motoda Eifu's and Mori Arinori's educational programmes in particular.[9] From Mori, who framed the series of Japanese educational ordinances in 1886, the Chinese Commissioners learned that education was the most important tool in the formation of public attitudes. Like the Japanese, the Chinese system was therefore statist in its orientation. The students were to learn the arts and sciences essential to the well being of the state. Compulsory education was enforced, because the state needed literate and patriotic citizens. School uniforms were required, because they identified the student with his assigned duty of studying for the sake of the state. As Mori had paid particular attention to teachers and teacher training, the Chinese School Laws also recognized teachers as special agents of the state. Along this line, Chinese teachers, previously free of overt control by the state, were now made civil servants. Normal school students were given state scholarships and were committed to teach for at least six years after graduation. In Japan, as Motoda Eifu, Emperor Meiji's Confucian lecturer, had taught, Confucianism continued to enjoy relevance in the modern world, particularly in the educational process. Hence, following the same line of thought, in the new Chinese system, as noted above, ethics was made a required course, military drill was included in the curriculum to strengthen moral education, and public schools were forbidden to teach materials considered dangerous to national peace or injurious to public morals, including Christianity. It is not surprising, therefore, that the "Educational Aims" prepared by the same Commissioners and decreed by the Imperial Court in 1906 strongly emphasized loyalty to the Emperor, reverence for Confucius, dedication to public welfare, and admiration for martial spirit as well as utilitarianism.[10]

To implement this new school system introduced from Japan, the Chinese also followed the Japanese model in establishing a Ministry of Education (*Hsueh Pu*) in 1905 as the central educational agency. In 1906, provincial associations of education (*chiao-yu hui*) were formed as in Japan to supplement local educational administration and to promote public education. In 1908, there was created in each of the municipal districts the Japanese-styled Educational Exhorting Bureau (*Ch'uan-hsueh So*) to promote the new schools. In 1909, a modern system of educational inspection was established, by which the empire was divided into eight inspectional regions as in early Meiji Japan, and in each province there was established the office of the Commission of Education to administer educational programs. The following American observation of the Japanese role in the establishment of educational administration in Ch'ing China is no exaggeration:

> About the time of the establishment of the Ministry of Education the Japanese Ministry of Education provided Japanese professors to give a five-weeks' course of lectures before the Chinese Ministry of Education and the commissioners of education who had been sent to Japan to study the Japanese system of education. Later, in 1906, the commissioners of education who had not been abroad were requested to visit Japan and examine the educational system of that country before beginning their official duties.[11]

Indeed, Japanese influence on China was not limited to establishing a modern educational system. The Japanese did much more. They educated Chinese students both in Tokyo and in mainland China by the thousands. The coming and going of the Japanese teachers and Chinese students between Japan and China, in Marius B. Jansen's words, formed "the first truly large-scale modernization-oriented migration of intellectuals in world history."[12] Many textbooks and teaching materials in the new schools were prepared from those already in use in Japan by returned students and Japanese teachers in China. Such leading publishing houses as the Commercial Press, Wen-ming shu-chu, Kuang-chih shu-chu, and Tso-hsin she were either establishments staffed with Japanese editors and technicians, or joint ventures of Chinese and Japanese.[13] Impressed with the Japanese influence in China, M. Rene Pinon wrote in 1905:

> This new China will be a Japanese China. It is under Japanese influence that all the reforms have been decided upon and accomplished.... In fact, in the normal schools which have just been founded, all foreign teachers are subjects of the Mikado.... It would be needless to dwell upon the enormous influence which cannot fail to result from this educational mission of the Japanese.[14]

And in 1906, Timothy Richard also pinpointed the Japanese influence very emphatically:

> However Pekin [sic] may regard Tokyo, it is plain that throughout the eighteen provinces Japanese influence had made enormous strides. Japanese travellers, commercial agents, teachers and drill-sergeants are to be found in the remotest parts of the Empire.... The best of the native Chinese papers are in Japanese control.... We expect nothing startling from the spread of Japanese influence believing that Japan's true policy is not to force China into a sham similitude of Western civilization or ideals, but to use the accessories of the Occident for the preservation of the fundamentals of Oriental life and polity.[15]

For our purpose, it should be noted that the feverish activity of the Japanese in Ch'ing China, and the Chinese dedication to absorbing and domesticating the ideological and technical features of Japan's modern model, all contributed to the development of education in China. As shown in Table 2, there was considerable expansion in the educational system throughout the country after the turn of the century.[16]

TABLE 2

Growth of Schools in China, 1909-1916

Year	No. of Primary Schools	No. of Students
1909	51,678	1,532,746
1911	86,318	2,793,633
1916	120,103	3,843,455

Year	No. of Middle Schools	No. of Students
1909	438	38,881
1911	832	97,965
1916	932	111,078

Year	No. of Higher Schools	No. of Students
1909	110	20,527
1911	115	40,114
1916	86	17,241

In Hupei province, where Chang Chih-tung, the promoter of Japanese-styled modern education, had served as governor-general for seventeen years from 1890 to 1907, the increase was particularly substantial (see Table 3).[17] Among the 1,504 modern schools in Hupei in 1907, there were 1,438 primary schools, which admitted 50,963 pupils.

In addition to the increase of schools and students, the School Laws of 1904, when fully implemented, also had a considerable impact on the individual student's capacity for learning. Following the Japanese example, the new system had imposed on the student an extremely heavy load. For instance, the School Laws required that the lower primary school pupil study Chinese classics for two hours per day, six days per week. In this particular course alone, the pupil was required to memorize a total of 100,800 words in five years. His learning load in this course was as shown in Table 4; the actual assignment for the pupil in this five-year course was to memorize the complete texts of the *Hsiao ching* (*Book of Filial Piety*, 2,013 words) and the *Four Books* (59,617 words), and a great part of the *Li-chi yueh-p'ien* (*Abridged Version of the Book of Rites*, about 78,000 words).

TABLE 3

Modern Schools in Hupei Province

Year	No. of Schools	No. of Students	
1891	1		240
1901	8	est.	1,000
1904	200		15,000
1907	1,504		56,671
1910	2,000	est.	80,000
1916	9,306		226,626

TABLE 4

Work Load, Lower Primary School, 1904

Year	Words read per day	Words read per year
First	40	9,600
Second	60	14,400
Third	100	24,000
Fourth	100	24,000
Fifth	120	28,000

Citing the Japanese practice of rote learning as supporting evidence, the Commissioners argued that the pupil's learning load in this five-year course was normal:

> In Japanese primary schools there are also reading courses, which require pupils to recite the lessons until they fully memorize them. Those with a slow mind are often retained in school until after sunset. In Japanese military academies, students are taught one to two thousand words in a two hour session of a reading course. The students cannot pass the course unless they can memorize all those words completely. That studying is not memorizing in

foreign countries is simply a false statement.[18]

The school system established in 1904 was repeatedly revised and modified to include elementary education for females, half-day elementary schools for adults, and three or four year schools designed with a simplified curriculum for children from underprivileged families. It should also be remembered that the state system of eduation was not the only means of acquiring an education in late Ch'ing China. Missionary schools and other private schools provided alternative opportunities.

The new school system represents a remarkable start in the development of education in modern China. But the results fell far short of the goals of the educational reformers. The development of elementary education in particular came slowly and not without opposition. The building and staffing of new elementary schools imposed a heavy burden on the villagers. This financial problem, together with the discontent with the new curriculum introduced from Japan, caused the village people to prefer the old style schools, which were to them more practical and economical. These schools seemed to emphasize a more familiar set of values and more pragmatic training according to the actual needs in village life. Su Yun-feng's study shows that the geographical distribution of the new primary schools in Hupei before 1911 was far from balanced; there were fewer schools in the mountainous northwestern regions than the richer eastern areas and the districts along the Yangtze River. And, as may be expected, a large number of the modern schools in Hupei were concentrated in the urban area of Wuchang.[19] The opening of 1,438 modern primary schools in Chang Chih-tung's Hupei in 1907 must be regarded as exceptional. Even then, there was room for only 50,963 pupils in a province of twenty-four million people, representing a school attendance rate of only .2 per cent.

Obviously the Japanized educational reforms did not produce literacy results in China equal to those in Meiji Japan. The reforms, however, developed a momentum that brought larger numbers to concede that literacy was not easy to achieve and that its development depended not only on educational reforms, but also on many other factors, including language reforms.

Chinese Language Reforms and Japan

Meiji Japan also contributed to the language reforms of the late Ch'ing. First, through indiscriminate translations and imitations, Chinese students in Japan introduced a massive infusion of neologisms into the Chinese language.[20] These new terms not only enriched the Chinese vocabulary, but also speeded up the adaptation of colloquial vernacular Chinese (*pai-hua*), in the place of literary Chinese (*wen-yen*), as the standard medium in writing.

Once introduced, these new compounds rapidly gained favor as new terms for ideas, concepts, and objects with which the Chinese were coming into contact for the first time in their quest for modernization. As a study shows, in the fields of politics, economics, and philosophy in particular, the majority of the terms borrowed from English, French, German, and Russian were in time superseded either by new creations in Chinese or by loanwords from Japanese.[21]

In 1958, Kao Ming-k'ai and Liu Cheng-tan identified 459 compounds of Japanese origin which are used in the modern Chinese language.[22] In the same year, Wang Li-ta cited 588 such terms.[23] Later, Saneto Keishu collected 830 Japanese loanwords, which were based on the findings of Kao, Liu, Wang, and other sources.[24] From a search into the publications of late Ch'ing and early Republican times in 1972, I myself added 233 more to the Saneto list, bringing the total to 1,063.[25] Even then, the list is certainly not exhaustive.

In her study of the introduction of socialism into China, Li Yu-ning also identified a total of 426 such terms, which she considered to be "essential in discussions of socialist ideas" in the Chinese context.[26] She classified these terms into three categories according to their origin: First, compounds made of Chinese characters that are found only in pre-modern Japanese and do not appear in classical Chinese; second, classical Chinese expressions first used by Japanese to translate Western terms; and third, terms created by modern Japanese. A few examples are listed in Table 5.[27]

TABLE 5

Modern Chinese Terms of Japanese Origin: Some Examples

A. Compounds made of Chinese characters that are found only in pre-modern Japanese and do not appear in classical Chinese:

Chinese	English	Japanese
ch'ang-ho	"occasion, case"	baai
chih-hsing	"execution, performance"	shikko
chih-p'ei	"management, control"	shihai
shou-hsu	"procedure"	tetsuzuki
yao-su	"element"	yoso

B. Classical Chinese expressions adopted by the Japanese to translate Western terms:

cheng-chih	"politics"	seiji
chi-chi	"active, positive"	sekkyoku
chu-hsi	"chairman"	shuseki
min-chu	"democracy"	minshu
tzu-yu	"liberty, freedom"	jiyu

C. Compounds coined by the Japanese from Western terms:

che-hsueh	"philosophy"	tetsugaku
cheng-fu	"government"	seifu
chin-hua	"evolution"	shinka
jen-sheng kuan	"view of life, philosophy of life"	jinseikan
k'o-hsueh	"science"	kagaku

In addition to the loan-terms, the Chinese also borrowed such Japanese suffixes or stems as *-teki* (Chinese, *-ti*), *-ka* (Chinese, *-hua*), and *-sei* (Chinese, *-hsing*) to coin new compounds denoting quality, substance, and the like. A few Japanese sentence structures were also introduced into colloquial Chinese. For instance, *tui-yu-* ("vis-a-vis") and *kuan-yu-* ("concerning") are said to be derived from *-ni taishite* and *-ni kanshite* in modern Japanese.[28]

These terms have posed many problems to the analytical linguist. Roy A. Miller has confessed that he does not know exactly what to call them:

They are not actually loanwords, since they are not partial or full imitations of foreign forms; they are not loan translations, since they do not really translate their originals, which in Japanese are themselves based on Chinese elements. Perhaps it is best simply to call them Chinese words based on Sino-Japanese originals.[29]

Wang Li also treats them as a special kind of new compounds, not as loanwords, since the principles upon which they are coined are the principles of literary Chinese as understood in both China and Japan. Miller even goes so far as to say:

The Japanese, in coining such neologisms, have in general been more Chinese than the Chinese themselves, and the results are certainly more Chinese than they are Japanese.[30]

The identification of these Japanese loanwords in Chinese, therefore, requires a special effort in examining the translations, writings, textbooks, and dictionaries in which they first occurred.

The aforementioned problems confronting the analytical linguist can be taken as testimony certifying the adaptability as well as popularity of these Japanese contributions to the Chinese language. Their massive infusion in a relatively short period of time had indeed significantly helped the development of *pai-hua*. Many terms of Japanese origin were considered as vernacular (in the sense that they are not literary), and hence criticized as "vulgar," "plain," "misleading," and "unsuitable" for literary writing by supporters of *wen-yen* in late Ch'ing and early Republican China. For instance, Chang Chih-tung, Chang Po-hsi and Yung Ching, the framers of the School Laws of 1904, denounced the "vulgarity" and "unsuitability" of such Japanese terms as *kuo-ti* ("national polity"), *wu-tai* ("stage"), *tai-piao* ("representative"), *she-hui* ("society") and *kuan-nien* ("concept"), and they forbade the use of them in schools.[31] Even revolutionary students in Japan also denounced many of these terms for their obvious "Japaneseness." Chu Chih-hsin, a famous revolutionary writer, had suggested in 1905 that the Japanese term *shihonka* ("capitalist") be replaced with a "pure" Chinese compound *hao-yu*, and *rodosha* ("proletarian") with *hsi-min* so as to include peasants.[32] P'eng Wen-tsu, while studying in Japan in 1915, even published a sizable book, entitled *Mang-jen hsia-ma chih hsin ming-tz'u* (*New Terms Likened to a Blind Man Riding a Blind Horse*), attacking the terms of Japanese origin for having caused unnecessary confusion in the Chinese language.

The proper and skillful use of these loan-terms from Japan, however, proved to be a blessing. Liang Ch'i-ch'ao, the great popularizer of new ideas and renowned writer who had stayed in Japan for over a decade, for instance, often used them in his writing. Liang's prose was commonly admired as "simple and clear," and being able to "carry an intensity of feeling that makes the reader follow him." In fact, Liang advocated colloquial writing and defended the use of these loan-terms as early as 1896, two decades before the vernacular movement took place.[33]

Indeed, the loan-terms were not only instrumental in the development of colloquial writing, but have continued to be pivotal in the Chinese vocabulary of today. An examination of the "Frequency Counts of the Basic Two-Syllabic Compounds in Modern Chinese" published in 1960 in mainland China will confirm this point.[34] In this massive survey of newspaper editorials, middle school textbooks and Mao Tze-tung's writings, covering writings of 1,044,501 words, 28 of the 88 compounds with the highest usage frequency counts (500 and up) are terms of Japanese origin (frequency counts are given in parentheses):

chu-i	(5533)	she-hui	(3307)	sheng-ch'an	(2044)
kung-yueh	(1493)	lao-tung	(1144)	wen-ti	(1124)
kung-ch'an	(1033)	tui-yu	(1009)	fang-men	(1003)
ssu-hsiang	(925)	tou-cheng	(919)	tzu-pen	(861)
min-chu	(806)	yun-tung	(753)	fen-tzu	(738)
nung-min	(727)	min-tsu	(719)	tsu-chih	(709)
tai-piao	(670)	cheng-chih	(638)	chi-hua	(594)
kai-tsao	(563)	cheng-fu	(562)	chi-chi	(536)
chiao-yu	(528)	k'o-hsueh	(500)		

In effect, the survey shows that 31.8% of the most frequently used two-syllabic compounds in contemporary China came from Japan.

On top of their influence on the vernacularization of the Chinese language, the Meiji Japanese also contributed to the other aspects of language reforms in China. They effectively convinced their Chinese contemporaries that the Chinese ideographs, given the complexity of their composition, were indeed a definite handicap in spreading literacy. In 1902, for instance, Izawa Shuji and Tsuchiya Hiroshi, renowned leaders of language reforms in early Meiji Japan, successfully persuaded their visitor, Wu Ju-lun, one of the most respected educators in China at the time, that China had to change the method of teaching Chinese, and that the adoption of the Japanese alphabet, the *kana*, as phonetic symbols in Chinese reading would be most practical. Following the advice of his Japanese friends, Wu petitioned to the authorities for such changes.[35]

Long before the Japanese, in fact, Western missionaries had attempted to use the Roman alphabet to teach Chinese. Yet the love of the ideographic script in China was so strong that the missionaries had little success in educating their Chinese converts in Roman script. However, as early as 1892, Lu Kan-chang had created the first native phonetic system by using semi-Roman symbols for the pronunciation of Chinese in the Fukien dialect. Lu's activities attracted considerable attention among intellectuals, and his method was soon imitated by many reform-minded Chinese. But Lu and his followers failed to achieve practical results owing to nationalistic pride and love for the ideographic script. As late as 1923, the Romanization system designed by the National Language Romanization Research Committee, of which such linguists as Ch'ien Hsien-t'ung, Y. R. Chao and Lin Yu-tang were members, failed to receive government support strong enough to popularize the use of the system.[36]

In contrast to the failure of Romanization, however, the Japanese *kana*-based syllabary designed by Wang Chao in 1900 was an outstanding success.[37] Wang, an exile in Japan after the Hundred Days of 1898, created an alphabetic scheme in which he used 62 *kana*-like symbols to transcribe Chinese ideographs in Mandarin. In his scheme, no more than two symbols were used to represent a syllable. These symbols, which Wang called the "Mandarin Phonetic Alphabet" ("*Kuan-hua ho-sheng tzu-mu*"), were expected to serve, like the Japanese *kana*, as an indication of the pronunciation of characters, but not as a substitute for them. Moreover, Wang and his supporters made it clear that the Japanese *kana* was itself derived from Chinese characters centuries ago. Hence, this device did not hurt Chinese nationalistic pride, nor did it compromise one's love for the ideographic script.

Wang maintained that it took only three to five days, or ten days at most, to learn his alphabet. Mastering this alphabet, one would be able to read alphabetized publications with ease. He asserted that it took only ten days to study the entire alphabetized *Four Books*, the original form of which would take at least two years for a diligent student just to learn to read.[38] It is not surprising that Wang's Mandarin Alphabet attracted a great deal of attention. Such renowned figures as Wu Ju-lun, Lao Nai-hsuan and even Yuan Shih-k'ai were among its most enthusiastic promoters. Wang's scheme was modified and simplified in the Republican era, promulgated by the government in 1918, and included in the curriculum of primary schools in 1920.[39] The system is still in use in Taiwan today. For over three-quarters of a century it has made a considerable contribution to popularizing a national spoken language and spreading literacy.

Other aspects of language reforms since the late Ch'ing, including systematic attempts to simplify and reduce the use of Chinese characters, were also influenced by the Japanese. Suffice it to say that the Japanese played a more important role than one would tend to think in making the Chinese writing system more accessible to the population at large.

Conclusion

The history of the adoption of Japanese ways in educational and language reforms at the turn of the century tells only a small portion of the story of Chinese modernization. It is nevertheless revealing. In many instances Chinese leaders overcame the habits of centuries and were ready to innovate, willing to take risks, and prepared to make compromises and meet challenges. Also, for some time they gained sufficient control over certain areas to be in a position to reward those who accepted the new changes. Hence we see the impressive development of education in Chang Chih-tung's Hupei province. And we also see the Japanese graphic loans and the *kana*-like syllabary absorbed into the Chinese language in modern times with relative ease and success.

But the new systems and the new values borrowed from Japan failed to penetrate all levels of society in China. Particularly, the common folk in the villages, who were made financially responsible for the development of elementary education, seemed to be reluctant to accept the changes as desirable and practical. Therefore the borrowed means and ways from Japan did not produce the same remarkable development by which Meiji Japan was characterized.

In hindsight, one may ask if the borrowed vocabulary was what China really needed during the late Ch'ing. Japan was on the road to becoming a highly centralized industrialized state, while the Chinese state was rapidly disintegrating. The state-building context in which the Japanese vocabulary was constructed embodied the ideal that late Ch'ing intellectuals aspired to, but that China could not achieve in the next few decades. In the Chinese cities, where modern culture and nationalistic feelings dominated, there was much enthusiasm for the new terms. The question remains if in the countryside the new loan-terms could be used by villagers in their daily lives, which were in many respects untouched by modernization. Their needs were perhaps more appropriately served by the older vocabulary. On top of the ever increasing anti-Japanese feelings after the Republic, this phenomenon adds to our difficulty in assessing the function of Japan in the educational and language development of modern China.

NOTES

1. Sun Ch'ang-wei, ed., *Ts'ai Yuan-pei hsiensheng ch'uan-chih* (Taipei, 1967), p. 705.
2. Since the publication of Feng-gang Wang's *Japanese Influence on Educational Reform in China From 1895 to 1911* (Peiping, 1933), there have been no serious studies of the subject.
3. Marius Jansen, *Japan and China: From War to Peace, 1894-1972* (Chicago, 1975), p. 150.
4. Kenneth Pyle, *The New Generation in Meiji Japan: Problems of Cultural Identity, 1885-1895* (Stanford, 1969); Donald Shively, ed., *Tradition and Modernization in Japanese Culture* (Princeton, 1971), pp. 77-119.
5. Quoted in Wang, *Japanese Influence*, p. 70.
6. Saneto Keishu, *Chugokujin Nihon ryugaku shi* (Tokyo, 1960), pp. 207ff.; Jansen, *Japan and China*, pp. 133ff.
7. For details see *Tsou-ting hsueh-tang chang-ch'eng*, collected in Shu Hsin-ch'eng, ed., *Chin-tai Chung-kuo chiao-yu-shi chih-liao*, 3 vols. (Beijing, 1962); Wang, *Japanese Influence*, pp. 68ff.
8. Shu, *Chin-tai Chung-kuo*, vol. 2, p. 419.
9. Donald Shively, "Motoda Eifu: Confucian Lecturer to the Meiji Emperor," in David Nivison and Arthur Wright, eds., *Confucianism in Action* (Stanford, 1959), pp. 302-33; Delmer Brown, *Nationalism in Japan: An Introductory Historical Analysis* (Berkeley, 1955).
10. Shu, *Chin-tai Chung-kuo*, vol. 1, pp. 220ff.
11. U.S. Bureau of Education, *Bulletin*, no. 15 (1911), p. 45; also quoted in Wang, *Japanese Influence*, p. 84.
12. Jansen, *Japan and China*, p. 149.
13. Saneto, *Ryugaku shi*, pp. 299ff.
14. Wang, *Japanese Influence*, p. 107.
15. Wang, *Japanese Influence*, p. 106.
16. Wang Feng-gang, *Chung-kuo chiao-yu shih* (Taipei, 1954). pp. 313-16.
17. Su Yung-feng, *Chang Chih-tung yu Hupei chiao-yu kai-k'o* (Taipei, 1976), p. 231.
18. Shu, *Chin-tai Chung-kuo*, vol. 1, p. 211.
19. Su, *Chang Chih-tung*, p. 213.
20. Saneto, *Ryugaku shi*, pp. 331-408.
21. Zdenka Novotna, "Contributions to the Study of Loan-words and Hybrid Words in Modern Chinese," *Archiv Orientalni*, no. 35 (1967), pp. 631-33.
22. *Hsian-tai Han-yu wai-lai-tz'u yen-chiu* (Beijing, 1958).
23. Wang Li-ta, "Hsian-tai Han-yu chung ts'ung Jih-yu chieh-lai ti tz'u-hui," *Chung-kuo yu-wen*, no. 68 (Beijing, February 1958).
24. Saneto Keishu, *Kindai Nitchu kosho shiwa* (Tokyo, 1973), p. 342.
25. My paper is outlined in Saneto, *Kindai Nitchu*, pp. 335-42.
26. *The Introduction of Socialism into China* (New York, 1971), p. 69.
27. Examples are from Li, *Introduction*, pp. 70-107.
28. Saneto, *Ryugaku shi*, p. 399.
29. *The Japanese Language* (Chicago, 1967), p. 260.
30. Miller, *The Japanese Language*, p. 261.
31. Shu, *Chin-tai Chung-kuo*, vol. 1, p. 205.
32. Li, *Introduction*, p. 31.
33. Philip Huang, *Liang Ch'i-ch'ao and Modern Chinese Liberalism* (Seattle, 1972), p. 6.
34. The counts were taken by Li Min *et al.*, and published in *Wen-tzu kai-k'o*, no. 1 (1960); details quoted in Saneto, *Kindai Nitchu*, pp. 330-32.
35. Wen-tzu kai-k'o chu-pen she, ed., *Ch'ing-mo wen-tzu kai-k'o wen-chih* (Beijing, 1958), pp. 24-29.
36. Chou Yu-kuang, *Han-tzu kai-k'o kai-lun* (Macau, 1978), pp. 26ff.
37. Chou, *Han-tzu*, p. 31.
38. Wang Chao, "Tzu-mu-shu shu" and "Chu tzu-mu-shu ti yuan-ku," in Wen-tzu kai-k'o, ed., *Ch'ing-mo wen-tzu*, pp. 32-33.
39. Chou, *Han-tzu*, pp. 39ff.

4
SHIMAZAKI TOSON'S <u>BEFORE THE DAWN</u>: HISTORICAL FICTION AS HISTORY AND AS LITERATURE

William E. Naff

The relationship between historical fiction and historical scholarship is always a strained one. Few of the admirers of Shimazaki Toson's classic novel *Before the Dawn* are prepared to argue that the work constitutes a perfect resolution of the conflicting standards and conventions of the two genres.[1] Its importance and validity are to be found in the balance that Toson was able to establish between the two.

Questions of genre constitute only one of the many categories of problems that confronted Toson in the writing of this fictional account of the years that followed the coming of Perry. *Before the Dawn* is not simply a work of fiction; it is also a documentation of the experience of the Shimazaki family in the middle years of the nineteenth century. Its long and complex agenda reaches far beyond the purely literary and historical, and Toson was remarkably successful in surmounting the additional risks and challenges created by that agenda. This success gives *Before the Dawn* a significance that is difficult to achieve either in works of conventional historical scholarship or in literary reconstructions of history.[2]

Although Toson never actually said so, it is implicitly clear from the work itself and from what he said in other contexts that he was consciously and deliberately setting out to create a new vision of the Meiji Restoration. He found the then-current received opinion of that time to be spiritually unsatisfying, intellectually untenable, and socially and politically regrettable. Japan in the 1920s was still struggling to free itself from the damaging misapprehension that the country had no usable past of its own and that it was totally dependent on European and American history for guiding precedents. This proposition had first been advanced by foreigners but it soon came to be widely propagated within Meiji Japan. Some people had in one way or another acquired a vested interest in it and others used its negative implications as a rationalization of xenophobia. The new vision which Toson wanted to create had above all else to be a valid product of Japanese experience if it was to counter the pernicious effects of such views. It could not be subservient to the European norms that had both sharpened and beclouded Japan's perceptions of itself in the three-quarters of a century since Perry's arrival nor could it serve either its creator or its readers properly if it merely provoked unthinking reaction against them.[3]

Toson's vision of the nineteenth century was a long time in maturing. He was fifty-seven years old when *Before the Dawn* began to appear in serial publication, and active preparations had already occupied him for more than a decade. One of the columns he wrote from Paris in 1915 for the Tokyo *Asahi* newspaper offers an informative glimpse into his thoughts and the nature of the vision that was already beginning to take shape in his mind:

> ... if only someone in our country would write a study of the nineteenth century! With what pleasure I should read it! We usually divide the century up between the Tokugawa and the Meiji periods but if we try to look at it as a whole it takes on a different meaning. I want to read a study of those times, beginning from around the death of Motoori Norinaga. I want to read of how the studies of the *Manyoshu,* the revival of the spirit of the old poetry, and the loving attention given to our language served as the basis for the sense of national identity that was just beginning to awaken around that time.... If, on the one hand, the scholarship of the Confucian academies displayed an infatuation with things Chinese in literature, in taste, and in morals, on the other hand, Dutch Learning was showing great vigor. The old and the new were living together in the greatest intimacy during the early years of the nineteenth century. I want to read about this. It is only about forty-five years since the systematic importation of Western culture began and there are those who say that today's new Japan was created in that brief period of time, but I feel that they are underrating us....
>
> In our country the nineteenth century was a time in which old things were being discarded while the new things

to replace them had not yet really been created. It was a time in which that great class known as "samurai" passed into oblivion. How can we ever count up the tragedies that resulted? I want to read about them. I want to read about how the Japanese language was consolidated through the great labor of unifying the written and spoken languages that was inaugurated by Futabatei Shimei and Yamada Bimyo. It was also around the end of the nineteenth century that the new poetry made its first tentative appearance....

For better or worse, we must know our fathers. We must know their times. If only there were someone to write the kind of study I want to read! What a vast number of topics we might find treated in it! It would not stop with mere comparisons of literature and the fine arts in their representations of the essence of the way in which the people of those times thought. It was Kitamura Tokoku who tried to seek out in the humor and satire of the light fiction of such writers as Sanba and Ikku the morality and the nihilistic tendencies present in the common people of that time. I want to read all about such things....[4]

The major concerns of *Before the Dawn* are all present in this article. It is already clear that the story will reach far beyond life in Shimazaki's own Kiso region and that it will not be restricted to purely social or political history. Toson's very frequent citations of the names of prominent people from Japanese intellectual and artistic life who have no immediate role in the plot serve as a ground figure that constantly draws the reader's attention back to the long, vigorous, and creative history of civilization in Japan. But the restoration of his own sense of connection with Japanese history, with his native region, and with the history and traditions of his family was also central to Toson's personal agenda. Themes developed out of those more personal concerns sometimes play against the ground figure and sometimes blend into it. The peculiar ambience of *Before the Dawn* arises out of the fact that Toson's stance was not that of the insider taking his readers on a guided tour of Kiso but rather that of a man long alienated from his roots who is now sharing with the reader his rediscovery of the people, customs, and countryside with which he had lost contact while still a small child. This homecoming had become possible only because he had at last come to terms with elements of his family history that had hitherto been too painful for him to confront directly: the bankruptcy and collapse of his distinguished old family, his father's tragic life, and his own failures as a son.

Almost all of Toson's entire output of fiction constitutes a single immense work. *Before the Dawn* deals with the same problems of connection; connection between himself and Japanese society and experience and connection between Japan and world history and culture which had always preoccupied him. He was an autobiographical novelist who seemed to have said about all that he had to say about his own personal experience and such a reaching back for the sources of his personal identity and public concerns was the next logical step. The content of Toson's writings is so intimately related to his personal life that it is necessary to review some of the salient points of his origins, education, and literary career in order to define the context and significance of *Before the Dawn*.[5]

Shimazaki Haruki, who later took the pen name Toson, was born in the village of Magome, a post station at the western end of the Kiso portion of the *Nakasendo*. The year of his birth was 1872, the fifth year of the Meiji era and the nineteenth year since the coming of Perry. He died in the summer of 1943, a little more than a year before the beginning of the air raids that were to devastate most Japanese cities.

His father Shimazaki Masaki was the seventeenth head of the Magome branch of the family and the last of a line of hereditary village headmen that went back to 1558 when the village was founded by Shimazaki Shichirozaemon Shigemichi.[6] The samurai status of the Shimazaki gradually faded away over the generations as their actual duties came to have less and less to do with samurai functions. Samurai status was formally restored during the lifetime of Masaki's father as a part of the declining Shogunate's effort to buy support in the countryside, but by that time the gesture had little significance.

Toson spent only a few years in Magome before his father sent him to Tokyo in 1881 to get him safely away from mounting family problems and to provide him with the new education for a new age that was then available only there.[7] He traveled in a party consisting of his eldest brother Hideo, Tomoya, the third of the four brothers, Toson himself, and another boy from the village. Five days of walking brought them to Oiwake, then the terminus of the new roads suitable for wheeled transport. There they boarded one of the stagecoaches newly imported from the United States for another two days of pounding and lurching over barely passable mountain roads.[8]

Once in Tokyo, the boy stayed with his sister and her husband, who coached him through his assimilation into metropolitan life. When his sister and brother-in-law returned to the Kiso he was placed briefly with a family acquaintance before entering the household of a downtown merchant as a *shosei,* one of the many promising but poor youths that people of substance in Tokyo were taking in and putting through school out of varying mixtures of idealism and shrewd self-interest.[9] His guardians, originally from Fukushima, the old administrative center of the Kiso, seem to have been exceptionally sympathetic but Toson nevertheless grew up away from home, a fact that determined that much of his life would be spent in trying to restore the sense of connection that was all but destroyed during his childhood and adolescence.

Shimazaki Masaki was already hopelessly alienated from Meiji life by the time of the birth of his last son. As a follower of the Hirata school of National Learning the new, European-style education that his son was to receive in Tokyo represented much of what Masaki found most repugnant in the new age, but he had long since come to realize, if not completely to accept, that his feelings could no longer be relied upon in dealing with life. In giving up his youngest child to the care of others he seems to have relinquished the last shred of the family responsibility around which he might have reconstructed his shattered sense of himself, but he recognized the necessity and he had never been one to put his own needs ahead of those of others. The critic Aono Suekichi has perceptively described Aoyama Hanzo, Masaki's alter ego in the novel, as

> ... a descendant in the seventeenth generation of Aoyama Dosai, the founder of Magome and ... the central pillar of that post station village. He was very conscious of that role and he was unsparing of himself in trying to guide the village safely through the disorder of the Meiji Restoration. Nor was that all. He was a person not bound by narrow readings of 'the way'; he had carried out a pilgrimage to Mt. Ontake to pray for his father's recovery, he was humble before his stepmother Oman, he respected his neighbors, loved his disciples and the village children.
>
> Why did Hanzo's life end in tragedy? For those very reasons. He was a disciple of Hirata Atsutane and Kanetane; an idealist who longed for a 'soul restored' (*naobi no mitama*),[10] and who suffered ceaseless pain from the disorderliness of the Meiji Restoration. What he did and what he carried out was misunderstood by others, his overflowing love for children and farmers not returned. He was a passionate man capable of such impulsive acts as tossing a fan into the imperial carriage in the mistaken impression that it was a part of the vanguard of the procession and he was a purist who would set the needs of his wife and children aside in order to serve the gods in

which he believed. He was also a man of simple and direct sentiment torn by the bankruptcy of his family and without any talent for economic things. He constantly berated himself as a fool and an incompetent.[11]

For all the sacrifices it entailed, Toson's early education was not quite good enough to get him through the entrance examinations for the public schools and colleges that constituted the only route to the most desirable careers in business and government. He was also deeply in love with European culture and eager to learn more English. These interests led him to become a member of the first entering class at the Meiji Gakuin, a Protestant mission school that by today's standards would stand somewhere between a preparatory school and a junior college.[12]

All the officials of the Meiji Gakuin except the president were Japanese although much of the teaching was done in English by foreign teachers recruited from among Scottish and American Presbyterians and American members of the Dutch Reformed Church. At this school Toson and his fellow students read the standard English writers. He acquired a lifelong love of Shakespeare and came to feel a particular familiarity and sympathy with the English Romantics, especially Byron and Wordsworth. Students at Meiji Gakuin were also introduced to the works of Charles Darwin and Herbert Spencer and imbibed heavily of a social-reformist, utilitarian brand of Christianity that usually stayed with them in some form even though few of them remained practicing Christians.[13]

Toson's literary awareness was first developed through his reading in English. Meiji Gakuin offered no instruction in Chinese and Japanese subjects, a characteristic shortcoming of such schools that in itself tells much of the spiritual and intellectual atmosphere of early Meiji education. Beyond the little bit his father had managed to teach him before he left home, Toson's education in this area was delayed and confined to outside tutoring and self-study. Among his later tutors in Chinese was the distinguished scholar and diplomat Kurimoto Joun, onetime Tokugawa official in charge of the port of Hakodate and diplomat for the Shogunate in its final days and the model for the character Kitamura Zuiken in *Before the Dawn*.[14] As he came to know Japanese literature, Toson found the plays of Chikamatsu and the poetry of Saigyo and Basho to be especially congenial. Basho's view of all travel and of life itself as pilgrimage was naturally sympathetic to the son of the keeper of a post station on a great national highway along which Basho himself had once traveled. Travel constitutes a recurring theme in Toson's life and works while the language and conventions of *joruri* are reflected both in his early closet dramas and in the form and diction of the poetry that brought him his first fame. His studies in Chinese brought him familiarity with the great T'ang poets and sufficient knowledge of *Hung lo meng* to publish an article about it a few years later.[15]

The tone of life at Meiji Gakuin was set by a stern and demanding Calvinist morality made even more rigorous by the samurai background of many of the school's leaders. Perhaps most disturbing and confusing of all to the young Toson was the fact that in this rigorously puritanical atmosphere, not too different from that generated by the stricter varieties of Confucianism, there was taking place the seemingly anomalous phenomenon of a social life in which men and women intermingled freely. The conventions that made this possible were so familiar to the American members of the school community that they were not really aware of them. The Japanese members of the faculty, many of whom had studied abroad, also seemed to have no outward difficulty in conforming but to an adolescent boy from the mountains of the Kiso who was growing up in downtown Tokyo with its rich overtones of pre-Meiji culture, the new conventions were both puzzling and alarming. "From the age of seven, boys and girls do not sit together" was the standard prescribed by Confucianism and the household standards maintained by Shimazaki Masaki had been thoroughly Confucian in practice.[16] In traditional life men and women worked together in propagating and maintaining the family and were often close companions in those roles but socializing tended to be sharply divided along gender lines. Although the rigor with which these standards were enforced varied widely from household to household (the young Toson was shocked by the casual admission by one of his Tokyo friends that he had slept in the same room with his girl cousins until well past puberty), any open departure from them was usually taken as *prima facie* evidence of sexual misconduct.[17]

In 1888 Toson was baptized into the Christian faith by the pastor Kimura Kumaji, who had been one of his first teachers of English in the years before Meiji Gakuin. In the novel *When the Cherries Ripen*, Toson describes the perception of Christ entertained by his alter ego, Kishimoto Sutekichi in terms that reflect both misapprehension and naivete.[18]

Sasabuchi Tomoichi suggests that the key to understanding Toson's youthful Christianity is to be found in Toson's rejection of the God of theology in favor of an incarnate and sensually perceptible God closer to the vision of the poet. In fact, Sasabuchi argues, Toson's Christianity was not really a religious experience but a poetic vision.[19] The conversion did not last long. The pubescent Toson soon discovered that although his instructors in his new faith seemed to teach that random sexual impulses were not to be found in worthy believers such impulses had nevertheless failed to disappear in him after his baptism. The very intensity of his will to believe precipitated a spiritual crisis and he withdrew from social life, growing morose and uncooperative. A sense of unworthiness and inability to measure up to Christian ideals led to a drift away from formal religious observance. The most notable immediate effect of this brief period as a Christian was that the alienation from traditional Japanese life that had begun with his departure from Magome and had deepened during his schooling in Tokyo was now completed by alienation from self. Yet, although his time as a practicing Christian was short, the influence of Christianity remained deep and permanent. In this as in many other aspects of his life, the nature of Toson's experience was paradigmatic for an important part of his generation of young Japanese intellectuals.[20]

Upon his graduation from Meiji Gakuin, Toson was abruptly brought back into confrontation with the problems of his family. His father's death was soon followed by bankruptcy. His elder brother Hideo sold the remaining properties in Magome and moved to Tokyo but his efforts to rectify matters yielded only a series of losses that continued until there was nothing more to lose.[21] Toson was caught up in conflicting obligations to his guardians and to his family. He passed his first summer out of school as a clerk in a new Yokohama branch of the retail business of his guardians but he was not at all suited to the work. He tells of retaining his sanity by hiding a copy of an English translation of Hippolyte Taine's *History of English Literature* under the counter where he could dip into it at every unobserved moment.[22]

At the end of the summer the unhappy young man gratefully accepted Kimura Kumaji's offer of a teaching position at the Meiji Jogakko, a women's school attached to the Meiji Gakuin. The salary was minimal, ten yen a month, but that still made Toson the only member of his family with a steady income. The new job went badly almost from the first. He soon fell in love with one of his students, setting off another attack of the paralyzing sexual guilt and confusion that had first overcome him as a student. The problem was exacerbated by strong moral convictions about his proper relation to his students and by sheer humiliation. The lineage of his family was at least as distinguished as that of the girl's but his present poverty and lack of future prospects made it impossible that her family would ever accept him as a son-in-law. He walked away from his job after only four months and passed most of the following year in a penniless wandering that started with a self-conscious retracing of the first part of the route of Basho's *Nozarashi kiko*.[23]

Once back in Tokyo with his conflicts somewhat cooled but far from resolved, he found his family even worse off than before. Repeated moves brought them into ever smaller and shabbier quarters where the few remaining pieces of good furniture from the old days looked more and more out of place. The low point was marked by a forced sale of all the household possessions to satisfy creditors. Kindly neighbors bought back some of the basic housekeeping necessities for them.

The family was still completely dependent upon Toson for sustenance and he was forced to ask for reinstatement in the job at Meiji Jogakko. The girl he loved had been staying on after graduation as an assistant, but she left to enter a marriage that her family had earlier arranged for her. She died soon afterward in the course of her first pregnancy. This hopeless and humiliating love resonated throughout the rest of Toson's life. It may even have had a role in determining his choice of a pen name.[24]

It was during these stressful years that Toson launched himself as a writer. His first publication, a translation of an article from an American magazine describing a visit by the original author to the home of Frances Willard, founder of the Women's Christian Temperance Union, appeared in the January, 1892 issue of *Jogaku zasshi*, a periodical associated with Meiji Gakuin. This was followed by other translations and original works both in this journal and in its more famous successor, *Bungakkai*, but all the while family misfortunes and personal difficulties were slowly grinding the life out of him.[25] He once again gave up his position at Meiji Jogakko, where his students had begun calling him "the ashheap" because of his haggard appearance and withdrawn manner. His family still had no income beyond what he could bring in. He was preparing to sell the last of his books in order to feed the family a little longer when a former colleague at the Meiji Jogakko told him of an opening at the Toho Gakuin, a Christian seminary in Sendai.[26]

In Sendai Toson found himself with a secure job, an adequate salary, and a viable distance from the relentless and demoralizing decline of his family and there he began to grow as a human being and as a writer. Within a few months he was publishing some of the poems that in August 1897 would form a part of *Wakanashu* or *Young Shoots*, his first volume of poetry. The title image carries traditional associations with the breaking of the winter and the revival of the earth in the spring when the meager late winter diet could be supplemented by the first fresh greens. The poems, for the most part a chaste and restrained celebration of the senses and of the glory and wonder of young women, overflowed with the joy of the breaking of a long winter of the soul. In their form and diction they echoed

Chikamatsu and the court poets but in their stance and voice they were new in Japanese literature.[27] They drew on Toson's earlier experiments which had in turn been deeply influenced by the work of his friend and mentor Kitamura Tokoku, who had committed suicide in 1894.[28] Much of their inspiration came from the English romantics whom both he and Tokoku had read at their different schools and from Dante Gabriel Rossetti, a recent discovery of Toson's circle.[29] *Wakanashu* was the first successful volume of the new poetry that had been trying to be born ever since the restoration and it remains the most widely read volume of verse to appear during the past century, constantly in print ever since its first appearance.[30] Three more volumes of poetry, some of them including short, lyrical prose sketches, brought Toson's career as a practicing poet to an end, although the careful and restrained use of language in his prose works continued to reflect his point of departure as a writer.

In the first manifestation of the somewhat prickly and unworldly stance that would always characterize him as a public figure, Toson did not capitalize fully on the spectacular success of *Wakanashu*. He did, however, take advantage of the modest economic fruits of his first book to resign from his job in Sendai, and once back in Tokyo he pursued a long-standing interest in European music by studying for a brief period at the Tokyo School of Music. While there, he became very close to the woman who was his violin teacher. This relationship had not yet been resolved when Kimura Kumaji arranged a marriage for him the next year and it was a complicating factor in the early years of that marriage. He joined the faculty of Kimura's new school in the mountain town of Komoro in western Nagano prefecture. The salary was meager to begin with and it steadily shrank during his tenure as the school struggled to stay afloat amidst increasing economic difficulties. In the next few years, he and his new wife, who had dreams of a literary career as well as an unresolved romantic attachment of her own, found themselves bringing up three little daughters in austere circumstances.[31]

During his years in Komoro Toson continued to read extensively in European literature in English translation and he kept up his Tokyo contacts, particularly with the writer Tayama Katai and the pioneer ethnologist Yanagita Kunio, both of whom kept him supplied with books.[32] He began to train himself as a writer of prose fiction. The reasons for the change are not altogether clear. Some point to circumstantial evidence that Toson had run out of poetic inspiration but it may be more important that while in those days novelists could sometimes support themselves by their writing, poets could not. After some interesting apprentice works set in the mountains Toson returned to Tokyo where in 1905 he published his first full-length novel with money borrowed from his father-in-law. By the time *The Broken Commandment* came out all three of his daughters were dead and his wife was suffering from night blindness due to nutritional imbalance. He has often been held responsible for the deaths--most notably by Shiga Naoya, who has a character in his short story "Kuniko" remark that *The Broken Commandment* could not possibly have been worth the lives of three little girls--but there is not sufficient evidence to support the charge.[33]

The romantic exhilaration and wistful longing that characterized Toson's poetry had vanished by the time he wrote his first novel. In its place was an often grim social commentary. Toson's critical posture toward the Meiji Restoration is usually dated from *The Family*, but his depictions of time-serving and cynical careerism among the educational and political bureaucracies in *The Broken Commandment* also foreshadow the more mature statements in *Before the Dawn*. Much of the internal energy of *The Broken Commandment* comes from Toson's personal life while the stance comes from *Hamlet*, the setting from the Komoro Gijuku and the Komoro district, and the general shape from *Crime and Punishment*. The framing of stories about Japanese experiences in readily recognizable borrowings from European classics was a popular challenge for writers which also seemed to answer an urgent need among their readers for reassurance about the presence of universal qualities in their own lives. The darkness of tone of *The Broken Commandment* matched a new mood in the country as the nineteenth-century European exuberance and optimism that underlay much of even the most painful of Meiji experience began giving way to twentieth-century pessimism and despair.

The autobiographical elements deeply embedded in *The Broken Commandment* came to the surface in Toson's subsequent writings. Although he was strongly predisposed both by personal inclination and by family and regional tradition to keep his own and his family's troubles and embarrassments to himself, his earlier reading of Rousseau's *Confessions* had solidified a growing conviction that concealment was not only dishonest and unwholesome but in the long run futile. The tension between an intensely private personality and an intellectual commitment to self-revelation did much to determine the shape of his career. *The Broken Commandment* explores the torment of Segawa Ushimatsu, a young man who tries to hide the dark family secret of his outcast origins, but the resonances of that story have as much in common with Toson's preoccupation with his own family secrets as they do with the sociological implications of outcast status. The issue of confession is handled on many levels; it ends with its protagonist making a public confession in the style of Raskolnikov, but it also involves a series of encounters between

Ushimatsu and Inoki Rentaro, the outcast political activist who displays Christ-like qualities and whom he reveres but with whom he finds himself unable to share his secret and whom in the end he denies.[34] An impressive first novel and an important social document, *The Broken Commandment* is also a first attempt to explore, at one step removed, the possibilities of autobiographical fiction. Both a popular and a critical success in its own time, it remains a landmark in the development of the modern Japanese novel.[35]

During his lifetime critics usually placed Toson among the Japanese naturalists but, as has been pointed out, the European strain in his intellectual furnishings drew much more heavily on the lineage of Rousseau than on that of Zola.[36] Japanese naturalism was inspired by the European school but it was in the end quite different. Toson was well acquainted with both the Japanese and the European versions of naturalism but he did not think of himself as a part of either.[37] Although he shared some of the interests of the Japanese movement, most notably its penchant for autobiographical fiction, it is the way that he expresses that autobiographical bent that most clearly distinguishes him from the naturalists. The characteristic product of the Japanese naturalist movement was the I-novel with its obsessively inward-facing focus on the personal life and state of mind of the author. In contrast, Toson's autobiographical interests constituted the point of departure for an ever-widening vision as his efforts to place himself in Japanese society expanded to include the problem of the place of contemporary Japanese experience in Japanese history and of Japanese history in world history.[38]

The Broken Commandment was followed in 1908 by *Springtime*, a novel which took its hopeful title from Botticelli and its grey mood from the trials and struggles of the author's early years. The tone is set at the very beginning by the singing of Ophelia's song by Aoki, the senior member of the group, as he tells his younger friends about a performance of *Hamlet* he had seen in the foreign settlement in Yokohama and it becomes a recurring motif throughout the story. *Springtime* is a fictionalized account of the time between two trains, the one in which Toson arrives back in Tokyo after his period of wandering and the one that will take him to Sendai. It is a convincing portrait of the longing and despair experienced by a group of sensitive and alienated young men living in the cultural and spiritual no man's land that awaited them following their graduations from Meiji Gakuin and other, similarly enlightened, progressive, and largely alien educational institutions of the day. The author's alter ego in the story is Kishimoto Sutekichi, who stands in awe of Aoki, his older friend and mentor. This character modeled on Kitamura Tokoku is idealistic, politically-aware, and hopelessly at odds with the society in which he lives. Certain of his qualities are echoed in other characters in other novels: most notably Inoki in *The Broken Commandment* and Aoyama Hanzo in *Before the Dawn*. In the final line of *Springtime*, the protagonist looks out of the window of the train as it leaves Tokyo for Sendai and reflects that "even people like me want somehow to go on living."[39] Some readers have seized upon this line and the stance it exemplifies as a prime example of what they find so irritating about this writer. Others have argued that the remark, for all its self-conscious heaviness, reflects the stubborn strength and courage that had enabled Toson to rise above his hardships and which had much to do with making his autobiographical explorations important to such a wide range of readers.[40]

The protagonists of the next two novels, *The Family* and *When the Cherries Ripen*, also carried the name Kishimoto Sutekichi. The surname, "Kishimoto," may carry resonances of the Tokyo neighborhood on the bank of the Sumida River where Toson grew up and of the highway that ran along the banks of the Kiso River before turning aside to pass through his childhood home, but it is "sute-," the first element in the given name, with its meaning of "cast-off," "rejected," or "abandoned," that is most suggestive. Life in Tokyo had cut Toson off from his home and family. When his mother and, later, his father, visited him in Tokyo he had nothing to say to them. His inability even to attempt to establish rapport with his father during their last time together was a galling memory in later years. Nor was it simply a matter of being alienated from the Kiso and all it stood for; his education at Meiji Gakuin had, for all its many admirable qualities, provided him with ideals that were in large part not so much rejected as simply not at issue in the larger Japanese society. Throughout his youth and well into his mature years Toson lived in poverty and loneliness and in circumstances that seemed to promise little other than more poverty and loneliness.

Toson's third novel was *The Family*, which deals with the aftermath a generation later of the events described in *Before the Dawn*. It completed serial publication in 1911 and appeared as a book later in the year. As in all of Toson's works, the range of reference was broad. Particularly noticeable are echoes of Havelock Ellis and of Tolstoy's *Anna Karenina* and "Kreutzer sonata." The story begins around 1898 and ends in 1910 when the protagonist and his wife have at last achieved a degree of tranquility in a difficult marriage which will end a few months later with her death from complications following childbirth. *The Family* is a low-keyed but powerful documentation of the inappropriate priorities and self-destructive malfunctions to which the traditional family system was subject amidst the spiritual and institutional dislocations of Meiji life. The collapse of two distinguished old provincial families, the unhappy marriage of the author's older sister and the disharmony and complications of his own married life are explored with great verisimilitude and with no concessions to any need readers might have to be entertained. Masamune Hakucho has observed that the author of the immensely popular *Wakanashu* had a ready-made audience that was eager to read anything autobiographical that he chose to write and that Toson was in no way inhibited from taking full advantage of that fact.[41] The uncompromising, though not literal, realism points forward to Toson's handling of historical reality in *Before the Dawn*, and it makes *The Family* an important record of the urban middle class of late Meiji, so much of which still had one foot in the city and one in the provinces and no firm ground in either place. Some critics have placed the beginning of the critical attitude toward Meiji that later emerges in *Before the Dawn* in this novel, but we have seen that it can be traced at least as far back as *The Broken Commandment*.[42]

Although Toson was profoundly alienated from Japanese life during much of his youth and early manhood, his alienation had not risen out of conscious rebellion, bitterness, or deliberate rejection of traditional values. His instincts were conservative but his education and his literary apprenticeship had led him and many of his contemporaries far afield from the common range of Japanese experience. As Toson was alienated from Japanese life by his education, Japan was itself alienated from its past by the upheavals of early Meiji. As Toson was in those years deprived of a sense of participation in Japanese life the cosmopolitan character of his education also made him keenly aware of how Japan was itself deprived of a sense of participation in the life of the world that had so forcefully moved in upon it. It was these two levels of isolation that informed Toson's life-long spiritual and intellectual quest for restored connection. He was deeply respectful of the possibilities of traditional Japanese values honestly and sincerely observed and his education and later experience provided him with abundant outside references by which to appreciate just what those values really were, but as an outsider in Japanese life it was appropriate that he would increasingly turn his attention to writing about a Japan that was also strongly committed to many of the values, hopes, and ideals that shaped the world of the late nineteenth century. Even though many of those values and ideals could be readily extrapolated from within the Japanese tradition, Japan in many ways remained an outsider in the greater world.

The next landmark in Toson's life was a sudden move to Paris in 1913 occasioned by the pregnancy of a niece who had come to help with the children after the death of his wife. The consequences of this renewed outbreak of his old confusion on sexual matters threatened not only his sense of himself but the viability of the public persona which constituted his stock in trade as an autobiographical novelist. In the failure in interpersonal relationships that it represented, it also served as a terrifying reminder of the failures that had marked his father's final years.[43] He left Japan feeling that he could never return; that he had destroyed all possibility of recovering himself in his homeland. In Paris he supported himself by writing for the Tokyo *Asahi* newspaper. His columns included more or less predictable fare such as sketches of Paris life, reports of the character and manner of living of his friend the Sanskrit scholar Sylvain Levy, and of premier performances of works by Debussy and Maeterlinck. They also reflected the usual expatriate's renewed sense of connection with his native country and there were frequent reflections on the alienation from Japanese life and experience of some members of the small Japanese community in Paris and disapproving comments on the general indifference to recent Japanese history both in Japan and in the world at large that culminated in the essay quoted earlier.[44]

Toson had expected to spend the rest of his life in France but the outbreak of World War I and the impossibility of supporting his many dependents from such a distance forced him to return home after only three years abroad. In 1919, three years after his return to Japan, he completed and published the novel *When the Cherries Ripen*, parts of which had appeared irregularly as a magazine serial while he was in France. *Cherries* is a work of fictionalized reportage but at the same time its lyrical treatment of reality is reminiscent of Basho's travel diaries. It draws on the period in Toson's life immediately preceding that treated in *Springtime*, and it includes reflections on student days at Meiji Gakuin, the first interval of teaching at Meiji Jogakko, and the heartbreak and humiliation of his first love. Pitched in a very low key even for a writer noted for low-key writing, it has been relatively neglected by critics and Toson himself was never satisfied with it. Yet in spite of some problems of structure it has a certain quiet charm and it has some revealing things to say about this crucial period in the history of Christianity in Japan. Meiji Gakuin was one of a number of Christian mission schools which were expected to train a new generation of Japanese Christian intellectuals to become leaders in the advance of Christianity as they pursued their various careers in the new Japan, an expectation that was in some ways markedly at variance with what actually happened. The tone of the novel is an uninsistent and yet wrenching blend of nostalgia and pain, going well beyond the degree to which such feelings are an almost inescapable part of looking back on adolescence.[45]

Toson's fifth novel, *New Life*, appeared in the Asahi newspapers between May, 1918 and October, 1919 and was published in book form at the end of the year. *New Life*, with the rather heavily calculated irony of its nod to Dante in the title, is not only Toson's most controversial work but the focal point for much of the fiercely partisan controversy that his life and career can still inspire.[46] At the time of its appearance Toson had for years enjoyed nationwide esteem as the embodiment of a national ideal: the poor boy who had succeeded against the odds through hard work and sound morals. Now he was making a detailed public confession of the obsessive attachment he had formed with a young niece. Nothing seems to be spared; the story is a chronicle of cravenness and dishonor. As soon as the pregnancy is discovered the protagonist moves the family across town to a new neighborhood where no one knows them and when that still does not offer sufficient cover, he flees the country. He is able to bring himself to inform his brother, the girl's father, only by letter and only after his ship had reached Shanghai.[47]

The coverup efforts, in which he was able to elicit his brother's complicity, were as effective as they were unsavory. Years seem to have passed before even his sister-in-law realized that her daughter had borne a child and given it out for adoption. When the protagonist finds himself unable to carry out his original intention to spend the rest of his life in France, he returns to Japan and, once home, fecklessly resumes the liaison. It seemed to the readers of the early installments that a national figure was committing slow suicide in public.

This merciless exposé of the protagonist's failings demonstrates that although Toson the man might have lost his moral bearings for a time, Toson the writer remained able to draw on the highest level of artistic integrity in reviewing his conduct. For all the extraliterary questions it raises and all the extraneous emotions that it generates, *New Life* forces the careful reader to make the emotional and intellectual investments that can be elicited only by a valid work of art. Even if such a reader does not always find Toson a comfortable companion, he will leave the novel humbled in his own judgments and with an admiration, possibly somewhat grudging, of the author's strength, resilience, and fierce moral commitment. When Toson later sets out in *Before the Dawn* to tell us a story that is replete with painful and still unresolved problems at all levels of national and private life he can do so as one who has long since earned our trust.[48]

As the 1920s moved into their middle years Toson was at last able to bring his personal life to order. The niece was moved out of his household and her father eventually took her away with him to

Taiwan. After recovering from what appears to have been a mild stroke, Toson made what was to prove a happy and successful second marriage to Kato Shizuko, a much younger woman who had been on the editorial staff of the short-lived feminist journal *Shojochi* which Toson had founded, investing a part of the modest wealth resulting from his share of royalties from the new uniform editions of modern Japanese literature.[49] Having at last achieved financial security, but also having read Kropotkin, Toson was finding his new-found wealth to be not an altogether comfortable experience, and there was much worry about its moral implications. Nevertheless, with the immediate problems of livelihood now firmly at bay, Toson could at last begin the final stage in the long struggle to come to terms with himself, his family and the Japan in which he lived. Up to now he had been kept away from Magome by the circumstances of his family's departure from the ancestral village. He had returned only once, to bring his mother's ashes home for burial late in 1896. Then, after only two nights in Magome, he walked for three days along the old Kiso Road, going as far as Fukushima. This experience inspired the brief "Kiso Valley Diary" (1897), the first of his prose works to celebrate the wild beauty and the austere traditions of the Kiso and a distant foreshadowing of the prologue of *Before the Dawn*.[50]

Toson did not again mention Magome prominently in any of his works until thirty years later, when his life was beginning to focus on preparations for the writing of *Before the Dawn*: he tells of buying a house there in 1925 and giving it to his eldest son, Kusuo. The business of reestablishing a Shimazaki presence in the home village occupied much of the next two years as he oversaw the repair and remodeling of the house and the purchase of farmland and agricultural tools and implements. These activities constituted a preliminary stage of research for *Before the Dawn*. Since all of the records and mementoes accumulated by the Shimazaki family over nearly three and a half centuries had been destroyed in the fire that ravaged the village in 1895, Toson was forced to rely on outside sources in the reconstruction of the life of his father. The most important of these were the diaries known as the *Daikokuya nikki*. They had been kept by Owaki Heimon Nobuoki of the Daikokuya, the next door neighbor of Toson's grandfather and the model for Satake Kimbei of the Fushimiya in *Before the Dawn*. Their discovery made it possible for Toson to reconstruct life in Magome at the level of honesty and integrity he aimed to achieve.[51]

Like most of Toson's other novels and like most important works of Japanese literature in the first half of the twentieth century, *Before the Dawn* first came out as a magazine serial but even the circumstances of that first publication were special. The initial installment appeared in the April, 1929 issue of the monthly journal *Chuo koron* and the remainder in successive quarterly installments until the October, 1935 issue. Book One was completed in 1932 and published in book form soon afterward. The same was done for Book Two after its completion and the two were then published in a revised, "definitive" edition later in that same year. This is the basis for all subsequent editions; a second revision was started but not completed.[52]

After the completion of *Before the Dawn*, Toson sharply decreased his literary output and, in spite of his retiring personality, began to take part in the public activities that fall to prominent writers. In 1936 he went to Buenos Aires as the Japanese representative to the world congress of the P.E.N. Club. After the conclusion of the meetings he visited the Japanese settlements in Brazil, then traveled to the United States where he visited the Boston area that was the setting of much of the literature his American teachers had taught him in the Meiji Gakuin, went to New York, which he viewed from the top of the Empire State Building, and flew to Detroit in a Ford Trimotor airplane to observe the assembly lines in the Ford Motor Company plants. A brief and disappointing visit to France concluded his final trip abroad.[53]

During the war, Toson stayed relatively clear of the public patriotic activities that men in his position were asked to participate in, pleading advanced age and preoccupation with a forthcoming work. He had originally planned to carry the narrative of *Before the Dawn* as far as the 1920s, but physical exhaustion and the unmanageable scale of such an undertaking made this impossible. He did not, however, abandon the project altogether; at the time of his death he was at work on the third installment of a second long work of historical fiction. Although too little of it was completed to enable us to know precisely what its author had in mind, it was clearly intended to be a sequel to *Before the Dawn*. The new novel, *The Gate to the East*, was named after a painting by Puvis de Chavannes that Toson had seen in Marseilles in 1936. The priest Sho'un is the central figure of the completed portion, which shares many settings and characters with *Before the Dawn*. Hanzo's daughter Okume and his old Edo friends Osumi and Takichi also make appearances. The difficulty of coming to grips with such a brief fragment is further intensified by the extreme constraints, reminiscent of those of the Tokugawa period and more effectively enforced, that were then being imposed on writers by the wartime government. Yet enough was completed to give the sense that *The Gate to the East* was, like *Before the Dawn*, addressed to not only a Japanese audience but to the worldwide audience that would have existed if only there had been enough general knowledge for that audience to be asking the right questions about Japan.[54]

Before the Dawn was the logical conclusion to Toson's literary career. Appearing during the years in which such writers as Tanizaki Jun'ichiro, Kawabata Yasunari, Yokomitsu Riichi, and Nagai Kafu were active, it remains the major literary event of its time. Still, many readers at first failed to grasp what Toson was doing. He had never before attempted anything so large or anything that might be called historical fiction, nor was there any precedent at the time for a literary treatment of recent Japanese history on this scale and with this degree of seriousness. Kume Masao made one of the most penetrating and significant attacks and spoke for many early readers when he complained of the endless bulk, the heaviness, and the pretension of the work. Kume insists that it is not a novel at all but "a novelist's discourse on history," with fragments that read like a novel scattered here and there in what is essentially a historical study. He maintains that it cannot be compared with the great historical novels of Ogai's final years.[55]

Kume's objections are not without merit but, being written as the fourth chapter of Book Two was just appearing, they were premature, more valuable as a statement of some of the risks that Toson took than of his success in meeting them. The question of the degree to which Toson actually succeeded in reconciling the conflicting demands of history and fiction has been argued ever since. It is unlikely ever to be completely resolved but the standard for the discussion was set quite early. A roundtable discussion of *Before the Dawn* appeared in the November, 1936 issue of *Bungakkai*. Its members included the playwright Murayama Tomoyoshi, who had just made a stage version of the novel, Hayashi Fusao, a onetime Marxist recently converted to the nationalistic and anti-modernist Nihon Roman-ha, several important novelists, and the critic Kobayashi Hideo, who contributed a thoughtful and cogent afterword. They agreed that Toson had resolved most, if not all, of the problems inherent in reconciling the literary, personal and historical demands that he had placed upon himself and that the work taken as a whole was not only a success but one of the outstanding achievements of modern Japanese literature. This remains the basis of the standard evaluation of the work fifty years later even though that evaluation has since undergone extensive refinements.[56]

There is now among historians a general consensus about most of the essentials of the Meiji Restoration in spite of often bitter disagreement about certain aspects of process or detail. A half century after its writing, *Before the Dawn* not only remains in agreement with most of the essentials of that consensus but has played a role in creating it. Its primary contribution is in its point of view, startlingly new at the time of writing, which is that of the rural intellectuals. That point of view is presented with a richness and conviction that is the product of the author's intense personal involvement. It is the passionate quality of that involvement, as well as the quality of the fictional fleshing out of the story where documentation must be supplemented by the imagination of the author in recreating the fine detail of a time past that most sharply distinguishes this novel from conventional historical scholarship. But the immediacy of the author's personal involvement also distinguishes *Before the Dawn* from the general run of historical fiction. Its being not only a work of literature but the testament of the Shimazaki family of Magome as prepared by its most famous member, makes it an historical document. If these qualities largely compensate for Toson's lapses in historical scholarship, they also remind us that most of Toson's contributions to historical understanding come out of his portrayals of Kiso life and Kiso people. He was not able to exploit consistently his perspective on the Meiji Restoration to bring the same freshness of vision to the other milieux of the story. His behind-the-scenes vignettes of Tokugawa politics and foreign relations are workmanlike and interesting but have been superceded many times since. His treatment of the Mito uprising remains fresh and vivid, perhaps still the best treatment of the subject in fiction, and the core of his story is unique and irreplaceable.[57]

The historical and ethnological background of the work has been extensively investigated by the historical anthropologist Haga Noboru, a specialist in grass roots intellectual movements of the eighteenth and nineteenth centuries. He shares with many other scholars the specific reservations that Toson's grasp of some aspects of National Learning was less than perfect and that there are a number of errors of detail in his description of the operating procedures of the post station system, but he quite convincingly argues that none of these shortcomings in any way negates the fundamental validity and importance of Toson's portrayal of late Tokugawa and early Meiji times.[58] In the course of his discussions Haga demonstrates that many of the modern objections to Toson's historical scholarship are themselves products of the response to *Before the Dawn*.

The historical value of *Before the Dawn* lies as much in the questions it raises about the nature of the Meiji Restoration as in the answers it proposes. The improved perspective of an additional half century prompts Haga Noboru to reverse Kume's premature evaluation and argue that Toson's achievement is even greater than those austere and cerebral works by Mori Ogai which are often, and with considerable justification, cited as the most distinguished achievements of Japanese historical fiction. Ogai probed deeply into some of the most sensitive questions about the nature of medieval and early modern Japanese culture and in the process he opened up new perspectives on familiar issues, but in *Before the Dawn* there was systematically presented for the first time a radically new vision of the Meiji Restoration. In that vision the driving force of the restoration came from the bottom up rather than from the top down as received opinion then had it. Toson further suggests that the primary cause of the frustration, disillusionment and tragedy that followed the restoration was to be found in the immediate reversal of this thrust from the bottom up by the new Meiji government once it had come to power.[59]

This proposition is quite clear in *Before the Dawn*. The emotional climax comes in the final pages of the first volume as Aoyama Hanzo literally dances in the street for joy when he learns of the imperial restoration. Kureta Masaka has just been through on his way to Kyoto and he has explained why the bottom-up character of this restoration will ensure that it will be an enduring one unlike the restoration of the fourteenth century which was promulgated from the top down and consequently collapsed with the first hint of unsteadiness in imperial rule. At the beginning of the second volume the new Meiji government cynically disposes of the problems created by Sagara Sozo's promise to cut the tax rates in half by declaring him an outlaw. This foreshadows the top-down posture that the restoration would soon assume. Haga argues that this vision of Toson's concerning the nature of mid-nineteenth-century Japanese experience has had an important influence on both the course of historical scholarship and of historical education in Japan.[60]

In the literary world the responses have been important if somewhat more difficult to document. One creative person who responded almost immediately to *Before the Dawn* was Murayama Tomoyoshi, a prominent figure in avant garde and proletarian literary circles. His stage adaptation was well received in its original 1936 production and in subsequent revivals. The reception of the 1955 film version by the director Yoshimura Kimisaburo was somewhat more muted but it is a powerful experience for viewers already familiar with the novel. Both Murayama's play and the work of such people as the Marxist critic Aono Suekichi reflect the fact that many of the earliest readers to appreciate the magnitude of Toson's achievement were from the political left. This was a group to which Toson was not hostile but which he also had no strong interest in pleasing. His connection with it was primarily through his second son Keiji and his third son Osuke, both of whom were active in proletarian artistic movements during the 1920s, and through his old friend Arishima Ikuma.[61]

Some of the harshest political and literary criticisms in the years following World War II also came from the political left, which had a vested interest of its own in bottom-up theories of the Meiji Restoration but from quite a different perspective. These criticisms include some simplistic objections that the points of view are for the most part limited to the very uppermost level of the agricultural classes. The story is, to be sure, about the Shimazaki family and it seems true that, until its decline at the end of the Tokugawa period, the Shimazaki family owned nearly sixty percent of the arable land of the village.[62] A novel with a different point of view would have been another novel altogether, one with its own strengths and weaknesses. Whether or not it might prove to be better than this one would be determined not by its subject matter but by the quality of its writing and the depth and integrity of the research and thinking that stood behind it. Toson has not left us enough concerning his political views to make discussion of the subject worthwhile, but his deep commitment to humane values is as clearly on record throughout the entire body of his work as are his human failings and imperfections. The highly perceptive and quite positive readings of his works by such Marxist critics as Aono Suekichi and Hirano Ken further demonstrate that what is at issue here are not really questions of ideology but of careful and attentive reading.[63]

For all its historical and political implications, *Before the Dawn* is above all a celebration of the humanity of its characters and of the richness, complexity, and diversity of the lives they lived during the final years of the Tokugawa Shogunate and the opening years of the Meiji era. Its dominant tone is lyrical and that tone is sustained even when the subject is external threat and internal political turmoil, the grinding hardship of maintaining the old post system, or the bitter disappointments that the new age brought to so many of those who had worked hardest and sacrificed most to bring it into being.[64]

Since its completion *Before the Dawn* has been followed by an immense volume of historical fiction, family and local histories, and publications that draw on the rich store of old diaries and household records and the remarkably complete official records preserved in most parts of the country. These works often illuminate the period from points of view that were not accessible to any of Toson's characters and the best of them serve to correct or augment Toson's historical vision, but *Before the Dawn* remains the standard against which all the others are measured. More than any other single work, it has informed the current Japanese national consciousness of this most dramatic and pivotal stage in the modern history of the nation.

Among the full-length novels *Before the Dawn* has inspired is Ema Shu's *People of the Mountains*.[65] Ema was a naturalist turned proletarian who, like many other leftist writers, was forced by the political atmosphere of the 1930s to take refuge in the countryside. He returned to his native Hida district immediately to the west of the Kiso where he collected materials and carried out the research for his massive story of a popular uprising that took place in Hida in early Meiji. Conceived as a rebuttal of Toson's version of the restoration in central Japan, its central figure is also a local official drawn after Ema's father. *People of the Mountains* was extensively revised after World War II when it was possible to speak more frankly about controversial historical themes. It has as yet enjoyed neither the critical and popular success nor the intellectual response accorded to *Before the Dawn*. An even more massive response to *Before the Dawn* is *Azumino*, a five-volume novel by the literary historian Usui Yoshimi. Its surprisingly successful unifying theme is the history down to the 1960s of The Nakamuraya, a Tokyo bakery and restaurant founded in mid-Meiji. For the greater part of a century the Nakamuraya has been an important gathering place for artists and writers, many of whom were given both moral and material support by Soma Kokko, the extraordinary woman who was long its driving force. The settings of the story include the country district near Matsumoto where many of the characters were born and from which the novel takes its name, and the Hongo and Shinjuku districts of Tokyo. *Azumino* is a valuable complement to *Before the Dawn*, but its interest is more specialized and, for all its immense cast of characters and great range of historical resonances, the response to it has been far smaller.[66]

None of even the most ambitious successors of *Before the Dawn* has made any attempt to challenge it directly on its own ground. The reception of *Before the Dawn* in the Kiso district suggests why. A late-twentieth-century visitor is seldom out of sight of some part of the text. Most often seen are the opening lines of the prologue with their powerful evocation of the ambience of this mountainous region which partakes of both the remote and the cosmopolitan, and their rich historical resonances that draw first upon the eighteenth-century *Guide to Famous Scenes of the Kiso*,[67] a work which draws in turn upon centuries of earlier writings about life and travel in the Kiso, going back to the early eighth century. Toson's lines appear on a monument in the garden of the Museum of Local History in Fukushima. They are on matchboxes and billboards, on plaques in the alcoves of guest rooms of inns; they are even on the packaging of souvenir bottles of sake sold on the platforms of nearby railway stations. The fame that Toson brought to Magome has made a tourist attraction of the once remote and obscure village. It is flourishing as never before in its history but its original character is all but swamped by a ceaseless flood of literary pilgrims and sightseers. Such popularity and ubiquity is a harsh test but Toson's words retain their force in spite of the overexposure just as Magome and the Kiso remain rewarding to visitors even when there may seem to be more of them than the region will comfortably hold.

Before the Dawn appeared in a time of growing spiritual and political unease. The interest aroused by the reports of perceptive readers of the serial publication grew steadily once the novel appeared in book form and there soon emerged a large and appreciative reading audience that ranged across the entire political spectrum to include the apolitical as well. There had long been a sense that Japan had taken a wrong turn at some point during the preceding century and in the years following World War I that feeling began to come to a head, although there was often intense disagreement about just when and in what direction the wrong turn had been made. Japan's limited participation in the war on the side of the Allies had created a number of new personal fortunes and a raging inflation that once again threatened to put the necessities of life out of reach for the poor. The once promising "Taisho democracy" was shaken by a series of scandals and the worldwide depression that ended the decade struck Japan early. Overseas markets dwindled and, as economic conditions worsened and the country continued to suffer real and imagined slights and insults from the other powers, faith in democratic institutions wavered and a growing number of influential people began to look to the military as a solution to both foreign and domestic problems. While the Japanese version of twentieth-century mass culture was taking shape around the newspapers, the radio, pulp fiction, and motion pictures, there also began to be talk of a "Taisho Restoration" and then of a "Showa Restoration" to complete the allegedly unfinished business of the Meiji Restoration.

The renewed dominance of national life by the military, most signally marked by the outbreak of hostilities in Manchuria in 1931, drew extensively on the canon of the National Learning movement as it attempted to rationalize its behavior. It is significant in the context of the times that Toson emphasized a contrary aspect of National Learning that held out the promise of a liberation from the dominance of the military class which it viewed as fundamentally un-Japanese and one of the most lamentable consequences of "Chinese-mindedness." In the process he somewhat exaggerates the role of the cooler and more generous thought of a Motoori Norinaga and understates the importance of the narrower and more militant teachings of Hirata Atsutane in informing the consciousness of rural intellectuals like Shimazaki Masaki.[68] It is difficult to determine just what proportion of this distortion comes from genuine misunderstanding and what comes as a response to family history and current national considerations, but both seem to have been at work.

The actual position of the National Learning movement on military matters was in fact ambiguous and unclear. Many members had been students of the martial arts; a substantial proportion were samurai. It was not things military as such which they opposed but the samurai monopoly on the bearing of arms which, the National Scholars charged, had introduced grave anomalies into national life. Although the samurai class suffered heavily in the Meiji Restoration, it was also the source of most of the new leadership in government and business and it was Japan's military successes over the fifty years preceding Showa that had, far more than her extraordinary social, intellectual, and economic achievements, gained the nation such respect as it then enjoyed from the world community.

Whatever their values or their points of view, thoughtful people in the Japan of the 1920s were ready to reflect upon Japan as it then was as against what it might have been. Few of the prevailing answers to the questions raised in the course of the Meiji Restoration seemed completely satisfactory and many of those questions were now being raised all over again. It was time for taking stock and *Before the Dawn* may have helped some of its readers to rethink their attitudes toward those crucial years that had done so much to set the terms in which the problems of their own times would have to be discussed. The second volume, with its ground tone of disappointment and disillusion, appeared not long after the collapse of "Taisho democracy" which, like the Meiji Restoration, had seemed to many to have been much more hopeful in prospect than it had been satisfying in practice.[69]

These current social, political, and historical concerns are part of the subtext of *Before the Dawn* but the primary emphases of the story itself lie on a different plane and are concerned with the recovery of a time now lost when the heritage of the Shimazaki family was still a part of everyday life. They are framed in the more fundamental considerations of hierarchy, formality, place, character, and time. Toson's careful and thoughtful handling of language always continued to reflect his early career as a poet while his cool and understated style reflected his social and literary posture. Many critics have described Toson's style as being founded on the formulaic language of the formal greeting or of formal social discourse (*aisatsu*).[70]

It is this quality of aisatsu that lends Toson's writing its tone of distance and formality, yet this should not divert attention from the richness of the original language of *Before the Dawn*. That language ranges from pure classical Chinese through Japanese versions of classical Chinese and various gradations of traditional mixed styles to the pure archaic Japanese of court poetry and the studied archaism of the eighteenth and nineteenth century writers of the National Learning movement. At one extreme the language is idiomatic in the minutiae of feudal documents, procedures, offices, rules, and orders and at the other it includes folk songs and dialect. Dialect is, however, more often hinted at than actually employed; a fully accurate presentation of Kiso speech would have imposed intimidating difficulties on the general reader. The native riches of language are further overlain with the unobtrusive Anglicisms and Gallicisms that remind us that Toson was a cosmopolitan as well as an intensely Japanese writer. Historical accuracy as well as the time in which Toson lived and his personal inclination tend to give his style a touch of the consciously elevated and refined. His characters speak with decorum, taste, and dignity. Like most great languages, Japanese has shared in the decline in the more humane varieties of literacy that has marked the last fifty years. Few Japanese readers today would be likely to agree that Toson had kept the promise made in the advance notice of *Before the Dawn* in the January, 1929 issue of *Chuo koron*, to undertake the writing of his "... fifth [sic] full-length novel in the plainest and easiest colloquial language possible...."[71]

It is in these areas that *Before the Dawn* possesses a historical and literary significance that is rarely discussed by Japanese critics. The immense range of language makes it a stylistic tour-de-force even though overt displays of stylistic virtuosity were utterly alien to Toson's mature personality.[72] The language inescapably reflects the hierarchical order that pervaded every aspect of traditional Japanese life and Toson's skill with that quality of the language, already somewhat attenuated in his time, is effective in creating the feeling of a time now past. The overall effect is one of gravity and formality-- of aisatsu. The formality that prevailed in all aspects of life was in part generated by hierarchical considerations that grew out of the social and political order, but it was also reenforced by personal feelings.

Juheiji and Hanzo's recently-discovered relative Yamagami Shichirozaemon is so deeply moved by the visit of Hanzo and Juheiji as to be almost perfunctory in his greetings when they arrive for a visit. He is impatient to bring his guests into a series of increasingly formal contexts that culminates in the austere elegance of the family tea room. It is there, where every nuance of speech and action can be perceived against the subtle gradations of conduct prescribed by the tea ceremony, that Shichirozaemon finds himself able to express his feelings most clearly and effectively. It is extremely difficult to suggest the richness of this aspect of traditional Japanese life through the medium of an English language which in current usage increasingly confines our lives to a grey and monotonous world created by a cold and timorous rejection of most of the gradations of formality through which enjoyment of and respect for the occasions of one's own humanity and that of others might be made manifest.[73]

But, if considerations of hierarchy and formality are all-pervasive, so too is a sense of place, particularly in the parts of the story that are set in Magome. The foreground characters of the novel were rooted in their home districts in a way that is almost beyond the reach of imagination a century later, whether in Japan or elsewhere, and it is in the context of that concern with the unique qualities of place that attention is given to the portrayal of character. No one is ever stereotyped or patronized or exploited for comic or political effect. Paradox is, of course, one of the constants of human experience and ranking high among the many paradoxes of the society Toson is portraying is the warmth and humanity that often prevailed within the interstices of the harsh limitations of its rigorous hierarchy and discipline. The number of people who would really want the Tokugawa order back is vanishingly small and it is not at all difficult to see why, but that order is still often capable of generating an honest nostalgia even among the most thoughtful. This is demonstrated by, among other things, the ongoing vigor and popularity of an immensely popular historical literature set in Tokugawa and earlier times that for all its popularity not infrequently achieves an admirable degree of intellectual seriousness. On balance--and when contemplated at a safe distance from its structural rigidities and built-in injustices, its sometimes cruel or indifferent officials and their often dehumanizing use of power, its famines, and its medical practices--the Tokugawa order can create the not always unfruitful illusion that it sometimes left more space for human dignity and was more clear about what is really essential to that dignity than do some versions of the modern order which replaced it.[74] The objection that Toson may nevertheless have been a bit too indulgent to the Tokugawa order is not without substance, but that indulgence seems to come out of family nostalgia rather than any sympathy for Tokugawa harshness.

Toson's portrayal of character, however deeply enriched by his experience of European literature and civilization, is in the end a product of the preoccupation with the specific that characterizes traditional Japanese culture. That preoccupation gave human individuality a position of central importance. The often remarked dominance of the group in Japanese life operates within a definition of the group as the context in which individuality is most effectively and felicitously expressed. It is only through the constant application of the most rigorous standards of social and professional discipline that the humanity of the individual can be realized. A particular concern with specificity is manifested throughout *Before the Dawn*. It underlies the constant emphasis on detail; it informs the depiction of the mountains, the forests, the rivers, the villages, the highway, and the farms, and it determines the way that people are trained, carry out their duties, and live, always under the sometimes burdensome and constraining scrutiny of those around them.[75]

This commitment to the specific and unique is also reflected in the treatment of time. All episodes and incidents are placed in the annual cycle by some image or reference reminiscent of traditional poetic usage. These may seem gratuitous in a given context but their cumulative effect is an essential part of Toson's art, an art which so often draws upon the deepest levels of Japanese literary tradition. The change in the reckoning of years, months, and time of day after the adoption of the international calendar and clock in 1873 effectively symbolizes the many disorienting shifts in reference points that were then taking place.

Before the Dawn has drawn inspiration from a broad range of world literature and it plays a role in the history of its country that is analogous to that played by certain literary masterpieces of certain other countries. Like all Japanese literary people of his generation, Toson was well-acquainted with the works of the German playwright Gerhardt Hauptmann whose *Vor sonnen aufgang* has certain parallels although, for all the similarity both of title and of certain aspects of plot, there are clear and important contrasts between the novel and the play. Hauptmann treats a provincial, *nouveau riche* family in the process of being destroyed by a presumably hereditary moral and physical squalor. Toson tells of a fine old provincial family that goes into precipitous decline as the negative aspects of its heritage collide with a new social and political order. He shares with Hauptmann the naturalist vision of a dark genetic legacy but for Toson that vision stands in productive tension with compassion and respect for the humanity of his forebears and for the lives they had lived in traditional Japan.[76]

While Hauptmann's play may have suggested something of the stance and point of view of Toson's novel, it does not seem to be the source of the title. Toson never really made clear anywhere exactly what he meant by "the dawn," and speculation has ranged to include even a family story that it was inspired by Toson's working habits.[77] There may also be a faint echo of Toson's description of his arrival in Sendai, which marked the end of the grim decade following his father's death, as "the dawning of life." The Sendai years marked the first step in the recovery of his own spirit and was therefore an indirect first step in the long process of restoring his family. The frequent comparisons of the coming restoration of imperial prerogatives to the promise of the breaking dawn in Book One are perhaps more directly relevant, but the most important source is probably the term *reimeiki* or "period of dawning," which Japanese literary historians date from around 1887. It was then that the first blind rush of foreign borrowing, carried out in a desperate quest for anything that might help to ensure national survival, began to be superceded by a time still tense and perilous but marked by the emergence of a new generation with both the time and the training to think more critically about the problem of European influence. There is also a passing reference in the title to the darkness that was gathering over Japanese life during the years in which the novel was being written, but the primary resonance of the title is perhaps to be found in the life of its protagonist Aoyama Hanzo who lived through the darkest times that Japan was to know until World War II, only to die just before first light.[78]

The greater story from which *Before the Dawn* is drawn is that of the second of the five attempts made by leading nations during the past century and a half to reconstitute themselves. Its position in modern Japanese literature is analogous to that of Mikhail Sholokoff's depiction of Russian experience in *The Quiet Don*. If, in spite of its tragic tone, Toson's story leaves a less harsh aftertaste than Sholokoff's, it is perhaps in part because the Japanese writer has at least a marginally more satisfying story to tell. For all the gratuitous loss and suffering, and all the missed opportunities that the Meiji Restoration entailed, it was less bloody in its inception and in its subsequent period of consolidation than were either the Russian or the Chinese revolutions, less destructive of the best of its cultural heritage, and more successful in realizing its immediate goals.

The creation of the modern Italian nation has few useful points of comparison or contrast and the only other one of the recent national reconstructions to predate Japan's was that of modern Germany. It was on the German experience that Japan drew most heavily in developing its new institutions since it was then closest to Japan's both in time and in the problem of creating a nation out of a multitude of feudal states. The top-down pattern of the German reforms that was imposed on the institutional development and style of the Meiji government came to be reflected also in the orthodox views of the history of the Meiji Restoration that prevailed almost unchallenged until the appearance of *Before the Dawn*. There have since been other parallels in the roles the two nations have played upon the world stage and in the way in which they have been perceived by the world, but those parallels have usually been more often apparent than real. It is Thomas Mann's *Buddenbrooks* that comes closest to playing a role analogous to that of *Before the Dawn* in defining the subjective tone of the German transition to a modern social and political order at the same time that it reminds us of the profound differences between the German and Japanese experiences.[79] As the two works show, Japan and Germany were able to retain many of their traditional ways of thought and much of their traditional social structure to draw upon in the new age. In both cases this was a source both of invaluable assets and of grave liabilities, but if the negative aspects of the Meiji Restoration place it heartbreakingly far from the humane ideals to which Aoyama Hanzo and his associates aspired and against which one might wish to measure all historical processes, its more positive aspects may still be favorably compared with the far higher prices that have so often been paid elsewhere for smaller gains.

In the end, Toson confronted the most complex and baffling spiritual and intellectual issues of his day with a remarkable degree of success. The extensive personal agenda which he brought to the work was an essential ingredient of that success. *Before the Dawn* is not only an acceptable, if imperfect, presentation of history but an important historical document in its own right. Even though Toson's reach may sometimes have exceeded his grasp it remains, for all its flaws, one of the major monuments of modern Japanese literature.

NOTES

1. The edition of *Before the Dawn* on which this discussion draws constitutes volumes XI and XII of *Toson zenshu* (Tokyo, 1965-1971). All citations of Toson's works will be from this edition, hereafter cited as *Zenshu*. This article is indebted to two works by Ito Kazuo: *Shimazaki Toson jiten* (Tokyo, 1972) and *Toson sho shi* (Tokyo, 1973). The context in which the discussion is set was influenced by Marius B. Jansen, *Japan and its World: Two Centuries of Change* (Princeton, 1980) and by Daikichi Irokawa and Marius Jansen, eds., *The Culture of the Meiji Period* (Princeton, 1985). See also Shimazaki Toson, William E. Naff, tr., *Before the Dawn* (Honolulu, 1987).
2. Immediately relevant to the present discussion is Mori Ogai's brief 1915 "Rekishi-banare to rekishi sono mama," *Gendai Nihon bungaku zenshu*, vol. VII (Tokyo, 1953), pp. 413-414 (hereafter GNBZ). There is no record of Toson's opinion of this essay but the standards that it describes are very much those that Toson followed although Haga Noboru points out that both the emotionalism of Aoyama Hanzo and Toson's intense personal involvement in the story set this work apart from Ogai's careful control of aesthetic distance. The specific nature of the relationship between fact and fiction in *Before the Dawn* is taken up in Haga Noboru, *Yo-ake mae no kutsuzo to kyozo* (Tokyo, 1984), pp. 40-153.
3. Haga, *Yo-ake mae*, p. 126, points out that such a revision was already under way in academic circles, that Toson could not possibly have been unaware of it, but that he did not draw on it. Toson's highly personal approach to history led to lapses in his historical scholarship which he often managed to rise above in his role as a creative artist.
4. "Zen seiki o tankyu suru kokoro," from "Haru wo machitsutsu," *Zenshu*, vol. IV, pp. 186-190.
5. For all its occasional floridity and sentimental excess, themselves powerful evocations of the time in which it was written, Muto Naoharu's *Yo-ake mae no sakusha* (Tokyo, 1936) is a solid and seminal study of Toson and *Before the Dawn* that is echoed far more often than it is cited in subsequent scholarship, in part because many of Muto's insights have become the givens of the field. For some helpful cautions, see Wada Kingo's methodological essay, "Shimazaki Toson no kenkyu" in Nihon bungaku kenkyu shiryo sosho, *Shimazaki Toson* (Tokyo, 1973), pp. 313-317 (hereafter Yuseido 1973), and "Tosonteki naru mono" by the same author in *Issatsu no koza, Shimazaki Toson* (Tokyo, 1983), pp. 1-12 (hereafter Yuseido 1983). Wada's *Shimazaki Toson* (Tokyo, 1966) is highly recommended as are Kieda Masuichi, *Shimazaki Toson* (Tokyo, 1943); Hirano Ken, *Shimazaki Toson* (Tokyo, 1957); and Shibukawa Gyo's work of the same title (Tokyo, 1966). Kamei Katsuichiro, *Shimazaki Toson ron* (Tokyo, 1953) is a classic study while Senuma Shigeki, *Hyoden Shimazaki Toson* (Tokyo, 1959) remains the standard critical biography. An important recent addition is Kenmochi Takehiko, *Toson bungaku josetsu* (Tokyo, 1985).
6. The history of the Shimazaki family is discussed in Senuma, *Hyoden*, pp. 20-29, and Haga, *Yo-ake mae*, pp. 50-53.
7. Haga, *Yo-ake mae*, pp. 54-56; Senuma, *Hyoden*, pp. 29-41; Kawazoe Kunimoto, *Shimazaki Toson* (Tokyo, 1965), pp. 18-45. Kitaoji Ken, "Oitachi--kisoji no tabi" in Kitaoji Ken, Ito Kazuo, and Hayasaka Raigo, *Toson ni okeru tabi* (Tokyo, 1973), pp. 61-93, traces the theme of travel in the life and traditions of the Shimazaki family.
8. Toson describes the trip in *Before the Dawn* and in greater detail in "Osanaki hi," *Bifu*, *Zenshu*, vol. V, pp. 391-395.
9. A description of his life as a shosei is to be found in *Sakura no mi no juku suru toki*, *Zenshu*, vol. V.
10. David Pollack, *The Fracture of Meaning* (Princeton, 1986), p. 50, renders this as "the power of rectification," a reading that brings out another dimension of the expression.
11. Aono Suekichi, "Yo-ake mae ron," in *GNBZ*, vol. 61, p. 467.
12. Kenmochi, *Toson*, pp. 170-172.
13. Senuma, *Hyoden*, pp. 79, 92. Sugimoto Tamisaburo, "Toson ga mananda koro no

meiji gakuin," *Toson kenkyu "fusetsu,"* vol. 1 (Tokyo, 1973), pp. 51-60 (hereafter TKF), and the early parts of *Sakura no mi no juku suru toki* depict the Meiji gakuin of that time. See also my unpublished paper, "Christianity in Japan, Some Literary Reflections."
14. It seems to have been Kimura Kumaji who put Toson in touch with Kurimoto Joun. See Senuma, *Hyoden*, p. 96. For Kimura's extensive influence on Toson's early life and career see Aoyama Nao, "Kimura Kumaji to Shimazaki Toson," *Yuseido* 1973, pp. 33-50.
15. Sasabuchi Tomoichi, *Bungakkai to sono jidai* (Tokyo, 1961), pp. 731-860, examines Toson's education.
16. Haga, *Yo-ake mae*, p. 22, discusses the paradoxical strength of Confucian mores among Hirata disciples and in Shimazaki Masaki's teaching and conduct.
17. *Zenshu*, vol. 5, pp. 427-428.
18. *Zenshu*, vol. 5, p. 558; Sasabuchi, *Bungakkai*, pp. 821-822. See also Sasabuchi, "Shimazaki Toson to purotesutanchisumu," in *Yuseido* 1973, pp. 18-32; Yoshimura Yoshio, *Toson no seishin* (Tokyo, 1979).
19. Sasabuchi, *Bungakkai*, p. 822.
20. See William E. Naff, "Shimazaki Toson: Life History as Archetype and as Commodity" in Edmund Leites, ed., *Life Histories as Civilizational Texts*, International Society for the Comparative Study of Civilizations Occasional Papers No. 1 (Carlisle, Pennsylvania, 1977), pp. 25-39.
21. The accounts of Hideo's disastrous stewardship given in Senuma, *Hyoden*, pp. 52-57, and in Saimaru Yomo, *Shimazaki Toson no himitsu* (Tokyo, 1966), pp. 31-37 are essentially in agreement. Saimaru Yomo, a physician and psychiatrist, is the granddaughter of Hideo, Toson's second oldest brother. See also her "Nani ga kakarenakatta ka (Toson no byoseki)," *Kokubungaku, kaishaku to kansho* (April 1983), pp. 208-215, in which she discusses some of the sources of Toson's sexual problems.
22. Senuma, *Hyoden*, p. 94.
23. Ito Kazuo, "Seishun no hyohaku," in Kitaoji *et al., Toson*, pp. 93-120, retraces the trip in detail, giving the literary resonances that in part informed Toson's choice of itinerary. It is also described in *Sakura no mi no juku suru toki, Zenshu*, vol. 5. The uneven early story "Utatane" (*Zenshu*, vol. 16), draws heavily on the experience of that time.
24. Shibukawa, *Toson*, pp. 3-10. Senuma, *Hyoden*, pp. 99-100, notes Toson's conflicting stances of negativism and idealization toward women. See also Kawasaki Takeichi, *Toson no ren'ai to furusato no bungaku--Shinsei yori Yo-ake mae made* (Tokyo, 1948).
25. Shimazaki Osuke, *Toson shiki* (Tokyo, 1967), pp. 5-144, consists of a highly-detailed chronological outline of Toson's youth that is very effective in bringing those times into focus.
26. Senuma, *Hyoden*, pp. 124-128.
27. For Toson's roots in classical Japanese literature, see Kubota Harutsugu, "Toson to Nihon no koten" in Ito Kazuo *et al., Shimazaki Toson--kamoku to tembo* (Tokyo, 1979), pp. 143-158. Kubota cites Toson's well-noted affinity for Genroku writers, particularly Basho and Chikamatsu, and the influence of the rediscovery of Saikaku by Japanese writers around the beginning of the 1890s. He notes the constant echoing of characteristic phrases from Basho throughout Toson's works, particularly those written at times of crisis, the importance to Toson of Basho's view of courtly elegance as exemplified by Teika and Saigyo, and of his recommendation to "not follow after the people of old but to seek what they sought (p. 147)."
28. Kitamura Tokoku had also attended the Taimei elementary school although he and Toson did not meet there. He later graduated from Tokyo Senmon Gakko, the forerunner of Waseda University. Tokoku wrote widely on poetry, drama, and criticism and completed a critical biography of Emerson shortly before his death. It was prepared for publication by Toson who also edited two separate editions of Tokoku's collected works, in 1894 and 1922.
29. For a discussion of Dante Gabriel Rossetti and his influence on the

development of new Japanese poetry, see Donald Keene, *Dawn to the West, Poetry, Drama, Criticism* (New York, 1984), pp. 226, 229-230. Keene speaks of Rossetti's influence on Ueda Bin and Kambara Ariake but overlooks his crucial influence on Toson even in the course of discussing the close affinity between Toson and Ariake. Fuji Kazuya, *Shimazaki Toson, Wakanashu no sekai* (Tokyo, 1981), is a painstaking analysis of the work and its sources. See also Michael Brownstein, "*Jogaku Zasshi* and the Founding of *Bungakukai*," *Monumenta Nipponica*, vol. 35 (Autumn 1980), pp. 319-336.
30. Keene, *Poetry*, pp. 191-215, gives a concise outline of the development of the new Japanese poetry and describes Toson's role in its creation.
31. Hayasaka Raigo, "Bungei no yo-ake--Sendai no tabi"; and Ito Kazuo, "Kansatsu to shisaku--Komoro no tabi" in Kitaoji *et al.*, *Toson*; Hayashi Isamu, *Shimazaki Toson--tsuioku no Komoro gijuku* (Tokyo, 1978).
32. Tayama Katai, *Tokyo no sanjunen*, *GNBZ*, vol. 97 (1958), pp. 339-341, tells of a visit he and Yanagita made to Toson in Komoro. Yanagita's work was influential in the development of Toson's perception of his ancestral home. See also Haga, *Yoake mae*, pp. 32-35.
33. Shiga Naoya, "Kuniko," *Shiga Naoya zenshu*, vol. 4 (Tokyo, 1955), p. 61. Senuma, *Hyoden*, p. 172, gives the cause of death of the eldest daughter as "tubercular meningitis," of the second daughter as "acute indigestion," and of the third daughter as "meningitis."
34. The personal qualities as well as the speeches and writings that Inoki shares with Kitamura Tokoku are often noted, but a second model is introduced by Mizuno Toshio, "*Hakai* ni tojo suru Inoki Rentaro no moderu, Oe Isokichi," *Yuseido* 1973.
35. Natsume Soseki's letter to Morita Sohei dated 3 April 1906 is regularly cited as an early evaluation that, if perhaps too kind, has nevertheless aged well:
"... I have read *The Broken Commandment*. It is an outstanding work which will be passed down to later generations as a novel of the Meiji era. Such works as *The Golden Demon* will be forgotten in twenty or thirty years. *The Broken Commandment* will not. I do not read many novels, but if a novel worthy of the name has been produced during the Meiji era, I think it is *The Broken Commandment*. You should make a strong introduction of Toson in this month's issue of *Geien*."
See Kenneth Strong, Jr., tr., *The Broken Commandment* (Tokyo, 1974); Edwin McClellan, *Two Japanese Novelists* (Chicago, 1969), pp. 79-93, gives an extensive critical discussion. Donald Keene, in *Dawn to the West: Fiction* (New York, 1984), pp. 256-257, gives a brief notice of the work.
36. See Kenmochi, *Toson*, pp. 47-66, for Toson's European sources; pp. 54-59, for the influence of Rousseau. Joseph Roggendorf, "Yoroppajin no mita Shimazaki Toson," *Bungei*, vol. 11, no. 12 (June 1955), pp. 23-29, also emphasizes the melodramatic, as against the dramatic, qualities of *The Broken Commandment*.
37. The most extensive study of Japanese naturalism is Yoshida Seiichi, *Shizenshugi no kenkyu* (Tokyo, 1961), which concentrates on Toson's earlier prose works. The second chapter of Frances Mathy, *Shiga Naoya* (New York, 1974), is a succinct introduction to the peculiar qualities of Japanese naturalism.
38. See Senuma, *Hyoden*, Kamei, *Toson ron*; Hirano, *Toson*. An interesting treatment is Umese Yoshihira, "*Hakai* no seiritsu--tennosei no ryokyoku kozo to Genji no michi--," *Shimazaki Toson kenkyu*, no. 7 (May 1981), pp. 57-66; *Shimazaki Toson kenkyu*, no. 8 (December 1981), pp. 18-27. Shibukawa, *Toson*, pp. 79-93, gives a fresh and lively reading. Strong, *Broken Commandment*, "Introduction," is an important English-language source, as is McClellan, *Two Novelists*, 79-93.
39. Yoshimura, *Toson*, p. 1, discusses the revulsion that this line has often aroused. He confesses that he once shared it, but says that with the coming of maturity he found that he could no longer despise Toson's heavy-handed and obstinate grip on life.
40. See Yoshida, *Shizenshugi*, pp. 77-111, for the impact of *The Broken Commandment*, the writing of *Springtime* as a response, the literary sources of that work, which range from Shakespeare to Turgenev, and its contemporary reception.
41. Masamune Hakucho, *Shizenshugi seisui shi* (Tokyo, 1948), pp. 77-80.

42. For an English version, see Cecilia Segawa Seigle, tr., *The Family* (Tokyo, 1976).
43. Haga, *Yo-ake mae*, p. 5, reviews some of the resonances of this side of Masaki's life in Toson's own life.
44. See above, note 3. The epigraph to *Haru o machitsutsu* is in English: "'It seems to me you have reached the same crisis which I had attained in the days when I was about to write *Brand*, and I am convinced that you, too, will know how to find the healing drug that can expel disease from your body. In energetic production lies an admirable cure.' From a letter of Henrik Ibsen." See also "Etoranzee," *Heiwa to Pari, Zenshu*, vol. 6, pp. 245-248.
45. See Akiyama Shigeo, "Shimazaki Toson no kyoshi-tachi--*Sakura no mi no juku suru toki* o chushin to shite--," *Shimazaki Toson kenkyu*, nos. 9-10 (August 1982), pp. 75-94. English commentators tend to be even less interested in the work than do those writing in Japanese. Keene (*Fiction*, pp. 265-267) briefly notes the work, and McClellan (*Two Novelists*, pp. 74-75) does the same. See also Naff, "Shimazaki," and my unpublished article, "Christianity in Japan, Some Literary Reflections." Senuma, *Hyoden*, pp. 224-229, reflects the usual reading.
46. Kenmochi, *Toson*, pp. 28-30.
47. Senuma, *Hyoden*, p. 217.
48. I am indebted to Hirano, *Toson*, pp. 52-143, for this reading of *New Life*. Hirano argues (pp. 127-128) that *New Life*, *The Tempest*, and *Before the Dawn* are outward manifestations of a lonely and intense internal struggle. Kenmochi, *Toson*, pp. 107-136, discusses the novel in terms of its relationship to Rousseau's *La Nouvelle Heloise*, mentioning Dante's *Vita Nuova* as a second source of inspiration. He notes that while Toson read the *Confessions* in English as a young man, the edition of Rousseau's novel in his personal library was in French. The depiction of Setsuko in the novel is overtly colored by her literary predecessors Heloise and Beatrice, but it is the *Confessions* that form the point of departure for the novel. See also Kanda Shigeyuki, "*Shinseiron* -- *Anna Karenina* to no hikaku ni oite," *TKF*, vol. 8, (Tokyo, 1973), pp. 9-19; Naff, "Shimazaki;" McClellan, *Two Novelists*, pp. 123-137. An important discussion of *Shinsei* in English is Janet Walker, *The Japanese Novel of the Meiji Period and the Ideal of Individualism* (Princeton, 1979), pp. 194-203.
49. *TKF*, vol. 9, includes a series of articles about this earnest, well-intentioned, and awkward venture in feminist publishing, by Tokumitsu Matsu (p. 14), Ito Kazuo (pp. 21-38), and Yamanaka Sawako (pp. 38-47), which examines the undertaking in the light of the incidents that had earlier given rise to *Shinsei*. The same issue also reproduces a number of short documents relating to *Shojochi*.
50. The "Kisodani nikki" was published in the October 1897 and January 1898 issues of *Bungakkai* and later appeared as a supplement to Toson's second volume of poetry, the *Hitoha-bune* of 1898; *Zenshu*, vol. 1, pp. 145-166.
51. The *Daikokuya nikki* takes its name from the *yago* or house title of the Owaki family, the models for the Satake family of the Fushimiya in *Before the Dawn*. *Zenshu*, vol. 15, contains the abridged version prepared by Toson as a part of his research.
52. Ito Kazuo, *Toson sho shi*, pp. 88-90.
53. Toson wrote of his travels to Argentina, the United States and France in *Junrei, Zenshu*, vol. 14.
54. *Zenshu*, vol. 14.
55. Kume's remarks appeared in the *Yomiuri shinbun* for 3 and 5 January 1933 and are reprinted in Yoshida Seiichi, ed., *Toson, Katai* (Tokyo, 1959), pp. 137-139.
56. Murayama Tomoyoshi, Shimaki Kensaku, Funabashi Seiichi, Abe Tomoji, Hayashi Fusao, Kobayashi Hideo, Kawakami Tetsutaro, Takeda Rintaro, "*Yo-ake mae* gappyo kai," *Yuseido* 1973, pp. 288-308. Muto, *Yo-ake mae*, gives an even more positive evaluation as it draws on Toson's earlier writings in placing *Before the Dawn* in his overall career.
57. Haga, *Yo-ake mae*, p. 151, notes that the novel's influence on historiography comes from Toson's grass roots approach to the Restoration and his handling of the Hirata school as a rural religion, even though he did not fully exploit those

approaches. See also "Oboegaki," *Zenshu*, vol. 15, an extensive memorandum on the writing of *Before the Dawn* that is distinct from the similarly titled piece from *Momo no shizuku* cited below, note 76.
58. Haga, *Yo-ake mae*, p. 6.
59. See Haga, *Yo-ake mae*, pp. 35-36, 42-43, where the author discusses Toson's failure to create a true grass roots history of the Restoration. On pp. 44-45, Haga discusses the significance of the early Showa political scene in setting Toson's agenda for the work. He argues that it is in not fully grasping the implications of the top-down form which the Restoration quickly assumed that *Before the Dawn* is weakest and that these failures led to errors in dealing with primary sources. Yet he concludes the discussion with the observation that the objections that he is raising only serve to make clear that *Before the Dawn* has even broader implications for Japanese history than Toson realized.
60. Haga, *Yo-ake mae*, pp. 40, 104-106.
61. Senuma, *Hyoden*, pp. 266-267, gives additional background for "Arashi" and "Bunpai." Shimazaki Osuke, *Chichi Toson to watakushi-tachi* (Tokyo, 1947), reports that Keiji became a part of the avant garde *Nika kai* in which Arishima was an important member, while Osuke joined Murayama Tomoyoshi and his *Mavo* group.
62. Haga, *Yo-ake mae*, pp. 35, 44, 54-56.
63. Haga, *Yo-ake mae*, pp. 50-52. On p. 115 Haga notes the fact that Toson's depiction of the Meiji Restoration as a change that came not from the top down but from the bottom up is sufficient to make him a target for bitter attacks from some Marxists. Note "Nomin no tame ni," from *Haru o machitsutsu*, *Zenshu*, vol. 9, pp. 210-212. Here, writing in 1925, Toson discusses the love for the land and for people of the land displayed by such writers as Anderson and Bjornson and reflects on the lack of reliable news of the condition of Russian farm people following the revolution. He quotes a line from Gorki to the effect that farmers are finished and that the time now belongs to the awakened classes, saying that he sensed cold tears behind the words. Yet in spite of all this, Toson's attachment to the land is so strong that he has sent his own son back to the old family home. He closes by saying, "Today there is an outcry for improving the self-awareness of farmers. What we want more than that mass outcry are good friends who will live with the farmers, to come to know their lives, and to enable those farmers who are being separated from the soil to return to it." This appears to be the intellectual context in which he sent his son Kusuo back to the soil in Magome.
64. Kenmochi, *Toson*, pp. 158-162.
65. Ema Shu, *Yama no tami* (Tokyo, 1985). In his discussion of the work (*Yo-ake mae*, pp. 91-97), Haga gives three of the author's possible motivations: 1) to rebut *Before the Dawn;* 2) to support a small journal of local history; and 3) to break out of the professional and political trap in which Ema found himself.
66. Usui Yoshimi, *Azumino*, 5 vols. (Tokyo, 1965-1979). Kenmochi, *Toson*, pp. 30-33, notes that Usui's work, like that of Ema, was intended as a rebuttal to Toson, but argues that in the end its most important contribution lies in what it has to tell us about the contrast in local culture between the mountain-encircled and impoverished Kiso region and the relatively lush and open farming country of Azumino.
67. The historical resonances of the opening passage and their roots in *Kiso meisho zue* are discussed in Hayasaka Raigo, *Yo-ake mae no sekai* (Tokyo, 1973), pp. 3-8. Senuma, *Hyoden*, p. 15, cites as the earliest accounts of the district the *Shoku nihongi* entry for the year 702 A.D. telling of the opening of a mountain road in Kiso and the *Sandai jitsuroku* entry for 713 telling of the difficulty of travel in Kiso.
68. In "Motoori Norinaga," *Momo no shizuku* (1936), Toson compares Norinaga's historical role in setting the stage for the Meiji Restoration to that of Rousseau in setting the stage for the French Revolution (*Zenshu*, vol. 13, p. 266). Haga, *Yo-ake mae*, pp. 84-88, emphasizes the impact on subsequent Japanese institutions and behavior of the Hirata school's populist approach to education in which the common people, no longer finding it possible simply to follow the orders of those on high when national affairs had become corrupt and confused, had to find a way of

coming to their own decisions and of trying to live in a pleasant and harmonious way. This is what National Learning offered. On p. 118 he reminds us that Hanzo's poem about American dollars reflected not a *kokugaku* but a "*sonno joishugi*" posture. Muto, *Yo-ake mae*, p. 5, asks, "... What did those people seek in National Learning? What did they seek and how? That is the question. Wasn't it the same thing that Hanzo of *Before the Dawn* sought in National Learning and that Kishimoto of *Springtime* and *New Life* sought in modern thought or in Protestant Christianity...?" Part I of Tetsuo Najita and Victor Koschmann, eds., *Conflict in Modern Japanese History* (Princeton, 1982), relates very directly to this issue, particularly pp. 81-106. Haga (p. 149) argues that Toson's motive for the writing of *Before the Dawn* grew out of his contact with French culture, and that his handling of this theme closely follows that of Hasegawa Nyozekan. The strong influence of Rousseau on Hasegawa's perception of Norinaga was particularly sympathetic to Toson, who in turn tended to make Hanzo more of a follower of Norinaga than the follower of Atsutane that he actually was. Again (p. 312), Haga notes that while Hanzo is made out to be a man profoundly under the influence of Norinaga, it is the resonances of Atsutane's teachings that characterize his poetry. Carol Gluck, *Japan's Modern Myths* (Princeton, 1985, esp. chs. 1, 8), explores the later implications and ramifications of the imperial ideology.

69. Compare Muto, *Yo-ake mae*, p. 7: "*Before the Dawn* was taken to its logical conclusion but the night that lies over this people and this society has yet to rise. The true dawn is still distant. The author has taken up one great problem but I believe that he has left to us and to succeeding generations a monument to his longing for a true dawning, recording for us those problems and the sound of the quiet but relentless approach of that dawning."

70. Hirano, *Toson*, p. 172, speaks of Toson's prose style as "a cold and severe (*reigen na*) style appropriate to one who had fallen into a hell of stillness (*kyokusei no jigoku*)." Roggendorf, "Yoroppajin," p. 25, describes Toson's style as marked by "tactfulness" (*tsutsumashisa*).

71. Reprinted in *Zenshu*, vol. 11, p. 543.

72. In "Oboegaki," *Momo no shizuku*, *Zenshu*, vol. 13, pp. 289-304, Toson discusses some of his problems with terminology and with deciding just how much elucidation of obscure terms to include in the text (see also *Zenshu*, vol. 11, pp. 595-596).

73. Muto, *Yo-ake mae*, p. 6, sums up Toson's use of language: "It is not enough to say that the author of *Before the Dawn* was a superb poet. Nor is it enough to say that he was a great artist. In him we see an historian who, with the deepest feeling, took up many of the problems attendant upon the great political, economic, and social changes following the Meiji Restoration and upon the tragedies they entailed."

74. Such nostalgia seems to lie behind the perennial popularity of such historical extravaganzas as Yoshikawa Eiji's *Miyamoto Musashi*, Yamaoka Sohachi's *Tokugawa Ieyasu*, Ikenami Shotaro's *Sanada Taiheiki*, or Nakazato Kaizan's *Dai Bosatsu Toge*.

75. See Nakamura Hajime and Philip P. Wiener, eds., *Ways of Thinking of Eastern Peoples* (Honolulu, 1964), chs. 34, 35.

76. Kenmochi, *Toson*, pp. 155-166, reports that Hata Toyokichi's translation of Goethe's *Faust*, Ikuta Choko's translation of Dante's *Divine Comedy* and Yonekawa Masao's translation of Tolstoy's *War and Peace* occupied prominent positions in Toson's personal library while he was writing *Before the Dawn*. Shibukawa, *Toson*, pp. 60-61, reports that Toson was also reading Tsuchii Bansui's translation of *The Iliad* during that time.

77. Haga, *Yo-ake mae*, p. 48, comments on Toson's remarkable reticence on the subject of the significance of the title.

78. Muto, *Yo-ake mae*, "Introduction," p. 4, appears to be reflecting a common reading of the title in the mid-1930s when he says, "The night over the present age and society is dark and deep. How shall I present myself as a critic of *Before the Dawn* to those who are now holding their breaths in the depths of that night, hoping for a true dawn, believing steadfastly that such a dawn will come?"

79. Roggendorf, "Yoroppajin," *loc. cit.*, compares *Before the Dawn* with *Buddenbrooks*, *The Forsyte Saga*, and *The New Machiavelli*.

5
FORECASTING A PACIFIC WAR, 1912-1933: THE IDEA OF A CONDITIONAL JAPANESE VICTORY

Mark R. Peattie

Among the most nettlesome questions relating to Japan's decision to open hostilities with the United States during World War II has been the problem of rationality of that decision in strategic terms. With the overwhelming evidence of the preponderance of American strength staring them in the face why did Japan's leaders go ahead with a strategy of extreme risk? It appears that their immediate state of mind, as well as particular circumstances and assumptions, led them to believe that they had no other choice, but these questions still leave open the question of rationality. Twenty years ago, Hosoya Chihiro, reviewing the whole process of Japanese decision-making in those last months of 1941, persuasively argued that the outcome was essentially irrational.[1] Yet it can be argued that if one looks at the Pearl Harbor decision only within the narrow time-span of the waning months of 1941 and entirely within the framework of decisions by a handful of men, the attack inevitably appears to be a sort of spasm of Japanese response to a set of particular and suddenly-posed strategic problems and alternatives. Viewed only from this perspective, the relationship of means to ends in Japanese policy, November-December 1941, will probably always seem "irrational."

It is the contention of this chapter, however, that public discussion in Japanese books and periodicals of the possibilities of a Japanese-American war for many years prior to the actual outbreak of hostilities may have contributed to an atmosphere which, by late 1941, made war with the United States seem more rational than we now suppose. These forecasts and predictions dealt with a number of the strategic problems encountered in the actual Pacific War, but the presumption here is not one of direct influence on actual military or naval decisions, nor does it claim that the predictions were entirely rational themselves. It is rather that the literature of the "coming war in the Pacific"--some of it fantastic and sensational, some of it reasoned and analytical--served to keep alive before the Japanese public the idea of violent collision with the United States, and further, to contribute to an acceptance of an offensive war, not only as possible, but also feasible.

Predicting a Pacific war, of course, was not just a Japanese activity. Actually, the names of Western writers who dealt with the subject--Homer Lea, H. G. Wells, General "Billy" Mitchell, Hector Bywater, and George Fielding Eliot, to name the most famous--are better known today, and some were familiar to readers on both sides of the Pacific at the time (Lea and Bywater, for example, were translated into Japanese). But the works of their generally more prolific and usually more maritime-oriented Japanese counterparts-- Mizuno Hironori, Ishimaru Tota, and Ikezaki Chuko--have only been studied within the past decade or so even in their own country.[2] For the most part, comment in English on their work has been dismissive or superficial.[3] Yet, since Japanese forecasting of a Pacific war, like descriptions of future war between western industrial societies in the nineteenth and early twentieth centuries,[4] reflects the need to mobilize public support in the face of a perceived threat, as well as providing a means of estimating the changes in Japanese attitudes to war, this literature clearly needs to be reconsidered.

The Japanese literature of a coming war with the United States developed in four general stages, each a response to a real or imagined crisis in Japanese-American relations. The first of these, which arose from the gathering estrangement between the two nations over issues of imperial and naval rivalry in the Pacific and the racial phobias on the American west coast in the face of growing Japanese immigration into the region, peaked around 1913. The second phase of Japanese war scare literature was provoked by the cluster of tensions between Japan and America immediately after World War I--the naval rivalries that emerged at the Paris peace conference, the hostile reaction to Japan's Siberian adventure, and the resurgence of anti-Japanese legislation on the American west coast--and lasted from the end of the war in Europe to the opening of the Washington naval conference in late 1921. The furious Japanese reaction to provocative American policies and actions in the mid-1920s--particularly the anti-Japanese immigration bill passed by the Congress in 1924 and the United States Navy's Pacific maneuvers in 1924-25--provided the impetus for the third wave of Japanese war scare literature.

The last and most intense period of Japanese speculation on the possibility of a Pacific war coincided with the Manchurian crisis of 1931-32 and the American diplomatic and naval response to it. In large part, as Hata Ikuhiko has pointed out, the war scare atmosphere of 1932 was a one sided affair, involving the agitation of the Japanese public by dramatic interpretations in the Japanese media of certain American initiatives, particularly the American announcement in May 1932 that the Atlantic Scouting Fleet would remain on station in the Pacific with the Pacific Battle Fleet. Seen in the Japanese press as an ominous concentration of American naval power against Japan, the demarche triggered a deluge of war scare publications over the next twelve months. Books, articles, fiction, non-fiction, and translations on the "coming war" subject flooded the Japanese reading world: seventeen books and thirty-six articles on the subject in 1932 alone.[5]

Then, rather quickly, the great surge in Pacific war forecasting came to an end. It may have been because of the announcement in Washington in February 1933 that the Scouting Fleet was to be withdrawn from the Pacific. It may have been because more sober assessments began to appear, such as *Amerika wa Nippon to tatakawazu* (*America Will Not Fight Japan*), by foreign affairs analyst Kiyosawa Kiyoshi, who is the subject of Shin'ichi Kitaoka's chapter in this volume and who, after returning from a trip to the United States, argued that the mood in the United States made it very unlikely that the two nations would go to war. Or it may have been the fact that the Japanese government, having become fully convinced that the United States was not secretly preparing for hostilities, in some way helped to bank the fires of public sensationalism on the issue.[6]

Prognostications of a war between Japan and the United States fell into three general categories, though a significant portion of the literature was a blend of either the first two or the second two classifications. The first of these consisted of works of pure fiction, usually of a sensational nature, served up by civilian authors who were minimally informed on the strategic and tactical issues involved and who obviously wrote for profit and entertainment. The second type comprised fictional works and propaganda pieces by retired, and occasionally serving, army and navy officers, who apparently wrote to rouse public support for a particular military policy--increased naval construction, civil defense against aerial bombardment, and the like-- by dramatizing the threat of the American hypothetical enemy. The final category was represented by serious analyses by informed civilian commentators and military and naval professionals which surveyed the range of strategic, tactical, and technological problems involved in a Japan-U.S. war.

The pioneer Japanese efforts at Pacific war forecasting were of the first type--largely the work of amateurs who had little knowledge of either the United States or the complexities of modern warfare, but who were energized by the apparent injustices heaped upon their compatriots in California and who were sensitive to an American presence in the western Pacific as an obstacle to their own nation's expansionism. Highly fanciful, these studies usually combined a smattering of commentary on the naval weapons, strategies, and tactics of both sides with a melodramatic narrative of a campaign against the United States. Typical of the genre were Shirokita Yasushi's *Nichi-Bei kaisen yume monogatari* (*A Fantasy of the Opening of War between Japan and America*), first published in 1913, and Oto Ryusen's *Nichi-Bei kaisen seba* (*If War Breaks Out between Japan and America*) which appeared the next year. Both authors served up dramatic accounts of Japanese conquest of American territory--the Philippines, Hawaii, and portions of the United States. Generally aware of the hardening dogma in Japanese naval circles that the outcome of the Pacific war would have to be determined quickly by a major fleet encounter in the tradition of Togo at Tsushima, both authors also dwelt upon a similarly decisive encounter between opposing lines of Japanese and American battleships. Though conscious of the preponderance of American material and numerical strength, they saw this as being more than offset by traditional Japanese fighting spirit.

Books like these, in which descriptions of Japanese naval glories and military conquests (usually of the Philippines and Hawaii, sometimes of the American Pacific coast) were substituted for meaningful analysis of strategy and tactics, were obviously less intended to inform the Japanese public of the strategic and material requirements for victory than to provide it with satisfying visions of Japanese expansive power and military ardor. Prospects of maritime war with the United States were exciting if nothing else, promising a quick, clean victory and the happiest of imperial results. As such they contrasted sharply with the more pessimistic fantasies concerning a second land war with Russia, influenced as they were by Japanese memories of protracted slaughter before Port Arthur.

The works of retired army and navy officers can also be found within the more lurid range of this literary spectrum. In 1921 businessman and former Army general Sato Kojiro (1862-1927) wrote *Nichi-Bei moshi tatakawaba* (*If Japan and America Fight*) to minimize what he considered Japanese fear in the face of growing American naval and industrial power. Sato not only dredged up all the old slogans, like *Yamato damashii*, which proclaimed the superiority of Japanese spirit over American industrial strength, but also added contemptuous assessment of American weaknesses--materialism and lack of moral fibre, the internal contradictions of race, class, and politics, the craven nature of its fighting forces--which would make it possible for Japan to face an American war with equanimity. Given what he considered Japan's invulnerable geographic position, Sato believed that Japan needed merely to adopt a defensive strategy, waiting on its own shores for an American fleet, struggling to cross the Pacific, harassed and panicked by Japanese naval attacks and running low on fuel, to enter Japanese waters. There, the Japanese fleet, fresh and close to its home bases and emboldened by the Japanese warrior spirit, could deal it a smashing blow.[7] While this was a strategic scenario shared in outline by the navy brass, its emotional and simplistic description in Sato's book could hardly have enlightened the Japanese public on the complexities and variables of such a campaign.

That same year (1921) Sato carried a number of his opinions even further in a fictional account of a conflict in the Pacific, *Nichi-Bei senso yume monogatari* (*A Fantasy of War between Japan and the United States*), in which America is brought to its knees by defeat at sea, aerial bombardment, and foreign invasion. Written with a minimum of analysis, Sato's war fantasy included many of the prejudices and misconceptions about American fighting ability which filled his other work. That it reflected the narrow frame of reference of a certain type of officer in the 1920s is attested to by a similarly far-fetched production, *Nichi-Bei sen chikakushi* (*The Japan-U.S. War is Coming*), written at the end of the decade by another retired general, Kato Seikatsu, who envisaged the Japanese conquest of continental America in a ten year war.

Yet other military professionals writing on the coming war in the Pacific did not share this optimistic view and were more anxious to alert the Japanese public both to the risks involved in such a conflict and to the vital requirements for a Japanese victory over the more powerful American fleet. One such author was Commander Mizuno Hironori (1875-1945), Superintendent of the Naval Archives of the Navy Ministry, and one of the few Japanese military or naval figures to write about the Japan-America war while on active service. Mizuno, who had been commissioned by the navy to assist in the completion of the official history of the Russo-Japanese War, in 1910 made a name for himself by writing the classic popular account of the Battle of Tsushima, *Kono issen* (*The Decisive Battle*). Four years later, writing under the pseudonym, "a naval commander," Mizuno drew up a fictional sequel, *Tsugi no issen* (*The Next Decisive Battle*), in which the annihilation of the Japanese Combined Fleet in a grand encounter with the American battle line in the Philippines leads to a catastrophic Japanese defeat, bursting the bubble of Japan's expansionist hopes. Mizuno's purpose in dashing off this fantasy (and, certainly, that of the Imperial Japanese Navy which let him publish it) was to rally public support for a massive increase in Japan's naval strength, specifically, the building of an "eight-eight fleet" (eight battleships and eight battle cruisers to be replaced in eight years). Without such an increase in naval power, Mizuno was trying to warn his readers, Japanese expansion was an illusion and the great naval encounter a foolhardy gamble.[8]

For all that, Mizuno's work can hardly be said to have been a careful or serious disquisition on the complexities of a possible conflict in the Pacific, since it differed from other examples of the lurid war scare literature of the day only in its pessimistic conclusions. But more thoughtful and analytical treatments of the subject appeared early in the next decade as professional military and civilian commentators began to ponder the uncertainties which followed the new naval arrangements prescribed by the Washington Treaty of 1922. Would Japan have true naval hegemony in the western Pacific now that America was forbidden to construct new bases there? Could Japanese submarines and light naval units make effective use of Japan's new island territories within its Micronesian mandate to ambush a westward-moving American fleet? What were Japan's chances in a major fleet encounter now that it had accepted a ratio in capital ships of sixty per cent of the strength of the United States Navy?

For most of the Japanese naval profession the bargain struck at Washington had been a bad one. Reserve Lieutenant Commander Ishimaru Tota (1881-1942) was one of those officers who believed that the sacrifice of the seventy per cent principle made for an unequal, oppressive, and therefore essentially unstable peace. To Ishimaru, who believed that heavy surface units would continue to be the backbone of the fleet, the supposed Japanese preponderance in the western Pacific might turn out to be an illusion at the time of a major fleet encounter. With Japan's current ratio of only fourteen capital ships to America's twenty-two, the main Japanese battle force would inevitably be defeated even if Japanese naval attacks on the main United States battle force west of Hawaii reduced it by thirty percent.[9] One of the few Japanese naval analysts to write openly of the continuing inevitability of war with America, Ishimaru outlined the various strategies which the Japanese navy, as the weaker of the two sides, would therefore have to use. Essentially, these focused on the rapid seizure of the Philippines and Guam as vital bases in the West Pacific and on a commerce-raiding strategy in which Japanese submarines, aircraft, and cruisers would harass American supply and communications lines in the Pacific. Yet Ishimaru was vague as to the ultimate success of such a strategy.[10]

Given the fact that the agreements reached at Washington failed to deal with a number of fundamental problems troubling the Japanese-American relationship, the eventual return of suspicion and enmity between the two nations should have been hardly surprising, but few in responsible positions in either nation could have predicted the speed with which American policies and actions were to inflame national passions and lead to another war scare in the 1920s. The humiliation of the American Immigration Act and the movements of the American Battle Fleet in the Pacific were trumpeted regularly in the Japanese press and became the subject of popular mass meetings. To these broadly-based feelings of national outrage were now added the inflammatory anti-American agitation of the ultra-nationalist right. In such an atmosphere did the Japanese literature of the coming war in the Pacific spring forth anew. Yet, in this third phase, Japanese war forecasting became less fantastic and adventurous and more somber, sophisticated and analytical.[11]

Recognition of the new strategic realities help to explain this trend. There was, in the first place, the chilling sense of national isolation now that the Anglo-Japanese Alliance had been relinquished and now that fresh doubts were being raised about the Washington Treaty system as an adequate guarantor of Japan's security. In considering the possibility of war with America, Japanese commentators now always had to assume that the United States might form an alliance with Britain, China, or the Soviet Union and thus turn Japan's industrial, military, and naval inferiority into a disastrous handicap. They realized, moreover, that certain American naval initiatives during the decade had made Japanese prospects for victory even slimmer. There was, in the first place, the shift in American naval concentration from the Atlantic to the Pacific when the United States Battle Fleet was brought to San Diego in 1922. Second, the long anticipated American offensive across the Pacific against Japan in the event of war seemed to have been given almost irresistible punch by the adoption of the so-called "ring formation," a tactical organization which shielded the main American force of capital ships within concentric rings of cruisers, destroyers, and submarines, and thus gave the American naval offensive formidable defensive powers against Japanese counter-attacks.[12]

But the difficulties to be faced by Japan in a war with the United States seemed to many Japanese commentators to go even beyond the question of weapons and tactics.[13] There were other, broader dilemmas, of which two loomed very large: America's continental position and its overall productive power. Geographically, continental America seemed unassailable. Even if Japanese naval forces could threaten Panama and the west coast of America, there was little reasonable expectation of a successful invasion of the United States, let alone the capture of its capital. The gap in productive power might also play a decisive role in the strategy of a Japanese-American war. Already overwhelmingly advantageous to the United States, this disparity could only grow worse for Japan in a protracted war.

Given these assumptions, the emerging consensus among these Japanese who wrote on the possibility of a Japan-U.S. war was that the best Japanese strategy lay in seizing the initiative at the outset of the war by pre-emptive attack and by the occupation of the Philippines and Guam early in the struggle. The former would throw the enemy off balance and the latter would not only give Japan control of the Western Pacific, but also present the United States with such an enormous task in the recovery of its lost possessions that it would sue for peace rather than expend the effort.

Yet Pacific war forecasting in Japanese books and journals in the 1920s generally assumed a tone of doubt that even these initiatives could guarantee Japanese victory. Though most assessments still centered on the probability of a great naval battle between capital ships--variously located off the Bonins, in the Carolines, or north of Luzon--few reached any forthright conclusions as to victory or defeat, in part because of the technological advances in aerial and subsurface technology.

Retired Admiral Kawashima Seijiro, writing in 1924, renewed Ishimaru Tota's alarms concerning the naval limitations of 1922 and declared America's considerable superiority in tonnage would permit the United States Navy to destroy the Japanese fleet piecemeal if the two were ever to collide.[14] Akamatsu Hiroyasu, another retired officer writing the same year, saw the United States holding most of the trump cards should a Pacific war break out, particularly the possession of advanced bases in the western Pacific and supposed American superiority in aircraft (particularly due to the existence of America's huge NC seaplane bombers).[15] Akamatsu was wide of the mark, of course. Far from being powerful bastions, the Philippines and Guam were highly vulnerable to attack and American analysts judged American airpower in the Pacific to be decidedly inferior in relation to that of Japan.[16] In *Kyokuto senso to Beikoku kaigun* (*A Far Eastern War and the American Navy*) military critic Hirata Shinsaku, viewing the United States Navy as a powerful weapon of American economic imperialism in East Asia, explored the strategies, doctrine, tactics, weapons, and leaders of that fleet. Hirata believed that it was in the American strategic interest to attempt a short, decisive war to prevent Japan from consolidating control of the West Pacific and from securing the resources of the Asian continent. Like Akamatsu, he saw the war centering on a struggle in the Philippines and believed that, should the Americans win it, they would storm northward to capture either the Ryukyus or the Bonins. Using either of those positions, the United States Battle Fleet would then try to lure the Japanese Combined Fleet into the final grand encounter--the Sekigahara of a Pacific war, he called it--which would feature not only a colossal gunnery duel, but a massive air battle overhead between carrier aircraft and float planes. Despite the Japanese ability to break the American "ring formation" and despite the heavy losses on both sides, Hirata predicted that the battle would end in a Japanese defeat, simply because the Americans would bring more ships and planes to the battle.[17]

To this trend of Japanese war forecasting in the 1920s which stressed the superiority of American naval strategy and weaponry, which viewed ambiguously Japan's ability to survive in a protracted war, and which more often than not predicted Japan's defeat in a great surface encounter, there were two significant and influential exceptions. One, embodied in the "Final War" theory of Colonel (and later, Lieutenant General) Ishiwara Kanji, was essentially continental in outlook and the other, represented by the writings of the naval critic Ikezaki Chuko, was still maritime in perspective.

Ishiwara's strategic views,[18] which he had begun to develop as a lecturer in military history at the Army Staff College, 1926-28, were placed in a vast historical framework--"The Final War"--in which conflict between Japan and the United States was seen as the ultimate collision between two penultimate stages of human civilization, one Asian (that is, Japanese) and one Western (that is, American). That final cataclysm--some decades beyond--would be a swift war of annihilation wrought by aircraft able to circle the globe without landing and capable of carrying indescribably destructive payloads.[19]

For some time before that, Ishiwara predicted, Japan and America would undoubtedly be locked in a protracted struggle which would harden each side for the final confrontation. In this exhaustive conflict, in which fighting might be waged only intermittently, industrial power and even diplomacy would be major elements in the belligerency. In a protracted war, Ishiwara was convinced, Japan could not depend upon her overseas lifelines to provide the nation with the essential resources to wage it. Quite possibly these maritime communications would be cut and the home islands blockaded. The only way to avoid this maritime dependence, therefore, was to imitate the continental strategy of Napoleon by harnessing the resources of the Asian continent, particularly those of Manchuria and North China. Such an effort would involve the creation of an industrial bastion centered in Manchuria, which would provide the resources and weapons with which to wage protracted war. Ishiwara was convinced that, once self-sufficient in Asia, as the United States was in North

America, Japan could not only stand against America, but, if need be, against the world.[20] For Ishiwara, therefore, Japan's military security lay on the Asian continent, not on the oceans. Like all Japanese strategists contemplating a war with the United States, of course, Ishiwara believed that Japan should endeavor to gain control of the Pacific by occupying the Philippines, Guam, and if possible, Hawaii. Yet in his official memoranda recommending strategies against the United States, he was utterly vague as to how the Japanese navy was to accomplish these bold initiatives. This rather casual approach to maritime strategy arose from his belief that, essentially, an American war would not be won or lost in the Pacific. To Ishiwara, the long anticipated great encounter at sea which would decide the war was a myth fostered by naval enthusiasts. It was a fundamental mistake, he insisted, to believe that Japan would lose the war if she lost control of the seas. To the contrary, Japan, even if driven from the Pacific, could carry on the fight quite successfully from its Asian stronghold while it raced to perfect the ultimate air weapon to win "The Final War."[21]

The novelist-turned-naval critic Ikezaki Chuko (1891-1949) provided a radically different perspective in the re-evaluation of the Japanese strategic dilemmas of the 1920s. Not only was he maritime in his orientation, but also less concerned with historical meaning and grand strategy and far more involved with the weaponry and tactical doctrine of what he saw as an essentially naval struggle. These problems he took up in a series of books which brought him sudden public acclaim: *Beikoku osoruru ni tarazu* (*The United States is not to be Feared*) published in 1929; *Nippon sensuikan* (*Japanese Submarines*), published that same year; and *Rokuwari kaigun tatakaieru ka?* (*Can We Fight with a Sixty Per Cent Navy?*) published in 1932.[22] Other books followed and by the mid-1930s Ikezaki's demonstrated grasp of naval history, strategy, doctrine, and technology, as well as his relatively dispassionate and scientific approach to Pacific war forecasting had assured his solid reputation as a naval critic.[23]

Ikezaki's *Beikoku osoruru ni tarazu* was the first really intellectual and analytical approach to the study of a Japan-U.S. war. His purpose in writing it was to dispel what he considered the illogical and unnecessary awe of American power among his countrymen. In rejecting arguments about the inevitability of a Japanese defeat in any collision with the United States, Ikezaki based his confidence on three major contentions: Japan's strategic advantage provided by its geographic location, the technological superiority of Japanese warships, and the tactical superiority of Japanese naval training. The first of these derived from the strategic situation of any Pacific war between the two nations: it would be fought west of Hawaii and would thus permit Japan to wage it from a nearly impregnable defensive position in that (in Ikezaki's view) Japan could neither be effectively attacked from the Asian continent by any land power nor blockaded at long range by the United States. Ikezaki based his second assertion on both the better balance of the Japanese navy in terms of warship types and on the superior speed of the Japanese battle line which gave it the opportunity to accept or refuse a major naval engagement. Finally, in considering the possibility of a major fleet action, should it be forced on the Japanese navy, Ikezaki concluded that Japanese superiority in crew morale, offensive spirit, gunnery, and torpedo tactics would more than make up for a quantitative inferiority in battleship main armament. While careful to avoid framing his argument in the mystical perspective of Japanese spirit *vs.* American materiel, Ikezaki simply concluded that numbers alone would not determine the outcome of a collision between the Japanese and American fleets.[24]

But to say that Japan could not be beaten to its knees by the United States was not to argue that the reverse was possible. Sweeping aside earlier war fantasies and their scenarios of Japanese invasions of the United States, Ikezaki limited his concern to what he considered would be reasonable objectives in a Pacific war: freedom of action in East Asia and the security of Japan's maritime communications with Asia and Europe. The strategy which Ikezaki advocated in winning a Pacific war and obtaining these objectives was simple: to acquire an invincible defensive position by seizing the Philippines and Guam at the outset of the war and holding them with adequate forces. Having in effect won the war by these initiatives, Japan would not need to undertake any further operations against the United States unless that enemy chose to try to carry the fight to Japan, in which case the Japanese navy operating from all but impregnable Japanese bases could, if it chose, venture out to meet the Americans with confidence borne of its superiority in technology and training.[25]

Ikezaki carried a number of his strategic speculations further in his more specialized studies on Japanese submarines. Like his first volume, its purpose was to show that Japan's inferiority in capital ships did not necessarily mean that Japan's overall defense was in peril and that indeed, under the conditions of the Washington Naval Treaty, it was the submarine which provided Japan with its most formidable weapon. Not only could Japan's huge I-class submarines raid American west coast ports and exploit the vulnerability of American trade routes throughout the Pacific, but repeated attacks by the navy's high speed attack submarines could reduce the size of any American battle fleet moving westward across the Pacific, a concept which reflected the emerging doctrine of interceptive operations worked out by Admiral Suetsugu Nobumasa, commander of the Combined Fleet.[26]

In 1932, Ikezaki shifted his focus from submarines to aircraft while continuing his cautious optimism about Japan's chances in a Pacific war with the United States. In his *Rokuwari kaigun tatakaieru ka?* he argued that the increasingly preponderant role of aircraft in a Pacific war would work to the advantage of Japan, not the United States. He based his assertion on three reasons: 1) the lack of American air bases in the West Pacific, where the war would largely be fought; 2) the increasing capabilities of air reconnaissance which lessened the chances of the grand battleship encounter which the Japanese navy might wish to avoid until it could pick a time of its own choosing; and 3) the opportunity provided by air power for a sudden pre-emptive strike against the United States.[27]

For Ikezaki, who was convinced that Japan's best chance in a Pacific war lay not in a decisive surface encounter, but in seizing the initiative at the opening of hostilities, this last point was particularly important. This meant, in turn, the most careful attention must be given to timing the opening of hostilities. As he was writing in the days when the United States Battle Fleet was still stationed on the west coast, Ikezaki urged a pre-emptive strike at the dock and storage facilities at Pearl Harbor to destroy them before the American battle line arrived. Such an attack, Ikezaki believed, would be so demoralizing that an American offensive drive might be effectively blunted before it even started across the Pacific. The hardest of hardliners, retired Admiral Kato Kanji, agreed and considered Ikezaki's discussion of these matters the finest part of the book. Writing to the author, Kato called Hawaii a "cancer in the Pacific" and declared that "To vacillate about beginning the war and to avoid fighting will make for a greater loss. To err by several days in the opening of hostilities will truly lead to a [strategic] no man's land."[28]

Ikezaki Chuko's speculations form an important public dimension of Japanese naval thought at the opening of the 1930s. To view his approach to the prospect of war with America as essentially reasoned and analytical, rather than fantastic and ideological is not to argue, of course, that his ideas did not include some fundamental misconceptions about the relative capabilities of Japan and the United States. Reflection on the course of the war from 1941 to 1945 makes these sufficiently apparent as to obviate discussion of them here.

Yet his writings are of interest not only for their thoroughness and wealth of detail, but also because they reflect certain emerging Japanese attitudes, including a criticism of the Japanese navy's obsession with big gun parity which prefigures the views of Yamamoto

Isoroku and air enthusiasts within the navy, the idea of a pre-emptive strike on Hawaii, and the concept of a negotiated peace based on a conditional Japanese victory. In stating these views Ikezaki contributed significantly to public discussion of the possibility of war with the United States on terms that were better than even.

With the onset of the Manchurian affair, the East Asian crisis of the early 1930s, and the last great wave of Japanese war scare literature other works appeared, of course, which had begun to influence the attitudes of the Japanese navy itself.[29] Navy reserve Lieutenant Commander Fukunaga Kyosuke's wildly sensational 1933 fantasy *Nichi-Bei sen miraiki* (*A Forecast of the Japan-United States War*), for example, drew enthusiastic comment from both admirals Kato and Suetsugu.[30] That same year war fever also inspired Mizuno Hironori to update his twenty year obsession with the great Pacific naval battle by stressing the role of aircraft carriers and naval air power in a Pacific war. His new study--half-fantasy, half-analysis--treated the usual Japanese offensives toward the Philippines and Guam, as well as carrier attacks on San Francisco and the Panama Canal. But these were to be side-shows compared to the decisive battle over Hawaii. To attempt to take what Mizuno considered the vital strong point of the Pacific with surface forces would be suicidal, in his view. "The only way in which to assault Hawaii is with an overwhelming air assault," he insisted.[31] Other works, like Hirata Shinsaku's *Warera moshi tatakawaba* (*If We Fight*), offered a pasticcio of information concerning the fighting forces of the two nations, as well as interesting speculation on possible operations--including carrier and submarine attacks on Hawaii--peppered with some singular notions of American fighting abilities (Western eyesight was less accurate than that of the Japanese because of eye color; Americans could not fight in the South Pacific because Westerners wilt in the tropics), and all served up in sensational style.[32]

More serious writers also continued to ponder Japan's prospects in a Pacific war, of course. Ishimaru Tota, who in 1931 had dismissed the prospects of war in his *Nichi-Bei hatashite tatakau ka?* (*Will Japan and the United States Really Fight?*), a year later concluded that Japan would be on the verge of war by 1935, if the United States succeeded in isolating Japan on issues involving Manchuria and Japanese naval security. His *Nippon tai-sekai senso* (*Japan's War Against the World*) reflected the deepening sense of desperation and international isolation felt by many in Japan. Faced with the possibility that a Japan-U.S. war might mushroom into a global war against Japan--certainly, Britain would join the United States, Ishimaru believed--Japan's best chance lay in a skillful meshing of non-military and military efforts: diplomacy to secure the neutrality of neighboring

Russia and China; psychological warfare to create disruptive agitation in Latin America, the Philippines and India; and a carefully integrated strategy to enable Japan to choose the best time to go to war. Selecting such a time would permit Japan to take advantage of surprise, the essential element in any war against a coalition led by the American colossus. "... The best way for a militarily inferior power to defeat superior enemies one by one," Ishimaru insisted, "is to open hostilities ahead of the enemy and fall like a thunderbolt on the unsuspecting foe."[33]

With the end of the crisis of 1932, the flood of Japanese literature predicting war with America flowed to a trickle. Though Ikezaki, Ishimaru, and one or two other serious writers wrote occasionally about the subject throughout the decade, Pacific war forecasting never again occupied a major place in the attention of the Japanese reading public. Prospects of war with the Soviet Union monopolized the headlines in 1933-34, and by the end of the decade, as relations with the United States moved toward their final crisis, the Japanese public was already too aware of the daily attrition of an actual quicksand war on the Asian continent to be interested much longer in either fantasy or speculation concerning a future conflict.

For two decades the literature of a coming war in the Pacific had kept alive the idea of a violent collision with the United States. In a number of ways it appears to have anticipated strategies actually employed by the Japanese in the first months of the real Pacific War: the sudden opening of hostilities by a pre-emptive air strike, specifically against American facilities in Hawaii; the early conquest of the Philippines and Guam; the effort to forge a secure position in East Asia and the West Pacific from which to bargain for a negotiated peace. Yet to the extent that it may have sensitized the Japanese public to the idea of a Japan-U.S. war, it would also seem to have perpetuated a number of popular misconceptions in Japan about the nature of such a conflict.

First, those who wrote about a Pacific war, by and large, never really understood the nature of America's industrial capacity for conducting war on a vast scale nor the American tradition of fighting wars to a victorious conclusion rather than to a negotiated settlement.

Second, Japanese commentators tended to view a Pacific war in isolation, without allowance for events elsewhere in the world which might influence the nature of the struggle. Even those, like Ishimaru Tota, who made a connection between a Japan-U.S. war and the larger framework of international relations, tended only to see the former affecting the latter. In actuality, of course, the setting for the Pacific War emerged as part of a global confrontation which began elsewhere in the world, a fact which was to have profound and unforeseen influence on Japanese policies from 1939 to 1941.

Third, for all the speculations in this literature on two of the most important technological advances of the first World War--the submarine and the airplane--Japanese writers never really grasped the extent to which these new weapons might weaken Japan's defensive position and destroy all hope of Japanese industrial self-sufficiency. While discounting the idea of an American surface blockade of the home islands, for example, none envisioned the extent to which American submarines would roam East Asian waters at will, interdicting the sea lanes, destroying the Japanese maritime fleet, and separating Japan not only from its extended conquests, but from the resources of the Asian continent as well.

Lastly, few of the sensational fantasies or even the more careful analyses of strategy really conveyed to the Japanese reading public the extent to which the destructive forces of modern war would be directly launched against them. Ishiwara Kanji had some conception of the fact, though his ideas on the "Final War" did not reach the Japanese public as a whole until a year or so before the Pacific War. Ishimaru Tota was one of the few who stressed the point that civil populations were no longer safe from a massive injury by a trans-oceanic enemy. Writing in 1932, he issued a warning to his readers that was both prophetic and uncommon in the literature of the coming Pacific conflict:

> Because Japan has never been exposed to an enemy attack upon her shores and since, for many years, America has not known the dread of foreign invasion, neither nation has really experienced the horrors of modern war. But in the next great war, awesome air navies, flying high over the heads of the defending forces, will launch attacks directly upon the enemy homeland.... Our complacency that the peace of the Pacific is preserved by its very vastness blinds us to the advances that science has made in war.[34]

NOTES

1. Chihiro Hosoya, "Twenty-five Years After Pearl Harbor: A New Look at Japan's Decision for War," in Grant Goodman, comp., *Imperial Japan and Asia: A Reassessment, Occasional Papers of the East Asian Institute* (New York, 1966), pp. 52-63.
2. See Hata Ikuhiko's analysis of Japanese and American war fantasies in his *Taiheiyo kokusai kankeishi: Nichi-Bei oyobi Nichi-Ro kiki no keifu, 1900-1935* (Tokyo, 1972), pp. 217-28.
3. English language commentary on the Japanese public literature of a possible U.S.-Japan war (as opposed to official plans, memoranda, and other confidential documents on the subject by Japanese military and naval professionals) has been meagre. Writing during World War II the military analyst Alexander Kiralfy dismissed all such writings as sensational or superficial. Alexander Kiralfy, "Japanese Naval Strategy," in Edward Meade Earle, ed., *Makers of Modern Strategy: Military Thought from Machiavelli to Hitler* (Princeton, 1944), p. 460. Saeki Shoichi, in a 1972 study, concentrated on the more fictional (and admittedly more sensational) works of the genre. See Shoichi Saeki, "Images of the United States as a Hypothetical Enemy," in Akira Iriye, ed., *Mutual Images: Essays in American-Japanese Relations* (Cambridge, 1975), pp. 100-114. John Stephan, however, in the third chapter of his superbly written *Hawaii Under the Rising Sun: Japan's Plans for Conquest After Pearl Harbor* (Honolulu, 1984), deals critically, if briefly, with a select number of both popular and serious works on Pacific war forecasting as they related specifically to Japanese consideration of a possible occupation of Hawaii.
4. I. F. Clarke, "Forecasts of Warfare in Fiction, 1803-1914," *Comparative Studies in Society and History*, vol. 10 (October 1967), pp. 1-25.
5. Hata, *Taiheiyo*, pp. 210-212.
6. Hata, *Taiheiyo*, p. 223; Ogawa Kanji, "Himerareta tai-Bei choho katsudo," in *Himerareta Showa shi*, special issue of *Chisei* (December 1956).
7. Sato Kojiro, *Nichi-Bei moshi tatakawaba* (Tokyo, 1921), pp. 3-14, 58-97.
8. Matsushita Yoshio, *Mizuno Hironori* (1960), pp. 26-27.
9. Ishimaru Tota, *Appaku sareta Nippon: Washinton kaigi no shinso* (Tokyo, 1922), p. 69.
10. Ishimaru, *Appaku*, pp. 65, 397-406.
11. Hata, *Taiheiyo*, pp. 154-55.
12. For details see Hata, *Taiheiyo*, pp. 234-35.
13. My assertions in this and the next two paragraphs are based on Hata, *Taiheiyo*, pp. 186-88.
14. Kawashima Seijiro, *Nichi-Bei issen ron* (Tokyo, 1925), p. 2.
15. Akamatsu Hiroyoshi, *Gunjin mitaru tai-Nichi to tai-Bei saku* (Tokyo, 1924), pp. 123-25, 132, 143-44.
16. See for example Jefferson Davis, *Japan: Air Menace of the Pacific* (Boston, 1927).
17. Hirata Shinsaku, *Kyokuto senso to Beikoku kaigun* (Tokyo, 1930), pp. 3-46, 75-78, 92-93, 122, 180-81, 243.
18. Ishiwara's views, while strictly speaking not a matter of public record in the 1920s, are included here because they eventually did come to have an appeal to a wide spectrum of officers within the army and to a number of civilian planners, particularly in Manchuria. His ideas, his career, and the influential role which he played in the major military and political events of the 1930s are explored in my *Ishiwara Kanji and Japan's Confrontation with the West* (Princeton, 1975).
19. Tsunoda Jun, ed., *Ishiwara Kanji shiryo*, vol. 1 (Tokyo, 1967), pp. 426-30 (hereafter cited as *IKS*).
20. *IKS*, vol. 1, p. 430; vol. 2, pp. 70-71.
21. *IKS*, vol. 1, p. 430.
22. In 1932 all three books were put together to form a single major study, *Taiheiyo senryaku ron*. All citations of these three studies are taken from that compendium, hereafter cited as *TSR*.
23. Nagai Tamotsu, *Ikezaki Chuko* (Tokyo, 1962), pp. 407-08.

24. *TSR*, pp. 97-118, 133-42.
25. *TSR*, pp. 91-92.
26. *TSR*, pp. 357-58.
27. *TSR,* pp. 398-99, 404, 408, 448.
28. Nagai, *Ikezaki*, pp. 249-250.
29. Hata, *Taiheiyo*, p. 222; Sadao Asada, "The Japanese Navy and the United States," in Dorothy Borg and Shumpei Okamoto, eds., *Pearl Harbor as History: Japanese-American Relations, 1931-1941* (New York, 1973), p. 234.
30. Fukunaga Kyosuke, *Nichi-Bei sen miraiki* (Tokyo, 1933), pp. iii-v.
31. Mizuno Hironori, *Dakai ka? Hametsu ka? Kobo no kono issen* (Tokyo, 1932), p. 15.
32. Hirata Shinsaku, *Warera moshi tatakawaba* (Tokyo, 1933), pp. 46-52.
33. Ishimaru, *Nippon tai-sekai senso* (Tokyo, 1932), pp. 309-10.
34. Ishimaru, *Nippon tai-sekai senso*, p. 390.

6
JAPANESE POLICIES AND CONCEPTS FOR A REGIONAL ORDER IN ASIA, 1938-1940

Kimitada Miwa

Introduction

It is the purpose of this essay to examine for the first time the different intellectual origins of Prime Minister Konoye Fumimaro's so-called "New Order in East Asia" proclamation of 3 November 1938 and the concept of a "Greater East Asia Co-Prosperity Sphere" which was made public by Foreign Minister Matsuoka Yosuke on 1 August 1940. Both were "idealistic," the former for its content drawing significantly on traditional concepts and values of the East Asian historical world, the latter for its high abstraction. But only when the latter was given a substance by a policy scientist like Royama Masamichi did it manage to assume a "realistic" appearance for policy purposes.

In the case of the former, it was as though at long last the idealism of Japan's non-governmental sector had overtaken the government, which had since the Meiji era consistently stood for realism. But in the case of the latter, it was the realism of Royama, a non-governmental policy scientist, which came to the rescue of a hollow policy statement. This dramatic turn-about was touched off--as we shall see below--by Saito Takao (1870-1949), a member of the Lower House of the Imperial Diet, who on 2 February 1940 made a severe verbal attack upon the Government from the floor of the Diet as a realist from the standpoint of power politics. But Saito's speech, and its aftermath, were products of a long intellectual process, with which we shall begin.

Modern Japan's Pan-Asianism

In studying the state of mind or attitudes that can be identified as "Pan-Asianism" in modern Japan, one must point out at least two independent and yet interlocking beginnings.[1] One of them sprang from the Japanese sense of a shared destiny as a part of Asia. This originated from the Japanese awareness of the historical world of East Asia with which, in the middle of the 19th century, Western nation-states wanted to begin relations--resorting to armed intimidation where necessary. The other was the awakening of Japanese nationalism as such: in addition to a group identity as being "Asian," generated when they were exposed to the above stimuli, came a response along the lines of the principles of the modern nation-states of the West. This latter form of Japanese nationalism eventually developed into Pan-Asianism as it combined with the pre-modern Japanese perception of themselves and their neighboring countries as forming a miniaturized counterpart of the Chinese imperial system with Japan at its imperial apex.[2] This in turn would be soon fused, in the age of rising militaristic expansionism in the 1930s, with the ancient concept of *hakko ichiu* ("eight corners of the world under one roof"), or expansion through Japan's imperial benevolence. In other words, this type of Pan-Asianism presented itself in history as an expansive overseas version of Japan's modern nationalism.

The notion of hakko ichiu was composed of the principles of "Imperial benevolence" and of assimilation. As such, it was a theory for the control of "alien tribes" which the Japanese had embraced since ancient times. But had it been always only this theory that the Japanese remembered when they were faced with other peoples? Whenever Pan Asianism is taken up in Japanese intellectual history, two treatises by Sato Shin'en (1769-1850), *Udai kondo tai ron* and *Udai kondo hisaku* (1823) are referred to, and one distinctive feature of these books is the philosophy of hakko ichiu which permeates them. But if Sato constitutes one extreme pole we can single out at least one other person, a contemporary of his, as constituting the other pole--a non-assimilatory approach to extra-Japanese "alien tribes." This was Matsuura Takeshiro (1818-88), who conceived of an international order starting from the genuine love of the Ainu, the last remaining aborigines of the Japanese islands.[3] He believed that what the Japanese must do for the Ainu was not to practice a policy of assimilation, but rather to respect and help preserve their tribal ways *in toto*.

Between these two poles, we may also discern a writer like Hayashi Shihei (1737-93). In his *Sangoku tsuran zusetsu* (1785), he put Yezo, the land of the Ainu (today's Hokkaido, most of Sakhalin, and the Kuriles), in the same category of foreign countries as the Ryukyus and Korea; in that spirit, he advised the Japanese to approach the Ainu from a posture of benevolence. He warned that when the time eventually came for the Ainu to decide to which side they should lean, the Japanese or the Russians (who had been continuously pressing southward), they might very well choose the Russians if the administrators and merchants of Japan kept on treating them as mercilessly and malfeasantly as they were.[4] His position was to establish Japan's sovereignty in the Ainu territories through the principle of popular sovereignty of the residents of the land, and thus secure political stability to the north of Japan proper. In contrast to Sato's strategy for the control of Eastern Siberia, by means of military conquest followed by the practice of "Imperial benevolence" of giving away rice and the like to the natives, it is noteworthy that Hayashi's advice was to begin with the "good and honest acts" of ordinary Japanese and leave the final outcome to the voluntary choice of the natives.

From what has been discussed above, if we were to draw a graphic distribution of the variety of modern Japanese ideas of and attitudes toward their Asian neighbors, they would fall along two dimensions: a vertical axis of group identity, of which the poles would be the Asian nationalism felt by the Japanese as Asians on the one hand and the expansive overseas version of Japan's modern nationalism on the other; and a horizontal axis, of which the poles would be the theory of control through assimilation and the non-assimilatory theory of preservation of indigenous tribal identities and co-existence with them. But this distribution began to fluctuate under the impact of the theory of China being not a "state but merely a civilization," which was touched off by the political instability that characterized China after the Republican Revolution of 1911.

Impact of the "China is not a State" Theory

At the beginning of this chapter I remarked that the 1930s in Japan were characterized by the adoption for the first time by the government of the idealism hitherto upheld by non-governmental personalities. Specifically, it was embodied in the policy of the "New Order in East Asia." But for this sort of political adaptation to take place, changes in the situation of China and accompanying changes in Japanese perception of China were prerequisite. The most fundamental among them was the Japanese perception prompted by the general political instability of the republican regime in Peking and by its failure to function effectively as a central government for all China. This led to the conclusion that "China was not a state but merely a civilization." I have discussed this problem elsewhere,[5] but in connection with the theme of this chapter it may be useful to state briefly its major points.

Among the Japanese proponents of such a view of China were men like Uchida Ryohei (1874-1937), a rightwing activist, professors of Kyoto Imperial University like Naito Konan (1866-1934), a world renowned historian of China, and Oda Man (1868-1945), an accomplished student of Chinese administrative law. What was common to all of them was the perception that Chinese political society and ordinary society were totally removed from one another; as a consequence, a modern nation-state could not possibly be formed there. In a memorial, *Shina kan* (*My View of China*), published on 1 October 1913, Uchida declared that the Chinese did not comprehend the concept of the "state." They were an "egoistic nation" on whose behalf the Japanese had been making efforts to "preserve" their country from internal rot and Western imperialism. But precautionary measures were required to keep Japan from being dragged down by China's embrace and becoming a victim in a "double suicide of lovers": by occupying Manchuria and Mongolia and turning them into bases for Japan's national defense, Japan could forestall the southern advance of the Russians and also prevent the Chinese from engaging in anti-Japanese activities.[6]

As Naito wrote in *Shina ron* (*A Discourse on China*), a book published in 1914, the Chinese lacked a "spirit of independence and patriotism relative to foreign countries." In China, he said, "there are no greater [subjectively] bodily organizations than a village community or an extended family."[7] From the point of view of China not being a state, the most salient characteristic of Naito's images of China was perhaps his homogeneous conception of what East Asian civilization was. In *Shin Shina ron* (*A New Discourse on China*), published in 1938, he stated that the development of East Asian culture "takes a definite course, irrespective of the differences of nations." Continuing, he wrote:

> For such reasons, if Japan and China had been united in a politically unitary state, it would not have struck the Chinese as peculiar at all even if the center of that culture were transferred to Japan and the Japanese became active on the Chinese political and social scene.[8]

Naito remarked that the Chinese were continuously rejuvenated through repeated invasions by different peoples from outside, and successfully maintained their "national mode of life" throughout. In this light, Japanese economic activities in China too should be appreciated as producing "unfathomable good effects." It was accordingly incorrect to denounce those activities categorically as "imperialistic" or "militaristic."[9]

Since his trip of investigation in China in 1906, Oda had emphasized the significance of the Chinese capability for self-government in the village community, while noting the absence of a "true political unity."[10] But less than a year after the outbreak of the 1937 Marco Polo Bridge Incident he published an essay, "*Fukakai na Shina minzoku* (The Inscrutable Chinese)," in the January 1938 issue of *Bungei shunju*, in which he supported the Japanese Government policy of seizing the five northern provinces of China and establishing an "independent and autonomous new regime" there.[11]

It is interesting to note that in 1938, in November of which their government would enunciate the "New Order in East Asia" policy, these two academic authorities implicitly supported the New Order by asserting peculiarities in the Chinese political culture from their own specialized, expert points of view. But as regards the intellectual continuity of the "non-governmental" sector from the 1920s to the 1930s, and the adoption of its "Pan-Asianist" ideas into national policy, the most exemplary scholar was Yano Jin'ichi (1872-1970). Toward the end of 1921 and in the early spring of 1922 Yano, a professor of East Asian History at Kyoto Imperial University, published two essays, "*Shina mukokkyo ron* (On the Absence of National Borders in China)" and "*Shina wa kuni ni arazaru no ron* (On China Not Being a Nation)." The central theme of these essays, that "China is not a nation," was incorporated into the so-called "Tanaka Memorial" of 1927, the authenticity of which has been rejected,[12] but which was regarded in the prewar period not only by the Chinese but also throughout the world as a blueprint for Japan's aggressive designs on the Chinese continent. That theme, in addition, inspired political scientist Royama Masamichi to new insight into the "reality" of China and, shortly after the Manchurian Incident of 1931, led him to publish a study of Japanese-Manchurian relations[13] premised on the "peculiarity" of Manchuria as a "peripheral zone of a nation."[14] It was Royama, as we shall see, who around 1940 blended these ideas with those of German geopolitics to come up with the concept of "Greater East Asian" regionalism.

To sum up, at least as seen in connection with Royama's new-found geopolitical interest (which eventually led him to make policy recommendations for substantiating the otherwise hollow governmental pronouncement of the "Greater East Asia Co-Prosperity Sphere"), Yano's thesis that China was not a nation was instrumental in making the "non-governmental" idealism of the 1920s surface in the 1930s as national policy. In this sense it became the theoretical premise for a regionalist concept designed to rescue Japan from its growing isolation in international opinion--an isolation paradoxically due in part to this very thesis.

On 1 March 1933 the Greater Asia Association was formed; Yano was not only a charter member, but even occupied a post on the board of trustees along with Prince Konoye Fumimaro, Hirota Koki, Matsui Iwane, Suetsugu Nobumasa, Hiraizumi Kiyoshi, Shimonaka Yasaburo, and Nakayama Masaru. Royama, on the other hand, was a leading member of the Showa Study Group when it was inaugurated in November of the same year; as early as 1935 he had begun advocating the use of geopolitical findings for the formation of a national policy. Both of these two groups were expected to function as a "brain trust" for Prince Konoye, but significantly enough there was practically no overlapping membership. A comparison of the two reveals that members of the Greater Asia Association were more traditional in their value orientation--Shimonaka, for example, upheld anti-modern theories of the state based upon the historical intellectual heritage of an indigenous village community. The Showa Study Group members were more distinctly oriented toward the scientism of modernization. As indicated by the frequent attendance of Ishiwara Kanji (1889-1949) at the functions of the Greater Asia Association, and also by the overlapping membership of Nakayama in Ishiwara's East Asian League (founded in 1938), the Greater Asia Association was more in line with the "Imperial Way Faction" of the military, while the Showa Study Group was more in line with the "Control Faction."[15] At any rate, what linked these two associations was that their members placed equally high hopes in Prince Konoye as a political leader and in their expectations that their own political ideas would materially affect the formulation of global policy. A further linkage between the two came in the form of Yano's thesis, which also inspired Royama's regionalism.

Applying the Principle of the "Just Way"

It had already been asserted many times by the 1930s that Japanese arguments for a cooperative Asian unity had come into being as a response to the "White Peril" as posed by the powers of Europe and America.[16] It followed naturally from the Japanese perception of the Western threat as a White Peril that this concern for unity took the name of "*Dai Ajiashugi* (Greater Asianism)" or "Pan-Asianism." As early as 1916, in the introduction to his book *Dai Ajiashugi ron* (*On Greater Asianism*), Odera Kenkichi (1878-1949) elaborated the position of Greater Asianism as a racial unity confronting the White Peril.

> Is it not strange that in the Europe which has come to control or overwhelm Asia the talk of the Yellow Peril is boisterously heard, whereas from among the colored peoples who have been conquered or intimidated by the white

nations little has been spoken of out loud about the White Peril? This, when the Yellow Peril is no more than an illusion while the White Peril is real.... Some people denounce Greater Asianism as being based on a narrow racist frame of mind. But racial prejudices are what the white nations have taught us. This trait is more especially pronounced among them. The fact that their arguments about the Yellow Peril are provocative and disdainful is proof enough, and the fact that in the New World discriminatory treatment is being dealt out steadfastly [to non-white ethnic groups] is substantial evidence. To speak of the White Peril and to advocate Greater Asianism cannot touch the malicious propagation by Europeans and Americans of the Yellow Peril and their calls for a white alliance. While the former is defensive, passive, and pacifist, the latter is offensive, aggressive, and imperialistic.[17]

Such Greater Asianism in the 1910s, deriving its cohesive force from racial sentiments as it did, pointed to a defensive regional alignment of one sort or another and not very much more than that. The Japanese were apt to believe that the Chinese shared their regional-racial sense of destiny and global outlook: a case in point is Sun Yat-sen's speech in Kobe, Japan, on 28 November 1924. The audience took Sun's talk as an appeal for Sino-Japanese collaboration for economic co-prosperity and joint security against the outside world. The title of Sun's talk as announced by the sponsoring Japanese newspapers was "The Problems of Asia," but he led off by noting that he was going to dwell on what he called "Greater Asianism." So his talk of the day is known by that name.[18] But contrary to what the name suggests, and indeed contrary to the expectation of the audience, the content of the speech--with its emphasis on what Sun called "Greater Asianism"--was not a call for a racial alignment against the White Peril. It was rather a proposal to eradicate the inequality that had hitherto been imposed upon oppressed nationalities not only in Asia but also in Europe. He called for the establishment of a new world order based on the East Asian moral principle of humanity and justice, or *wang tao* (the "just way"). When even the Soviet Union was propounding wang tao, asked Sun, "is Japan going to be a willing handmaiden of Western imperialism or is it going to choose to become the great bastion of East Asia's 'just way'?"

The Greater Asia Association's predecessor was the *Han Ajia Kyokai* (Pan Asia Association), established in 1932. The latter expanded its activities when it was joined by such notables as Matsui Iwane (1878-1948), then a lieutenant general, and was renamed in light of the Greater Asianism of Sun Yat-sen.[19] In spite of its name, however, there is no sign that this organization adopted Sun's ideas of the "just way." The philosophy of wang tao was indeed accepted in principle as a basis for regional unification, such as an Asian league premised on the fact of an historical East Asian world. But the Association could hardly go so far as to work with the alleged wang tao of the Soviet Union. On the contrary, its attitudes toward the USSR were those of ideological distrust and historical hostility. In this respect, it stood for a regionalism which was sharply different from Sun's Greater Asianism. This fact can be clearly seen in the charter of the Association. According to this document the "independent state of Manchukuo" was considered a "new just-way state," but one which had come into being as the "last defense fortification of East Asia against the global conquest of the Occidentals."[20] It was openly posed against the imperialistic expansionism of Soviet Russia.

In addition to the above argument, from the personal history of Shimonaka (whose activities as an ideologue of autonomy for agrarian communities were followed by a passionate involvement in the activities of the Greater Asia Association), we may characterize his and his colleagues' Greater Asianism as a combination of "East Asian ethical values" and "East Asian anarchism."[21] As such it was distinctly indigenous to Japan, and clearly different from Sun Yat-sen's way of thinking. This characteristic can be observed more or less intensely in all the members of the Association, and it is in sharp contrast to the members of the Showa Study Group, who developed their thought around certain ideas imported from the West. The comparison can be brought into an even sharper contrast if we pair Shimonaka with Ryu Shintaro[22] and Nakayama with Royama.

Nakayama and Prince Konoye's Proclamation of a New Order in East Asia

The New Order in East Asia Proclamation was made by the Japanese Government on 3 November 1938. Two days earlier, on 1 November, it had been adopted by the Cabinet, and on the following day it had been reported to the Emperor at the Palace by Prime Minister Konoye. The draft of this proclamation is said to have been written by Nakayama Masaru in Peking.[23] Nakayama had been teaching East Asian Politics as a faculty member of the just-established Nation Building University (Kenkoku Daigaku) of Manchukuo. This professional post had been given him, so it seems, through Ishiwara's good offices.[24] At the time he purportedly wrote the draft declaration, Nakayama was accompanying the oldest son of Konoye, Fumitaka, and one of his classmates from the Peers' College in Tokyo, Hosokawa Morisada, on a one-month trip in China. In the draft proclamation the Japanese Government was to propose to China and Manchukuo that they make concerted efforts with Japan to establish a new order. As a preliminary to this, Japan was to rectify its own mistake committed when, on 8 January of that year, it had denounced Chiang Kai-shek, saying it would henceforth not deal with him. In the new declaration the Japanese Government would say that "it is not going to reject ... even the Nationalist Government" in Chungking.

If indeed Nakayama had been asked to prepare a draft of such grave importance, one might presume that there should have been a very special and intimate relationship between him and Prince Konoye. But actually theirs was not an old tie. It was only in the summer of 1937 that Nakayama had the opportunity of seeing Prince Konoye close up.[25] Nevertheless, Nakayama and Prince Konoye were related to each other in a curiously special way. Nakayama had attended school between 1915 and 1918 at the To-A Dobun Shoin (East Asia Common Culture College) in Shanghai which had been established in 1898 by the To-A Dobun Kai (East Asia Common Culture Society) headed by Prince Konoye Atsumaro, the father of the Prime Minister.[26] This was the only Japanese college of political economy that publicly ensconced the teachings of Confucius as the basis of moral education. Its educational aim, as phrased by Nezu Hajime in 1901, was that "we are determined to preserve China's integrity and to map out plans for the permanent security of East Asia and the unending peace of the world."[27]

Nakayama was born in 1895, the son of a peasant in Kumamoto Prefecture on Kyushu Island. By the time he was out in the world making his own living, he had begun thinking about how to pursue his belief in agrarian values. In a 1930 essay, he wrote about an old man among his relatives. He called him the "archetype of a small landed farmer in decline," the type of man in whom one found "both laborer and manager put together." In this type of man, he wrote, "you find plenty of good will and the spirit of independence of a producer." He adored this type of man from the bottom of his heart.[28] His fervent desire for communitarian social change, emanating from his agrarian-oriented values, was emphatically stated when he wrote:

> From the point of view that the best of the Japanese race must be preserved, too, it is really unbearable to watch agrarian villages in decline. Should there be found appropriate means to defend agrarian villages against urban exploitation, no matter what sort of theories or methods they may be, I would be glad to come running to serve the

cause even if physically I may happen to be weak and wounded.[29]

By the end of the 1930s this sort of "agrarianist" response to the social problems of Japan had become the prototype of the new order to be established in East Asia. It was a call to return to a classical East Asia, a new-found antithesis to the modern industrial society of the West.[30] And it could be accomplished by first destroying that order of international law of the European system of nation-states which had been forced upon East Asian countries since the mid-nineteenth century, and then by replacing it with an "international new order"[31] in accordance with the "real force of history."[32] The essay in which Nakayama referred to the "real force in history" and an "international new order" is dated July 1937, three days after the beginning of the Japanese general offensive in Northern China, when it became apparent that the plans to localize the Marco Polo Bridge Incident of 7 July had not produced the expected effects. In spite of its terminology, the argument he pursued here followed not the logic of power politics but rather Nakayama's view of humanity and civilization in East Asia. Calling Japan a catalytic "new *pei ti* (northern barbarian),"[33] he concluded that its fundamental role could be reduced to "*musubi*,"[34] literally signifying "tying together," "uniting," or "concluding":

> It is the short-sighted assessment of an antique collector to see Japan as an admixture of things peculiar to a colony. The beginning of a new harmony can be found in what strikes an observer at first glance as mere disorderliness.... It goes without saying that the cultures of Europe are incapable of rescuing themselves any more, much less the world at large. The new potential power lies with the third civilization. It makes both Eastern and Western civilizations come alive through "musubi," or harmonious combination. This is what can produce a new order in China, and Japan may rightfully serve as a catalyst for this combination.[35]

Having set the role of Japan in world history as that of creating a "third civilization," Nakayama remarked that what Japan sought was an economic bloc "which is a new trend in the world," a form of regional solidarity. Japan "does not desire to carve out even a patch of land, and does not intend to kill a single innocent man." It only wanted to see China "return to East Asia," and "in cooperation with China, Japan" wanted to "lay the foundation of world peace" by means of the "third civilization."[36]

The idea Nakayama expressed in this essay--that Japan did not desire even a single fragment of territory in China and would not take away the life of any of its innocent citizens, but only ask it to return to East Asia--was incorporated into Prime Minister Konoye's proclamation of 3 November 1938. Konoye declared Japan's war aim thus: "what Japan desires is the establishment of such a new order as to assure stability in East Asia in perpetuity."

(Parenthetically, "Konoye's proclamation" on the New Order in East Asia actually refers to two documents: those of 3 November and 22 December 1938. The latter document, according to Nakayama, was originally drafted by Colonel Horiba Kazuo on the recommendation of the General Staff. When it was shown to him Nakayama, upon his own judgment, entered a phrase in the draft that what Japan wanted to get from China was "neither pieces of territory nor indemnities."[37])

The So-Called "Anti-Military" Speech of Saito Takao

On 2 February 1940, on the floor of the House of the Representatives of the Imperial Diet, Saito Takao (a representative of the opposition *Minseito*), delivered a question highly critical of the Government of Prime Minister Yonai Mitsumasa (1880-1948). Its main thrust was directed against the Government's idealistic aim to seek the termination of the China conflict through the declared principle of "no annexation and no indemnities." Despite its bellicose tone, given its context the question was a sharply "anti-military speech";[38] as a consequence, Saito was expelled from the Imperial Diet and his name was deleted from its rolls. The *Asahi* newspaper, in its issue of the following day, for example, reported the event with such headlines as "Representative Saito Makes a Slip. Will it Lead to His Expulsion? Army and Political Factions Alike Extremely Resentful" and "There Can be no Settlement of the Conflict Which Denigrates the Japanese People's Sacrifices--Saito Questions the Prime Minister." According to the paper, Saito's questioning went as follows:

> ... in settling the conflict, one thing that we should never forget is the multitude of sacrifices our people have had to pay while it has continued.... We cannot conceive of the substantive content of a settlement of the conflict which forgets these sacrifices.

Continuing, Saito traced the origins of what Prime Minister Yonai called the "staunch and unshakable" principles for the settlement of the conflict to the Konoye Proclamation, and listed them as follows:

1. Respect for China's sovereignty.
2. No annexation and no indemnities.
3. Economic cooperation.
4. No curtailment of the privileges and interests of third powers in China.
5. Withdrawal of Japanese troops from all parts of China except for Inner Mongolia.

Having made these points--with which the military officially agreed--Saito proceeded to pin Yonai down: "Do the Japanese people have to take care of all the military expenditures which have been spent up to today and, in addition, all that inestimable amount which it may very well cost in the indefinite future"[39]--and yet implicitly look forward to nothing concrete in return?

Obviously these words of question and answer must have been recorded officially in their entirety, but the published version in the *Kampo sokki roku* (*Official Stenographic Record*) contains so many censored words and sentences that it is difficult for us to understand accurately what Saito really meant to say. At any rate, the Disciplinary Committee of the House of Representatives deliberated on the case and on 7 March the plenary session of the House resolved to strike Saito's name off its roll by a vote of 305 to 7.

A full record of the oral questions and answers was published in the postwar period, and a delicate but significant shift in the evaluation of Saito may very well result from how one now reads the document. In my opinion, Saito was a rare Japanese, one who analyzed international politics from a realistic point of view and criticized the Cabinet accordingly at a time when the Japanese as a whole (both in and outside the Government) were misled by nativistic idealism. For those dreaming of the construction of a new international order based on such principles as the spiritual culture of the Orient and government by the "just way" of Imperial benevolence, Saito's criticism of the Government--using the vocabulary of the Western political science of power politics--must have appeared blasphemous, coming amid a conflict which was known to the people as a "holy war." Professor Yabe Teiji of Tokyo Imperial University, for example, a leading member of the Showa Study Group (and as such close to Prince Konoye and exerting a sizable influence on his formulation of policy), wrote in his diary for 3 February as follows:

> Yesterday in the House of the Representatives, Saito Takao questioned the Government about its manner of settling the [China] conflict and said something, so it appears, to the effect that it would make meaningless why

we had been engaged in the war. He was denounced as being malignantly opposed to the Imperial armed forces and blasphemous of the proposed New Order, or as helping to confuse the people as to their war aims.[40]

This statement was representative of one intellectual's immediate response to these confusing developments; the following is a less ambivalent reaction by one who was familiar with Saito and also close to the nativistic idealism of the "New Order in East Asia." Kimura Takeo (1902-1983) was a member of the House of Representatives who sat on the Disciplinary Committee that considered the case of Saito. Kimura had organized the East Asian League Association in 1938, with Ishiwara Kanji at its head. Believing in the idea of *minzoku kyowa* (multinational cooperative harmony), Kimura had supported Konoye's New Order proclamation, and construed Saito's criticism as a materialistically motivated argument for a crass power-political settlement. "The notion that Japan should support its life at the cost of China," said Kimura, "is absolutely incompatible with the moralistic national policy which reflects the founding spirit of Japan." With the establishment of the "independent" state of Manchukuo, one could be confident that, instead of exploitation of China by Japan, a "mutuality of interdependence" would make them "both coexist and prosper." From this emerged the notion of a New Order in East Asia that incorporated the principles of "no annexation" and "no indemnities." Thus Kimura criticized Saito, who had denounced the Konoye Proclamation in calling "the war meaningless, if it seeks to acquire neither territory nor indemnity."[41]

Royama Masamichi's "Regionalism"

As seen above, in the Konoye Proclamation of a New Order in East Asia, we find strong strains of the nativistic sense of unity with China and the peculiarly East Asian principle of Imperial benevolence, as held by men such as Nakayama Masaru. But to establish conclusively why, at this very point, Nakayama had to be called in to ghost-write the Proclamation, we must still more widely explore the historical record. According to Nakayama, Konoye came to realize the necessity of presenting to the world the concept of a New Order as a national consensus of the Japanese when, in the early summer of 1934, he was visiting the United States on the occasion of his oldest son Fumitaka's graduation from Lawrenceville School near Princeton, New Jersey. Colonel Edward M. House, who as the right-hand man of President Woodrow Wilson had helped establish the so-called Versailles system of world peace, remarked to Konoye that if Japan should deny the validity of the international order established by the Washington

Conference of 1921-22, then in its place Japan should propose a new order which would elicit the understanding of other nations. Apparently Konoye took his cue from this remark.[42]

Although it may be rash to say that the Japanese expression for a new order was a direct translation of the term used by House, a rather intensive exchange of opinions did follow between Konoye and House as to what content such a new order should have. Their views were expressed, respectively, in "Wanted--A New Deal among Nations" by House and "How to Secure Lasting Peace" by Konoye in the 14 October and 7 December 1935 issues of an American periodical *Liberty*. "Just as social peace cannot prevail without some adjustment of the capitalistic system," wrote House, "so international peace cannot be preserved without drastic territorial adjustments." So writing, he asked Great Britain, the United States, and the Soviet Union to reconsider the matter, and hoped for a revival of international justice. In contrast, Konoye warned the major powers, hinting at the probability that their stubbornness would force "have not" nations like Japan to resort to their own logic and rise in arms against the "haves."[43]

Konoye's was a revolutionary logic of radical change in the old order--a sort of theory of "class conflict" among nations. But it is not difficult to find in it some ideas stemming from the principle of Imperial benevolence which had been a traditional norm of government in East Asia. Thus we may infer that later in the 1930s it was not so abrupt for Konoye to accommodate Nakayama's ideas for a "new order." When Konoye went to the United States in 1934 he was accompanied by Royama Masamichi. The latter was made painfully aware that there were no persuasive ways to explain Japan's position to the United States. He saw that the arguments of the so-called Pan-Asianists, which were based upon closeness in geography and blood relations, and which referred to the "facts" of the Japanese and Chinese "using the same ideographs and being of the same racial stock" or "being separated only by a narrow strip of water," might magically lead the Japanese to daydream of Sino-Japanese solidarity, but they lacked the scientific force to convince either the nations of the West or even the Chinese themselves, who constituted the postulated partner of Japan in that new order. It was German geopolitical thought that drew Royama's attention when he was wondering what would best remedy this deficiency. Interacting with the Yano thesis that China was not a state--a view which had already drastically affected Royama's views of the Chinese continent--German geopolitical thought would develop into his own distinctive theory of regionalism.

Geopolitics as a science was first introduced in Japan by

Fujisawa Chikao's "*Rudorufu Cheeren no kokkagaku ni kansuru gakusetsu* (Scholarly Theories on Rudolph Kjören's Study of the State)," published in 1925 in volume 25 of *Kokusai ho gaiko zasshi* (*Journal of International Law and Diplomacy*). According to Professor Mitani Taichiro, from about 1933 on Royama began to insist that "as the foundation on which a foreign policy is to be formulated," not only universalistic international law and treaties but also "politico-geographical conditions" were important. "To meet this need" it was, he said, highly recommended to study the "geopolitical manner of thinking."[44] Indeed it was in November of that year that Abe Ichigoro's *Chiseigaku nyumon* (*An Introduction to Geopolitics*) was published as the "first full-fledged introductory book on German geopolitics."[45] Nevertheless, it was not until much later that Royama himself used the term "geopolitics" or "geopolitical," or referred to the founder of German geopolitics, Karl Haushofer (1869-1946) in his own scholarly publications on the nature of policy science. It was after 1940--not during the "New Order in East Asia" phase of national policy, but with the advent of the "Greater East Asia Co-Prosperity" period.

How did Royama's attraction to geopolitics--under whatever rubric--come about? Could it not be that Royama found in the economic thought of German geopolitics a cue to overcome the simplistic arguments for Sino-Japanese solidarity based upon nativistic belief in shared culture and racial affinity? But he was not altogether smitten by geopolitics either, because he was repulsed by another of its characteristics, the fact that it appeared not essentially different from the concerns of the "old" imperialism. For example, German geopolitics was sharply and appropriately criticized in 1936 by Ohara Keishi in his *Shakai chirigaku no kiso riron* (*The Fundamental Theories of Social Geography*). To Ohara, German geopolitics was "nothing but an idealistic expression of German capitalism in its process of reconstruction and statist development, and it was to play the part of a scientific weapon to strongly expedite the advance thereof."[46]

Komaki Saneshige (1898-), a professor at Kyoto Imperial University, was inspired likewise by German geopolitics, but he too saw its imperialistic character as anachronistic, along the lines mentioned above. So he tried to distinguish his own theories by calling them the geopolitics of *kodo*, sometimes translated into English as the "Imperial Way," but more precisely signifying the notion of "just and benevolent government by the *Tenno*," the Emperor of Japan.[47] Royama, in contrast, consciously tried to avoid this type of sentimental and romantic argument for a Japanese return to Asia. He held the regionalist elements of German geopolitics in high esteem and yet, right from the outset, he was critical of the very foundation on which German geopolitics was built, namely, geographic materialism and the ethical organic theory of the state. What appeared imperative to him was to establish and explain a national policy which could not be accused of being the same as Western imperialism. The Japanese "must be prepared," said Royama, "to accommodate the nationalist desires of Asiatic peoples, and to weave them into a world policy which is readily distinguishable from Western imperialism."[48] Komaki, on the other hand, propounded in effect dogmatic expansionism in the name of the Tenno's justice and benevolence. His was a type of agrarian anarchism which in practice would deprive the Asian nations involved of their self-reliance and self-government. In contrast, what Royama was proposing was an open-ended regionalism, a theory for building a mutually complementary regional economy through the voluntary participation of peoples within the region.

It was in the summer of 1938, upon his return from China, that Royama wrote an article entitled "*To-A kyodotai no riron* (The Theory of an East Asian Cooperative Body)," in which German geopolitics was presented as discussed above. This article was published in the November issue of *Kaizo* (*Renovation*); that is to say, it was presented to the public immediately prior to the pronouncement of the New Order in East Asia by Prime Minister Konoye. And Royama was a leading member of the Showa Study Group, Konoye's "brain trust." From this it is natural to speculate that the central theme of the policy pronouncement flowed from the Study Group in general and Royama in particular. One might even conclude that the author was indeed none other than Royama himself. But if we accept Nakayama's contention that it was originally written by him in Peking and dispatched from there to Tokyo, it becomes necessary to essay some other interpretations. The following is my own.

First of all, the New Order in East Asia proclamation was a consequence of Konoye's own political considerations. The scientific validity of the theory for an East Asian cooperative body might be indisputable to him, but it could not be expected that it would be appreciated as a basis for action by the Japanese masses. Its geopolitical strain would promptly invite negative reaction from the intellectuals, in light of the aforementioned critique by Ohara, since the intellectual milieu in Japan was still generally opposed to Hitlerian trends toward sheer territorial aggrandizement. Was it not wiser to present the proposal not in terms of the scientific reasoning of economics but rather in tradition-rooted and emotion-bound expressions of neighborly relations and racial affinity? In conclusion, therefore, could it not be anticipated that, if theories of the rule of Imperial benevolence taken from the cultural history of East Asia-- instead of the regionalistic expressions of economic rationalism--were applied, their readier appeal to the sense of international justice and national mission of the contemporary Japanese would produce the desired support for the policy? If so, it follows that the task of ghost-writing the policy pronouncement might have thus devolved on Nakayama, a principal member of the Greater Asian Association (whose name, one will recall, drew on Sun Yat-sen's idea of Greater Asianism) and a representative graduate of the East Asia Common Culture College of Shanghai. Royama himself authored a passage which indirectly substantiates this line of reasoning: in the March issue of *Kogyo kokusaku* (*National Industrial Policy*) he wrote that since he believed that a "regional theory" based on the "regional relations of Japan with the continent" alone must be the "theoretical target" of the theory for the creation of an East Asian cooperative body, he had decided "not to give a leading position to the question of race and culture." Because of this stand, he was not altogether sure whether "the Japanese would easily agree to this type of theory for the East Asian cooperative body."[49]

As a result, the scientific regionalism of Royama was disguised with traditional Japanese views of Asia based on Konoye's political considerations. As such it was expected to have a readier appeal to the sentiments of the Japanese public. It was also hoped that it would have a similar effect on the Chinese. The big difference between Royama's regionalistic thinking and the prevalent romantic notion that the Japanese and the Chinese shared one destiny and constituted one community was demonstrated clearly when, immediately subsequent to Foreign Minister Matsuoka's remark about the Greater East Asia Co-Prosperity Sphere, Royama suddenly began to make explicit references to "geopolitics" and Karl Haushofer.

In addition to Royama, there were a number of men in the Showa Study Group who expounded the concept of the East Asian cooperative body. One common feature of their arguments was that they were not commingled with the wang tao philosophy which Nakayama upheld, defined as "a just way, a way of virtue, and as applied to the individual a way of sincerity." In place of this Oriental philosophy, their arguments were rooted in economic rationalism. This characteristic can be observed most symbolically in an article, "*To-A keizai kyodotai no seisaku* (The Policy of an East Asian Economic Cooperative Body)" published in the December issue of *Chuo koron* (*Central Review*) by Kada Tetsuji (1895-1964), a professor at Keio University who was active in the East Asian Bloc Economy Study Section of the Showa Study Group. He wrote that although it was called an "East Asian Economic Cooperative Body, its intent is not to subjugate East Asian countries to serve Japan at the cost of their individual character." On the other hand, "Neither is it meant," he concluded, "for Japan to practice *jen*, the Confucian virtue of humanistic justice, if it were feared that to do so would jeopardize Japan's own security and existence."[50]

The Greater East Asia Co-Prosperity Sphere: A Slogan in Search of Substantiation

Now at last we turn our attention to the concept of the Greater East Asia Co-Prosperity Sphere *per se*. The core of this concept had been already aired in a radio speech by Foreign Minister Arita Hachiro (1884-1965) of the Yonai Cabinet on 29 June 1940. Arita, too, was a member of the Showa Study Group. Prior to this, on 18 April, Yabe recorded in his diary:

> Yesterday Foreign Minister Arita declared that [our government] entertains a profound interest in the present situation of the Dutch East Indies, which is about to undergo a change on account of the European war. It seems apparent that the "Southern Policy," the study of which the Showa Study Group has recently completed, stimulated that interest.[51]

This observation seems to support the speculation that the regionalist thinking of the Showa Study Group influenced Arita to use the *idea* of a greater East Asia co-prosperity sphere for the first time, even if the concept had not yet been given that verbal formulation. It was Matsuoka Yosuke (1880-1946) as Foreign Minister who used those words *officially* for the first time.[52] Foreign Minister Matsuoka released a statement at 12:30 p.m. on 1 August 1940 which read partly as follows:

> For years I have been propounding that it is the national mission of Japan to propagate to the world the way of the Tenno, the Emperor of Japan. To put it from the international political point of view, the way of the Tenno is nothing but to allow every nation and every people to enjoy what is due to them. In other words, as applied to the present foreign policy of our country, it means nothing more than establishing a greater East Asian co-prosperity sphere by linking Japan, Manchukuo and China together as a first step starting from this great spirit of the Imperial Way.[53]

Matsuoka then went on to explain that this "greater East Asia co-prosperity sphere" was the same as what had been known formerly as the new order in East Asia sphere or "East Asia stability sphere." But he also added that it was so wide as to "include such southern regions as the Dutch East Indies and French Indochina."[54]

The *Asahi shimbun*, a national daily, headlined the news report as "The Establishment of a Greater East Asia Co-prosperity Sphere--Cooperation with Concurring Countries." In the same issue, another news report announced an impending "decisive battle between Great Britain and Germany which will revolutionize world history in the 20th century." The next day, the same paper covered the outlines of Soviet foreign policy as delineated by Foreign Minister Molotov under the heading, "There Are Chances for Improving Soviet-Japanese Relations--Molotov Views Japan's New System as Profoundly Important."[55] In the fast-changing international environment of Japan that such news reports indicate, Matsuoka had given expression to the notion of a greater East Asia co-prosperity sphere shortly after noon on 1 August and in the evening had met with German Ambassador Eugen Ott, at which time he took the initiative of sounding out German attitudes concerning a triple alliance among Japan, Germany and Italy.[56] As far as Matsuoka was concerned, this alliance was to constitute a "Eurasian continental alliance" including the Soviet Union in addition to Japan, Germany, and Italy, and as such it was conceived as a tool for opening formal negotiations with the United States. It is prudent to refrain from making any definitive assessment as to how deeply geopolitical thought was ingrained in Matsuoka's mind at this point, but the relationship between Matsuoka's statement of 1 August and Royama's initial use of the word "geopolitics" in his own writings on policy formulation appears to have been close and significant.

In November 1940, at a lecture meeting held under the auspices of the Institute of Pacific Relations at Sophia University in Tokyo, Royama addressed the audience on the subject of "Extended Regionalism in Greater East Asia: A Geopolitical Analysis." To him, "to construct a greater East Asia co-prosperity sphere" was a question of how to bring into existence an "extended regionalism" or "extended economic region." He explained what he had already had in mind, making references to Haushofer freely for the first time.[57] Soon thereafter he published an article, "A Geopolitical Analysis of a Greater East Asia Co-Prosperity Sphere," in the March 1941 issue of *Kaizo*. He stated emphatically the "need for a geopolitical analysis of a greater East Asia co-prosperity sphere," and proposed to make the most of such sciences as geopolitics, in addition to hitherto employed scientific methods, to enhance analytical accuracy. "I for one," he said, "have been making efforts to construct a regionalistic globalism, based on geopolitical analysis, such that it may provide a foundation for our continental policy, as it has developed in the most recent decade from the outbreak of the Manchurian Incident through the China conflict."[58] Continuing, he confided that "The Theory of an East Asian Cooperative Body," published in the fall of 1938, was one manifest result of such concern and effort.

According to Royama, it was acceptable to see either Matsuoka's statement or the "establishment of the new order in greater East Asia" as presented in the *Kihon kokusaku yoko* (*Essentials of National Policy*), which had been made public earlier the same day, as official Government policy. But the content of this policy was "much too abstract and unfathomable."[59] So he, an actor outside the Government, took it upon himself to give it substance by employing a scientific methodology. Royama pointed out two basic problems that confronted the concept of a greater East Asia co-prosperity sphere: even as a simple extended regionalism it consisted of two rather different regions, and these regions overlapped the economic regions of the United States or Great Britain. In other words, in reality the proposed extended region was not a coherent economic region, and in order to bring about such an economic region, the first step must be to establish it as a political region. This contention followed from the trifling economic interaction between Japan and the proposed extended region, which was in sharp contrast to the Balkan area in the extended economic region which Germany was then attempting to form: mutual complementarity there amounted to nearly 50 percent of their respective economic transactions.[60] Japan's economic (and therefore theoretical) deficiency was not so bad in the case of the East Asian region alone, but it was acute in the case of South and Southeast Asia.

In the above analysis one can see a man outside the Government trying to feed "realistic" content into its "idealistic" policy framework. And it is ironic that the very policy statement itself was formulated in the aftermath of the "realistic" criticism that was directed against the Government by another "non-governmental" person, Saito. To this criticism the Government had responded with the concept of a super-region, a greater East Asia co-prosperity sphere, by dropping the principles of "no annexation" and "no indemnity" from the New Order in East Asia and transforming and extending it. In the same vein, in response to Saito's warning against the "power politics" of the Western powers, the Government proposed to practice the way of the Tenno. Accordingly, the universally applicable designation for their own country, *Teikoku* ("the Empire"), as still used in the New Order in East Asia proclamation, was promptly dropped in favor of the more particularistic term *Kokoku* ("the Land of the Tenno"), which was already in the *Essentials of National Policy* when it was adopted by the Cabinet on 26 July 1940. In this document (made public as mentioned earlier on 1 August), we find many other examples of particularistic and ethnocentric terms and concepts like the phrase, "the great spirit of founding the nation to bring eight corners of the world under one roof (hakko ichiu)," indicating a move away from internationalization as defined by the advanced western nation-states.

These particularistic concepts must have looked not only much too abstract but also unscientific to Royama who, out of scientific and economic concerns, had decided to employ geopolitical ideas with precision. The concepts must have appeared like dangerous tricks which could mislead Japan into devastating crisis. However, from the point of view of the geopolitics of the "Imperial Way" as advanced by men like Komaki, these policy pronouncements accurately reflected or represented their own beliefs. In other respects as well these policy statements are the end product of an intellectual current which originated with a document prepared by the Investigation Bureau of the Foreign Office in December 1936. This document, entitled "*Nihon koyu no gaiko shido genri koryo* (General Principles Peculiar to Japan for the Guidance of its Diplomacy),"[61] elucidated an evolution, along the lines of wang tao, that "transcends small differences" and upon which a league of East Asian states could be built. Furthermore, in August of the following year, Foreign Minister Ugaki Kazushige (1868-1956) had been presented with a memorial by a group of eight so-called "young, progressive career diplomats" of the Foreign Ministry. Their statement used archaic Japanese words and concepts, giving it a strong nationalistic aura: "We, as employees of the Foreign Ministry who are expected to serve as vanguards of the high commissioner (of the Tenno) who is entrusted with the task of propagating the way of the Tenno" have long since considered what platform or principles should guide the "diplomacy" of this land of the Tenno, and have come up with a "set of basic propositions."[62] In this manner, policy recommendations composed of nativistic values and concepts were emerging from within the Foreign Ministry itself in the name of the idealistic way of the Tenno, or kodo.

Royama never explained how and why the designation Japan used for itself, Teikoku or Empire, was replaced by Kokoku or the Land of the Tenno. But as far as we can see, Teikoku was dropped for fear that its implications would be confused with those of its derivative, *teikokushugi* ("imperialism"), which had become synonymous with Western practices of armed preponderance and colonial exploitation. In its place the name Kokoku was chosen; it was expected to signify Japan as the one and only practitioner of the Way of the Tenno as the essence of the East Asian tradition of wang tao.[63]

Japan had declared war in the past against the Chinese, the Russians, and then the Germans using documents signed by Emperors

Meiji and Taisho using the title *Kotei*, the same term that Japanese used for not only a Chinese or Korean Emperor but also Western emperors like Kaiser William II or Czar Nicolas II. However, on 8 December 1941, when at last Emperor Hirohito declared war on Great Britain and the United States, that long-established custom was discarded in favor of signing the document simply with Tenno, the one and only such sovereign in the whole world. With this, I would argue, the idealistic transformation on the governmental level was completed. Royama did make some final efforts to put realistic substance into this official frame of mind. For example, on the eve of Pearl Harbor he was still promoting the activities of the War Economy Study Corps of the War Ministry and collaborating with its chief, Colonel Akimaru Jiro. Even after the outbreak of the war, he went to the Philippines where he engaged in a field study of the Filipino concept of national polity and other issues of political culture to see if Japan's concept of national polity and related political notions made any sense to the Filipinos--a prerequisite if the Japanese were to make the concept of a greater East Asia co-prosperity sphere work at all. His findings were negative.[64] These activities testify to the scientific attitude of Royama, a convincing example of sober and positive realism on the part of one Japanese outside the Government. Their eclipse testifies also to the victory of idealism, which penetrated the Government from without and warped national consciousness in a manner resistant even to the most realistic of critiques, as we shall see below.

NOTES

1. Miwa Kimitada, "Ajiashugi no rekishiteki kosatsu," in Hirano Ken'ichiro, ed., *Nihon bunka no henyô* (Tokyo, 1973), pp. 387-90.
2. Miwa Kimitada, "Japan Neither East nor West but All Alone," in Hilary Conroy and Harry Wray, eds., *Japan Examined* (Honolulu, 1983), p. 385.
3. Miwa Kimitada, "Nihon no sekai rempo undo wo sasaeru dochakusei," in Kawata Tadashi and Miwa Kimitada, eds., *Gendai kokusai kankei ron* (Tokyo, 1980), pp. 233-34.
4. Hayashi Shihei, *Hayashi Shihei zenshu*, vol. 2 (Tokyo, 1944), pp. 662, 669-79.
5. Miwa Kimitada, *Kyodotai ishiki no dochakusei* (Tokyo, 1978), chs. 2, 3.
6. Kokuryu kurabu, ed., *Kokushi Uchida Ryohei den* (Tokyo, 1967), p. 538.
7. Naito Konan, *Shin Shina ron* (Tokyo, 1938), author's preface, p. 10.
8. Naito, *Shin Shina ron*, p. 266.
9. Naito, *Shin Shina ron*, pp. 273-74.
10. Banno Masataka, *Kindai Chugoku gaiko shi kenkyu* (Tokyo, 1970), p. 423.
11. Banno, *Kindai Chugoku*, p. 428.
12. John J. Stephan, "The Tanaka Memorial (1927): Authentic or Spurious," *Modern Asian Studies*, vol. 12 no. 4 (1973), pp. 733-45.
13. Royama Masamichi, *Nichi-Man kankei no kenkyu* (Tokyo, 1933); Gomi Toshiki, "1930 nendai Nihon no shin kokusai chitsujo koso--Royama Masamichi no baai," *The Journal of International Studies*, vol. 2 no. 2 (July 1979), p. 12.
14. Mitani Taichiro, *Taisho demokurashii* (Tokyo, 1974), p. 238.
15. Ishiwara, a major Imperial Way Faction leader, masterminded the Manchurian Incident of 1931, but was staunchly opposed to Japan's military actions in China after 1937. For a full account see Mark R. Peattie, *Ishiwara Kanji and Japan's Confrontation with the West* (Princeton, 1975).
16. For example, see Peter Duus, "Nagai Ryutaro and the 'White Peril', 1905-1944," *Journal of Asian Studies*, vol. 31, no. 1 (November 1971), pp. 41-48.
17. Odera Kenkichi, *Dai Ajiashugi ron* (Tokyo, 1916), pp. i-ix.
18. Miwa Kimitada, "1924 nen hai-Nichi imin ho no seiritsu to Bei-ka boikotto," in Hosoya Chihiro, ed., *Taiheiyo Ajia ken no kokusai keizai funso shi* (Tokyo, 1983), pp. 171-72.
19. Heibon sha, ed., *Shimonaka Yasaburo jiten* (Tokyo, 1971), p. 243.
20. Dai Ajia kyokai, ed., *Dai Ajia kyokai nempo* (Tokyo, March 1934), p. 1.
21. Shimonaka Yasaburo, *Bannin rodo no kyoiku* (Tokyo, 1974), pp. 561-62.
22. For the contrasting "pacifist" ideas of Shimonaka and Ryu, see Miwa, "Nihon no sekai rempo undo," pp. 234-37, 241-42.
23. Nakayama Masaru, *Nakayama Masaru senshu* (Tokyo, 1973), p. 280; *Asahi shimbun* (3 November 1938); Yabe Teiji, *Konoye Fumimaro* (Tokyo, 1976), p. 367.
24. Nakayama, *Nakayama Masaru*, p. 278.
25. On this occasion, Ozaki Hotsumi of the *Asahi* and Yoshioka Bunroku of the *Mainichi* were also called in. Nakayama observed that in the presence of Prince Konoye, Ozaki appeared very condescending. See Nakayama, *Nakayama Masaru*, p. 273.
26. Nakayama, *Nakayama Masaru*, pp. 275-76.
27. Nakayama, *Nakayama Masaru*, p. 261.
28. Nakayama, *Nakayama Masaru*, p. 364.
29. Nakayama, *Nakayama Masaru*, p. 365.
30. For an illuminating treatment of agrarianism in prewar Japan see Thomas R. H. Havens, *Farm and Nation in Modern Japan: Agrarian Nationalism, 1870-1940* (Princeton, 1974).
31. Nakayama Masaru, *Tai-Shi seisaku no honryu* (Tokyo, 1937), p. 24.
32. Nakayama, *Tai-Shi seisaku*, p. 36.
33. Nakayama, *Tai-Shi seisaku*, p. 35.
34. Nakayama, *Tai-Shi seisaku*, p. 49.
35. *Loc. cit.*
36. *Loc. cit.*
37. Nakayama, *Tai-Shi seisaku*, p. 281.
38. For example, see Kyoto daigaku bungaku bu kokushi kenkyu shitsu, ed., *Nihon*

kindai shi daijiten (Tokyo, 1958), p. 215.
39. *Asahi shimbun* (3 February 1940).
40. Yabe Tenji, *Yabe Teiji nikki*, vol. 1 (Tokyo, 1974), p. 285.
41. Ishikawa Masatoshi, *Seiji naki seiji* (Tokyo, 1963), pp. 187-89. See also Miwa, *Kyodotai ishiki*, pp. 63-76.
42. Nakayama, *Nakayama Masaru*, p. 280.
43. Miwa Kimitada, "Taiheiyo jidai to Amerika," Time Life Educational Systems, ed., *Anatomy of U.S. Business* (Tokyo, 1972), pp. 79-81.
44. Mitani, *Taisho demokurashii*, p. 265.
45. Hatano Sumio, "'To-A shin chitsujo' to chiseigaku," in Miwa Kimitada, ed., *Nihon no sen kyuhyaku sanju nendai* (Tokyo, 1980), p. 18.
46. Takeuchi Keiichi, "Nihon ni okeru geoporitiiku to chirigaku," *Hitotsubashi Ronshu*, vol. 72, no. 2 (1974), p. 186.
47. Miwa Kimitada, *Chihoshugi no kenkyu* (Tokyo, 1975), pp. 223-26.
48. Royama Masamichi, *To-A to sekai* (Tokyo, 1941), p. 197.
49. Royama, *To-A to sekai*, pp. 141-42.
50. Takahashi Hisashi, "To-A kyodotai ron: Royama Masamichi, Ozaki Hotsumi, Kada Tetsuji no baai," in Miwa, ed., *Nihon no sen kyuhyaku sanju nendai*, p. 76.
51. Yabe, *Nikki*, vol. 1, p. 302.
52. Yoshii Hiroshi, *Showa gaiko shi* (Tokyo, 1971), p. 118.
53. *Asahi shimbun* (Evening, 2 August 1940).
54. *Loc. cit.*
55. *Loc. cit.*
56. Yoshii, *Showa gaiko shi*, p. 118.
57. Taiheiyo kyokai, ed., *Taiheiyo mondai saikento* (Tokyo, 1941), pp. 2-57.
58. Royama, *To-A to sekai*, pp. 364-65.
59. Royama, *To-A to sekai*, p. 362.
60. Taiheiyo kyokai, ed., *Taiheiyo mondai*, pp. 51-54.
61. I am indebted to Professor Watanabe Akio of Tokyo University for this document. See also Watanabe Akio, "Kindai Nihon ni okeru taigai kankei no shotokucho," in Nakamura Ryuhei and Ito Takashi, eds., *Kindai Nihon kenkyu nyumon* (Tokyo, 1977), p. 147.
62. Ugaki Kazushige, *Ugaki Kazushige nikki* (Tokyo, 1971), vol. 3, p. 1255.
63. It could have been for the sake of deprecating men like Colonel Ishiwara Kanji, who had been the proponent of wang tao, that Matsuoka Yosuke insisted that Japan had kodo, the Japanese Imperial way, and that that alone would suffice for optimum construction of the state of Manchukuo. Matsuoka had long claimed authorship of the concept of kodo, of which he wrote in 1941: "I believe that the hub of the grand task of raising Asia to save the world is Japan's Imperial way." See Matsuoka Yosuke, *Ko-A no taigyo* (Tokyo, 1941), p. 275.
64. Masamichi Royama and Tatsuji Takeuchi, *The Philippine Polity: A Japanese View* (New Haven, 1967).

7
PROPHET WITHOUT HONOR: KIYOSAWA KIYOSHI'S VIEW OF JAPANESE-AMERICAN RELATIONS

Shin'ichi Kitaoka

James W. White, translator

Introduction

It is already more than 40 years since the Japanese critic Kiyosawa Kiyoshi (1890-1945) died three months before the end of the Pacific War. If he is remembered at all today it is most likely, first, for his *Ankoku nikki*,[1] a diary written during the war. A penetrating, liberal critique of the war, it has been widely read and highly praised since it was first published in 1948. Among students of the political and diplomatic history of modern Japan, he is also known for his *Gaiko shi*,[2] expanded into *Nihon gaiko shi*.[3] This was not only the best diplomatic history of modern Japan written before 1945; it is a work unsurpassed even today in insight, balance, and narrative beauty.

However, Kiyosawa was not solely a diplomatic historian or diarist. His diplomatic studies in fact began only after restrictions on freedom of expression made publication of his works for a general audience difficult, and he devoted himself to his diaries after even scholarly works became difficult to publish. Criticism was his *metier* and even his conceit: "If we [Kiyosawa and his fellow critic Baba Tsunego] are not critics, who else is?"[4] The objects of his commentaries ranged far and wide, from Japanese politics, foreign policy, society, and thought to international relations, but his specialties were diplomacy and the United States and, hence, Japanese policy vis-a-vis America. Edifying and criticizing his government and fellow Japanese regarding policy toward America were the foci of his most strenuous efforts. And in the words of Baba Tsunego, "Around the time of the war he was the only one whose perceptions of America really were on target."[5]

However, it was precisely this field in which prewar control of expression was most severe. In sharp contrast to the U.S., where Japan experts like Joseph Grew and Eugene Dooman were put in important positions, there was no scope for the activities of Kiyosawa, who could do nothing but turn to historical studies and subsequently to his diary. It was a tragedy not only for Kiyosawa but for Japan as well.

Today Kiyosawa's commentaries on Japan-U.S. relations are practically unknown in Japan; indeed, a comprehensive critique of them is yet to appear.[6] It is the primary object of this essay to analyze these commentaries, test them against international realities of the day, and place them in the context of contemporary domestic public opinion. However, this essay is not solely concerned with Kiyosawa himself. Its second objective is to clarify the reasons for the accuracy of his perceptions of America and, by implication, the reasons why so many other intellectuals' appraisals of the U.S. were distorted.

The Immigrant Experience

Kiyosawa was born in the village of Kita Hodaka, Azumi county, Nagano Prefecture, in 1890, to a relatively prosperous farm family. Upon graduating from elementary school in 1903 Kiyosawa entered a tiny private school run by Iguchi Kigenji, who was a disciple of Uchimura Kanzo and a "Non-Church" Christian. Under the strong Christian influence of Iguchi, over 40 of his students traveled to America in 1905-1906, to spread their faith. Kiyosawa left Japan at the end of 1906; he worked his way through Tacoma High School and subsequently attended Whitworth College and the University of Washington. He was, however, basically self-educated, and never graduated from college. He began working for the Japanese-language newspaper *Hokubei jiji* at about the time he graduated from high school, and his articles soon came to enjoy a high reputation in the immigrant community: "during the two years he headed the Tacoma bureau of the *Hokubei jiji* he wielded the most influential pen on the West Coast."[7] Later Kiyosawa moved to the Japanese-language newspaper *Shin sekai* in San Francisco, and until his return to Japan in 1918 he continued his activities as a newspaper writer. Indeed, it is likely that his reason for returning home was a hope, as a journalist, to reach an even wider audience.

As it happened, Kiyosawa's arrival in the U.S. coincided with the cresting of the first wave of the anti-Japanese movement, set off by the debate over attendance by immigrants' children at public schools in San Francisco. As Kiyosawa described it in a letter home in 1907, "Everywhere one hears voices calling for war with Japan.... The treatment of Japanese in this country is shockingly shabby. You hear things like 'Jap bastard!' everywhere. They greet us with every conceivable sort of contempt."[8] The issue was laid to rest temporarily by Japan's unilateral restriction on emigration in the Gentlemen's Agreement of 1907-08, but the roots of anti-Japanese sentiment were deep and in 1913 California passed the Alien Land Law, which placed severe restrictions on land ownership by Japanese.

For the immigrants, these conditions made their homeland the object of inexpressible longing. As Kiyosawa later wrote, "It's hard to imagine just how blessed, how wonderful Japan seems when you're in a foreign country."[9] The government of his homeland was, however, not overly solicitous of its emigrants. What did shock the Japanese government was not the persecution of the emigrants per se, but rather that nationals of the "Great Power" Japan were receiving discriminatory treatment. The government was primarily interested in protecting its prestige as a first-rate power, even at the cost of sacrificing the welfare of the emigrants. Moreover, the emigrants were embarrassed by and fearful of the indignation and emotional response of their government to this impugning of its honor. For the rest of his life Kiyosawa maintained an attitude of mistrustful distance from the government, a product of his experiences while an emigrant.

It is doubtful that the Japanese government could have done anything to protect the emigrants even if it had tried. Japanese diplomacy focused on Washington, but the ability of the federal government to intervene in state politics was very limited. Kiyosawa was perfectly aware of this. In an essay written in 1914, in the immediate aftermath of the passage of the Alien Land Law, Kiyosawa dispassionately analyzed every conceivable hypothetical diplomatic solution to the problem, and concluded that each was impossible of realization.

He was, however, not pessimistic about the immigrant problem in the long run. He saw as one reason for the persecution the industriousness of the immigrants, which threatened the jobs of American workers. Another was that many of the immigrants had no intention of settling in America; they remitted most of their wages, built closed communities, and did not associate with Americans. That such behavior should be rejected was unsurprising. He was sure that if the immigrants could avoid losing their strength--their industriousness--while correcting their failings--for example by resolving to settle permanently, investing in the U.S., and interacting positively with Americans--then they would surely become reconciled with the Americans and flourish. The reasons for this were, first, that as long as the West Coast remained rich in economic opportunities there would be a demand for a high-quality work force. If the Japanese immigrants were excluded, immigrants from such places as eastern and southern Europe would replace them; the Americans would then appreciate the quality of Japanese workers, and reconciliation would become possible. Second, Kiyosawa noted the high rates of marriage and birth among the immigrants; their children, born in the U.S., would have the rights of American citizenship, and if they used these rights then the restrictions on land ownership would not be so terrible. In sum, Kiyosawa believed that the factors which would determine the future of the immigrants were economic, not political, regardless of Japanese governmental protection or American persecution.[10]

Subsequently, due to the adoption of measures such as the prohibition of mail-order marriages, one of the factors supporting Kiyosawa's optimism crumbled, and later Japanese immigrants were unable to achieve striking progress. Still, those Japanese who had already arrived in the U.S. did in the end achieve success, and Kiyosawa's prediction was thus in general outline on the mark.

In any case, the above typifies the way that Kiyosawa saw relations between peoples on a dimension apart from interstate relationships. Such a position was quite exceptional; in the Japan of his day, the progress of the people was conceived of only within the framework of national progress. But Kiyosawa's position, as we shall see, became the fundamental basis of his foreign policy views.

The Retreat from International Cooperation, 1920-1931
1. Perceptions of America

Kiyosawa returned to Japan in July 1918; in 1920 he joined the *Chugai shogyo shimbun* (the predecessor of the *Nihon keizai shimbun*) and began his literary career in Japan. In 1927 he moved to the *Asahi shimbun*, but left in 1929 to become a freelance critic. The decade between Kiyosawa's return to Japan and his becoming an independent commentator was the high-water mark of internationalism in Japan. Beginning with the establishment of the Japan League of Nations Association in 1920, a variety of groups actively espousing pacifism and international cooperation appeared or grew, and many opinion leaders joined them. This movement was heavily infused with pro-American sentiment. In fact, the key members of the pacifist-internationalist groups and the U.S.-Japan friendship groups were largely the same people.[11] The U.S. had not joined the League, but in hosting the Washington Conference (1921-22), sponsoring the Kellogg-

Briand Pact (1928), and contributing to the stability of Europe with the Dawes (1924) and Young (1929) plans for German reparations, it remained as ever a champion of international cooperation. On the other hand, Japan had more problems with the U.S. than with any other powers, and thus it was natural for Japanese internationalists to emphasize harmony with the U.S. above all else.

However, in the late 1920s the internationalist tide began to ebb. In the summer of 1931 even the hitherto liberal *Asahi shimbun* began to support a hard policy line on Japan's position in Manchuria. By September, when the Manchurian Incident occurred, persons openly propounding international cooperation had already become rare.[12] By March 1933, when Japan left the League, the only person to criticize the move publicly from an internationalist perspective was Kiyosawa. The proponents of U.S.-Japanese friendship had also begun to disappear. Why did the internationalist pro-Americans change their tune or fall silent? And why did Kiyosawa alone not do likewise?

The first major shock to the internationalist position came from the U.S. Japanese Immigration Exclusion Act of 1924. Despite the fact that immigration from Japan had already been strictly limited, this law categorized Japanese as "non-naturalizable aliens" and banned further immigration. The Japanese were stunned: public opinion boiled over, protest meetings were held, and the major newspapers issued a joint statement condemning the U.S. A number of suicides even took place in protest. The shock to the internationalist pro-American group was equally deep: even Shibusawa Eiichi, most important of the major figures in all the internationalist groups, and Nitobe Inazo, the central figure among internationalist intellectuals, expressed their deep distress and anger. Coming from persons so known for their moderation, such expressions were extraordinary. Nitobe's response is well known: he resolved not to set foot on American soil until the law was changed. Until firmly requested to visit the U.S. by his government in 1932 he repeatedly refused invitations to visit the U.S. and, in going back and forth to Geneva in his capacity as Vice Secretary of the League of Nations, avoided passing through the U.S.

The reason internationalist pro-American groups were so shocked by events was that they had held an image of America as lover of humanity and justice. It is said that Shibusawa had acquired an image of the U.S. as a country of "just and humanitarian" principles from his study of the Japan policy enunciated by Townsend Harris, which had been sharply at odds with the aggressive policies shown by England and France during the Opium War.[13] Nitobe, a junior of Woodrow Wilson while a graduate student at Johns Hopkins University, had sympathized deeply with the ideals of international peace and cooperation expressed by Wilson as president. This attitude was shared by many of the young men who respected Nitobe greatly.

Such idealistic understandings of the U.S. had always had their rivals. The criticism that the pacifism and international cooperation trumpeted by America were nothing but ideological camouflage for the status quo national interests of the American and English "haves" had been around for a long time. The young Konoye Fumimaro's *A Rejection of Pacifism Anglo-American Style*[14] was typical of the genre. Given this context one can understand how disillusioned the internationalist pro-Americans were by the Exclusion Act, and how it weakened their position.

In response to the Exclusion Act, Kiyosawa took a tack completely different from that of the internationalists. His first book, *Beikoku no kenkyu*, appeared in the immediate aftermath of the Law, amid a flood of anti-American works.[15] He was, of course, hardly uninterested in the immigration problem. As he put it in his Introduction: "As for the exclusion question, I lived myself in the center of anti-Japanese feeling for a long time, and felt the outrage of persecution; I even worried whether, in discussing this, I would be able adequately to express the burning anger and feelings of blame which fill my heart." Nevertheless, Kiyosawa did not go along with the seething climate of anti-American opinion. On the contrary, he thought it essential to calm this opinion and restore harmonious U.S.-Japan relations. It was for this reason that he published *Beikoku no kenkyu*.

The foremost reason why Kiyosawa emphasized Japanese-U.S. cooperation was because the U.S. was a mighty economic power. To him, the economic development of the U.S. was *the* major phenomenon of the twentieth century. It was an event without parallel in world history; there was no international relationship not influenced by it to a profound degree. Particularly for Japan, which faced America across the Pacific and depended critically on its exports to America, amicable relationships with the U.S. were utterly essential to future growth. In *Beikoku no kenkyu* Kiyosawa repeatedly stressed that America was first an economic phenomenon and only secondarily a political one. This was in clear contrast to the internationalist pro-Americans, who paid primary attention to the "political" America. If the most symbolic American was for them Wilson, for Kiyosawa it was Henry Ford.[16]

Of course, Kiyosawa was not the only one who took note of America's economic power. However, in contrast to the typical Japanese stress on the size of the country and its wealth of resources, he put the emphasis on human and social factors such as efficiency, diligence, low level of armaments, and the youth of the population (due to the large immigrant population). Additionally, he put much greater stress on spiritual factors such as the pioneer spirit and faith in one's own abilities. Unlike those preoccupied with American economic activity, who fell easily into the belief that Americans were a nation of mercenaries, Kiyosawa explained that the apparent American love of money was in fact the view that making money was a way of expressing and fulfilling one's capabilities and not simply enslavement by Mammon.

This attention to spiritual factors also characterized his observations on politics. In overviewing the American political system Kiyosawa stressed the traditions of the Pilgrim Fathers and the framers of the Constitution. He was of course not blind to the problems of contemporary American politics. Drawing on Bertrand Russell, Kiyosawa noted the absence in America of the European tradition of autonomous corporate groups and the consequent tyranny of public opinion and the ease with which minority freedoms could be violated. This danger had been greatly enhanced by such trends as the disappearance of the frontier, the concentration and acceleration of industrial organization, and the influx of immigrants. Immigration and racial problems and Prohibition were examples of this. However, at the same time Kiyosawa offered the example of the strength of anti-exclusion sentiments even in the anti-Japanese hotbed of California, and argued that wholesome forces not subservient to the tyranny of public opinion were always extant. It was here that Kiyosawa saw the soundness of the moral power which supported the foundations of American politics. Accordingly, Kiyosawa proposed the following:

> The agonies that Japan goes through over the U.S. are also the agonies of the U.S. herself. America's intelligentsia and leaders exert themselves to lead the impetuous masses wisely, but they also have the moral courage to express their views resolutely. These two elements have been in conflict ever since America's independence; no matter how many weaknesses America has, it usually manages to be fair, and we must put our faith in this characteristic.
>
> We should keep an open mind, and we should lend our strength to those Americans who love justice. Our hope is that they not let America go astray. We should link up with America's best elements, make clear to them the common ground we share, and attack the pro-war faction and inflammatory elements from both sides.[17]

Thus there was a broad gap between Kiyosawa's image of America and that held by other internationalist pro-Americans. This was partly because the internationalist pro-Americans were mostly graduates of the imperial universities, and came from an elite of imperial university professors, high-level bureaucrats, and business leaders deeply tied to the government. Such people had first studied and then visited America, where they associated with other elites (such as university professors, high officials of the federal government, diplomats, and Wall Street bankers) and created their images of America accordingly. Kiyosawa, by contrast, was self-taught, had no ties to the government, and had lived at the bottom of American society as an immigrant. He knew many Americas and was inclined neither to idealize American democracy or Wilson, nor to become disillusioned with them. Thus Kiyosawa, amid the retreat of the internationalist pro-Americans, did not relinquish his arguments for U.S.-Japan concord--indeed, he strengthened them.[18]

2. Changing Images of Manchuria and China

Amid the waning of international cooperation following the passage of the Exclusion Act, in 1925 the Institute for Pacific Relations (IPR) was established. It was organized by intellectuals from a number of countries interested in the problems of the Pacific region and its Japanese branch, the JIPR, was from the late 1920s on the major base of the internationalist pro-Americans.

The core of JIPR membership were former students of Nitobe Inazo. Their emphases were on Japan-U.S. relations, and especially immigration questions, within the Pacific basin. It mattered little to them at first whether the IPR concerned itself with the China question,[19] since it did not seem to them that there were any issues involving China which threatened the security of the Pacific. They felt that China--and especially Manchuria--was essential to the future prosperity of Japan, and they accepted Japan's China policy as a whole.

Consequently when, in the late 1920s, Japan's interests in Manchuria were threatened by Chinese nationalism and by the rise of the Soviet Union, they were impelled toward hard decisions: should they renounce Japan's interests in Manchuria and pursue the path of international cooperation, or should they abandon cooperation and appeal to force of arms in order to protect these interests? And how should they deal with the fact that the Kwantung Army had already launched military operations? Despite the fact that until this moment they had been the staunchest supporters of international cooperation, almost all of them fell silent or chose rather to support Japan's interests in Manchuria. This marked the decisive collapse of the internationalist position in Japan.

But once more Kiyosawa remained steadfast, because he--unlike the other internationalist pro-Americans and most of his other countrymen--did not believe that Manchuria was of crucial importance to the prosperity of Japan. In 1924 he had visited Korea, Manchuria, and China; in 1925 he again visited Korea, Manchuria, and Siberia. His observations appeared in the *Chugai shogyo shimpo*, and in several essays as well.

In one essay Kiyosawa analyzed the notion of Japan's "special position" in Manchuria; he pointed out that it had no basis in international agreements and that therefore it was problematic how stable a position Japan could build there.[20] Further, Japan's capacities there were limited: "Last year, and the year before that, I visited Manchuria. I was amazed: with the exception of the South Manchuria Railway, the economic position of Japan in Manchuria--which people here at home who don't really know what's going on there think is practically an extension of Japan--is extraordinarily weak. Japan's strength is entirely based on the railway, and almost everything else is nothing but ancillary consumer operations. I was quite disappointed that there was really nothing worth seeing."

And Kiyosawa saw instability even in the future of the *Mantetsu*, as the railway was known. In the first place, it was operating a great many enterprises in addition to the railroad, but only the railroad itself and the Fushun coal mines showed a profit. Moreover, in 20 years the Mantetsu presidency had changed 10 times, reflecting the inconsistency of government's policies for running it. Moreover, influences from domestic political parties had crept in and a tendency for the company to be used as a source of political funds had become blatantly clear, with scandals coming in train.

In addition to instability within, there was an external threat. Nationalistic Chinese saw the Mantetsu and Kwantung Province as symbols of the invasion of China by Japanese imperialism and sought their recovery. Moreover, the USSR having weathered the chaos of its revolution, it was predictable that the East China Railroad would revive and become a competitor of the Mantetsu. Third, it could also be predicted that the labor problems then growing in central and south China would spread to Manchuria. It was quite conceivable that ideological influences from the USSR would spread to Manchuria as well. In sum, Kiyosawa perceived that the underpinnings of Japan's "special position" were quite weak.

In contrast, he had been impressed by the extremely hardworking Chinese of Manchuria, who were making steady progress in their own enterprises. In them Kiyosawa saw the Japanese emigrants in the U.S., putting down roots and building prosperity through hard work in the face of racist persecution. If America were unable to restrain the prosperity of the Japanese immigrants even when exercising its sovereignty to do so, how on earth was Japan ever going to restrain the development of Chinese people who weren't even within its own territory? Although he avoided any explicit assertion, Kiyosawa clearly thought it possible that Japan would be expelled from Manchuria by the industrious Chinese. It is also probable that his sympathies lay more with the Chinese, who kept silently at work without caving in to Japanese persecution, than with the Japanese in Manchuria, who even with government protection were unable to achieve any substantial development.

In mainland China too, the thing which most struck Kiyosawa was the industriousness of the Chinese people. Immediately upon entering China, "I was struck with admiration for how hardworking the Chinese people were, how they worked, oblivious to fatigue, as if they were born to work." More than anything else, he attributed to the people's diligence the fact that, although Chinese politics in the 1920s were in utter chaos, China had not decayed, much less collapsed. "I believe that the growth or decline of a nation is determined by whether its people produce much or not, that is, whether they work or not," he stated, and he argued that China's future was bright.[21] Most Japanese saw only China's political disorder and had little faith in the prospect for future growth; even those who recognized her economic potential put primary emphasis on natural resources. Kiyosawa's priorities were in just the opposite order.

As one may see, Kiyosawa's youthful experiences as an emigrant influenced his views of Manchuria and China, and of foreign policy in general. Productivity, based on the industriousness of the people, constituted the foundation of the growth of nations and peoples; political factors were of only secondary importance. Thus he adjudged Japan's Manchuria policy to be built on sand, and predicted that sooner or later China was going to control Manchuria and build a unified China. Moreover, the rich China of the future would be of great value to Japan. If China were to be an enemy then it were best that she were weak, but if one thought of her as a trade partner, then the stronger and richer the better. It was imperative that Japan change from a geopolitical policy based on the former assumption to an industrially-focused policy based on the latter.[22] Therefore, Japan's insistence on her interests in economically dubious Manchuria and Mongolia and her derogation of Sino-Japanese relations, which disadvantaged the far more important China market, seemed exceedingly unwise to Kiyosawa. Thus he advocated a negotiated restoration of Manchurian and Mongolian interests to China.[23]

But Kiyosawa opposed excessive emphasis on China. He saw Japan as less dependent on China than England was on Europe, and rejected the view that Japan could not survive without China.[24] This followed from his industrially-based concept of international relations, in which China figured as a trade partner secondary to America.

China's current political instability also figured in his reasoning. Kiyosawa was extremely apprehensive of the xenophobic and anti-imperialistic forces driving Chinese politics, which exceeded ordinary nationalism. Such a foreign policy, which ignored international agreements and clamored incessantly about the recovery of rights and would sanction any means thereto, could not contribute to international order. Kiyosawa felt that in order to check such blind xenophobia the only option available was for Japan, Britain, and the U.S. to cooperate closely. Therefore the targets of Japan's China policy should in fact be Britain and the U.S., and it was more important that Japanese diplomats in China be experts on America and England than on China.[25]

Kuroshio ni kiku, published in 1928, was a collection of Kiyosawa's major essays on foreign affairs from the 1920s. As the title--*Listening to the Pacific*--suggests, Kiyosawa did not treat Japan's relations with the U.S., China, Russia, and England as sets of bilateral ties but rather as a system of international interrelationships. First and foremost came cooperation with America. He proposed that amicable relationships with China could best be built by preventing an explosion of Chinese nationalism--optimally through adding England to the basic U.S.-Japan concert--and gradually relinquishing Japan's interests in Manchuria. In this way Japan might expect to grow economically, mainly through trade, primarily with the U.S. and secondarily with China.

In contrast, the internationalist pro-Americans represented by the JIPR basically supported Japan's China policy, including her special interests in Manchuria, but still hoped to improve relations with America. The precedence they gave to these special interests over international conciliation was due to the perceptions of Manchuria and China noted above, and to their lack of any integrated grasp of Japan-U.S. and Sino-Japanese relations.[26]

3. The Shock of the Great Depression

A mortal blow was delivered to the post-World War I international order by the American Great Depression of 1929. Its effect on Europe was more direct and deep, but its impact on Asia was great also. The story of how Japan's export-dependent economy--especially its rural sector--sustained a shock which became a major stimulus to the political rise of the military needs no retelling here.

But hardly less important than this was the collapse of the image of America as the champion of the postwar international order and the quintessence of economic prosperity. Concomitantly the intellectual prestige of Marxism--despite its political suppression--reached its acme in Japan. Many intellectuals argued that the inevitable collapse of capitalism had begun. Events seemed to augur the demise of liberal democracy and the bankruptcy of internationalism. Even those who still saw the necessity of cooperation with America and the virtues of America as a model saw them becoming far less credible. Former proponents of international concord, and especially cooperation with the U.S., were thrust upon a dilemma, and recanted entirely or fell silent.

By chance, Kiyosawa was--after an absence of 10 years--in the U.S. when the Depression began.[27] He was not, however, overwhelmed by it. He criticized the excessively theoretical arguments emanating from Japan, especially those of the Marxists. He argued that, depression or no, many workers still owned automobiles and ate steak, and it was a mistake to underestimate America's strength. It was of course not that he was unaware of the massive difficulties facing the American economy. He felt that there were problems, especially on the distributive side of the American economy, and predicted that some sort of control--the introduction of some type of socialism--was inevitable.[28] But he had no doubts about the productive capacity of the American economy or the hardworking popular spirit which supported it. Although in later days Kiyosawa spoke of himself as a sort of socialist, his was a socialism of distribution but not of production--indeed, he consistently opposed the kind of forcible bureaucratic control later adopted in Japan.

Another factor in his view of the Depression was Kiyosawa's differentiation between policy liberalism and a more basic liberalism-- as he called it, liberalism of the mind. To the argument that the eclipse of the British Liberal Party amounted to the demise of liberalism, he countered that even though there were policy differences between the Conservative, Liberal, and Labour parties, all were ultimately founded on liberal principles.[29] This was a position which he had long held, and after 1930 he expressed it more often and more clearly; it was in the context of the Depression, through his continuing debate with the Marxists, that he re-evaluated his own liberalism. Despite being attacked as anachronistic, Kiyosawa repeatedly asserted the classical liberal views that the freedom of the individual was the goal; that not restricting others was more important than avoiding restrictions on oneself; that one should respect others' views and not blindly assert one's own righteousness; and that to all these ends freedom of speech was absolutely essential.[30]

In any event, far from being irrevocably influenced by the Depression, he used the occasion to look more deeply into his own previously held beliefs and to confirm them. However, most Japanese intellectuals were powerfully influenced by the seeming ruin of

America, which laid the basis for the sharp shift in their attitudes with the outbreak of the Manchurian Incident.

The Manchurian Incident and the Isolation of Japan
1. The Manchurian Incident and the Shanghai Incident

Kiyosawa returned home in October 1930. However, in April 1931 he again left for America, and did not return until July 1932. Between 1930 and 1932 major changes occurred in Japan. In October 1930 Prime Minister Hamaguchi's Minseito cabinet had just ratified the London Naval Arms Limitation Treaty, over the resistance of the Naval Staff and the Privy Council. The Hamaguchi Cabinet was the most progressive of all Japan's prewar cabinets, and its Foreign Minister was the leading internationalist Shidehara Kijuro. Thus ratification of the Treaty was a victory for party government and for the policies of international cooperation. But it was their last victory. In November 1930 Hamaguchi was shot (and died in August 1931); the successor Wakatsuki Cabinet was unable to cope with the Manchurian Incident and fell in December 1931, and the Inukai Cabinet which followed it collapsed over the May 15 Incident in 1932. During the same period there were two unsuccessful coup d'etat attempts by elements in the military (in March and October 1931), and both former Minister of Finance Inoue Junnosuke and business leader Dan Takuma were assassinated by right-wing terrorists in 1932. Abroad, the Manchurian Incident occurred in September 1931 and the Shanghai Incident in January 1932, and the puppet state of Manchukuo was established in March 1932. The era of party government and international conciliation was a thing of the past.

It was only natural that Kiyosawa should be critical of the Manchurian Incident. In *Gaiko shi* he expressed this opinion, albeit indirectly:

> When it comes to writing about the Manchurian Incident and subsequent events it is impossible for me to repress an intense feeling of misgiving. There is about this affair none of the calm of writing history *qua* history. At present the possibility of presenting fairly the positions and realities of both sides is limited. Moreover, it is quite impossible freely to analyze and evaluate the situation.[31]

At the time of Kiyosawa's return to Japan the possibility of war with the U.S. was being debated. He was solicited to write a book titled "Will America Fight Japan?"; he wrote hurriedly and three months later published *America Will Not Fight Japan*.[32] He did not believe that the Manchurian Incident need lead to war with America, and his title expressed his attempt to calm public opinion by propounding this view. There could be no Japan-U.S. war because, first, Japan depended too heavily on America economically to be able to fight with her and had nothing to gain from such a war. Second, given America's history, public opinion, and political system--especially the foreign policy role of the strongly isolationist Senate--she would never go to war over Asian issues.

But Kiyosawa was apprehensive on two points. The first was Secretary of State Stimson's non-recognition policy. In January 1932 Stimson explicitly stated that the U.S. would not recognize any situation created through methods which violated the Kellogg-Briand Pact. Kiyosawa felt it unwise to judge worldwide events in such indiscriminate fashion and criticize states accordingly, thus giving rise to emotional reactions which would close off possibilities of political resolution.[33] And the Stimson Doctrine *did* sharply exacerbate Japanese public opinion, fueling serious consideration of the possibility of war with the U.S.

The other point which caused Kiyosawa deep worry was the Shanghai Incident. American public opinion, relatively placid at the outset of the Manchurian Incident, worsened decisively over this affair, and Kiyosawa was shocked at the dramatic change. To carry the war to Shanghai, with its many foreign residents and multiplicity of foreign interests, was extremely dangerous. Japan had acted precipitately and was slow to offer explanations after the fact. Stimson had ignored Japanese public opinion, and Japan had now ignored America's.

America Will Not Fight Japan, despite its title and thrust, had a strongly pessimistic tone. The conclusion was particularly ominous: if by chance war broke out it would be due *both* to the accession to political power in either country of a faction desiring war and able to channel opinion (most importantly, middle class opinion) on a belligerent course, *and* to a direct attack by either country upon the other. At the time he wrote both seemed inconceivable eventualities, but events followed this scenario closely in 1941.

2. Withdrawal From the League

The announcement of Japan's withdrawal from the League of Nations in March 1933 finalized the departure from the internationalist foreign policy line begun with the Manchurian Incident. In articles in *Chuo koron* entitled "Questions for Foreign Minister Uchida"[34] and "An Opinion for Ambassador Matsuoka"[35] Kiyosawa criticized government policy toward the League. Both articles elicited dozens of personal messages of agreement and encouragement, but the public arena was then completely dominated by a hard foreign policy line and no one expressed views parallelling Kiyosawa's.[36]

"Questions for Foreign Minister Uchida" was written at the time of the climactic debate over the Manchurian Incident in the Assembly of the League. Kiyosawa was critical of the Incident, but on this occasion his primary focus was the clumsiness of Uchida's diplomacy. In particular he criticized Uchida's excesses of inflexible terms like "absolutely" and "always." When Stimson used similarly hardline language he had been received with applause at home; Kiyosawa could see him painting America into a corner, but even his language could not be compared to the "bitter end diplomacy" of Uchida, who proclaimed that even if "Japan were reduced to scorched earth" she would not withdraw from Manchuria. With the appointment of Matsuoka Yosuke as Special Plenipotentiary to the League this posture became even more unyielding. Kiyosawa characterized his as "grandstand diplomacy" which cheered "relatives" in the gallery immensely but had not the slightest impact on the foreign judges making the real decisions.

The reason Kiyosawa focused on tactical ineptitude was that he believed it possible to reach a compromise with the League over Manchuria without large-scale damage to Japan's position. The Lytton Report was not advantageous to Japan, but it was decisively different from and softer than the Stimson line, and was an adequate basis for compromise. For this reason, Kiyosawa was greatly distressed by Japan's departure from the League. Perhaps it was because "An Opinion for Ambassador Matsuoka" was written in the midst of his shock at the withdrawal that the essay stands out for the sharpness of Kiyosawa's pen and the boldness of his argument. Predicting that Matsuoka would be welcomed on his return like a conquering hero, Kiyosawa recalled the abuse showered upon Komura Jutaro when he returned from the 1905 Portsmouth Conference and praised Komura's resolute belief--despite his expectation of criticism--that diplomacy could not be based on mass psychology. As Kiyosawa addressed Matsuoka and his colleagues:

> We have no quarrel with a parliamentary system based upon the voice of the people. However, when the nation faces a crisis is it not the duty of individuals, and especially leaders, to transcend public opinion temporarily and sacrifice themselves for the nation? In the past our country certainly did not want for such leaders....
>
> But where are there men with such patriotic integrity today? Are they not groveling before King Mob, panic-stricken, and trying only not to displease him?
>
> Why is this? You were not always this way....

By praising the wisdom and courage of Komura and other Meiji leaders he implied that the foreign policy of Matsuoka and Uchida had failed; he also criticized them explicitly as "sycophants of public opinion." In the introduction to *Gaiko shi* Kiyosawa summarized one consistent characteristic of earlier Japanese foreign policy: "popular opinion was always hard-line, while government policy was always prudent." Now he was compelled to say that "since the Manchurian Incident, and especially since the China Incident, Japan has had no foreign policy at all."[37] One of the primary reasons for this was that foreign policy leaders like Uchida and Matsuoka had lost their courage and become handmaidens of public opinion.

But Kiyosawa did not simply limit himself to criticism. In the same work he urged, as emergency steps, (1) a guarantee of peace with the U.S.; (2) the adoption of a non-aggression treaty with the USSR; and (3) amelioration of relations with China by attempting to avoid mutual provocation for the time being. He went on, quoting from the Imperial Rescript of withdrawal from the League:

> The advancement of international peace is what we evermore desire and our attitude toward enterprises of peace shall sustain no change.
>
> By withdrawing from the League and embarking on a course of its own, our Empire does not mean that it will stand aloof in the extreme Orient, nor that it will isolate itself thereby from the fraternity of nations. It is our desire to promote mutual confidence between our Empire and all other powers and to make known the justice of its cause throughout the world.[38]

From this passage Kiyosawa inferred that the Emperor's intent lay in the reconstruction of international relations (even if not in the context of the League). Behind this one can see Kiyosawa's fear of a Japan which had lost all internationalist characteristics running amok in Asia.

3. The Rise of the "Asian Monroe Doctrine"

With the passing of the League withdrawal issue, the *pro forma* resolution of the Manchurian Incident with the Tangku Truce of May 1933, and the replacement of Uchida by Hirota Koki as Foreign Minister, the next four years--up to the outbreak of war with China in July 1937--were a sort of interwar lull. A variety of currents roiled the surface of Japanese foreign policy during this period, but the tide underlying them all was one of growing Asianism. Just as

Kiyosawa had feared, withdrawal from the League had left Japanese foreign policy bereft of universalism and internationalism, and opened the way for the rise of Asianism.

In October 1933 the Five Ministers' Conference (comprised of the Prime Minister and ministers of Foreign Affairs, Finance, the Army, and the Navy) reached the following foreign policy decision: "Our goal is to realize concert and mutual help between Japan, Manchuria, and China under Imperial leadership and, in this way, to secure permanent peace in Asia and contribute to the promotion of peace throughout the world."[39] This decision was noteworthy in its departure from the earlier concept of a Japanese-Manchurian bloc and positing of a "*Sino*-Manchurian-Japanese bloc." Until now Japan had recognized the existence of a universal world order and had simply asserted that Manchuria was a special area to which the principles of the order were inapplicable; with this decision Japan denied the very existence of a universalistic world order and began to stress the establishment of a particularistic regional order in its place.

On 17 April 1934, at a press conference, Foreign Ministry Information Bureau Chief Amo stated, "Japan is resolved to carry out her destiny of preserving peace and order in East Asia."[40] This was a natural extension of the Five Ministers' decision; nevertheless, it was interpreted as an "Asian Monroe Doctrine" and had worldwide repercussions. In its implication that Japan could not stand by and watch other countries supply arms to China or carry out other politically significant activities there, the Amo Statement did share the concepts of the Monroe Doctrine. Indeed, there were many who had explicitly called for such an Asianist foreign policy: the U.S. claimed to occupy a leading role in the Americas by virtue of the Monroe Doctrine; Japan's role in Asia was analogous; American interference in Japan's Asian affairs was therefore unreasonable. At first glance this seemed a plausible argument, and those who flatly refuted it were few. Kiyosawa was one of these exceptions.

Beginning in *Beikoku no kenkyu* he referred repeatedly to the way the U.S. issued unilateral fiats not based in international law (and reinterpreted them as it served her pleasure) and interfered unjustly in other countries' domestic politics, and to the antipathy this behavior engendered in other countries--especially those in Latin America. Unilateral declaration was not entirely without norms: "International affairs ... if an actor clings resolutely to a position, energetically, over a long period, then in time that position tends to become recognized ... one example of this is the Monroe Doctrine; another, albeit a more narrow one, is Japan's special interests in Manchuria and Mongolia."[41] The major question was one of time: almost 100 years had elapsed before the Monroe Doctrine was recognized in the League of Nations

Charter and thus acquired legal status; by contrast, Japan's special position in Manchuria and Mongolia had not accumulated a sufficient weight of years. And it was unlikely that Japan's leading position in regions extending beyond Manchuria and Mongolia would ever win the support of other countries.[42]

Ironically, however, at the very time that Monroeism had become recognized, it had begun to change. After World War I, with the spread of the idea of self-determination of peoples, feelings rose in Latin America and even the U.S. had difficulty intervening as openly as before.[43] Then President Roosevelt announced the Good Neighbor Policy and established a non-interventionist policy vis-a-vis Latin America. Observing the concrete consequences of this policy, Kiyosawa concluded that by the end of 1933 Monroeism had so substantially changed that it had in fact been discarded.[44] To Kiyosawa Monroeism was unattractive in principle and had become untenable in practice; since even its American originators were in the process of reforming it, what Japan should be studying was not Monroeism but America's process of reform.

4. International Isolation

Although Asianism was becoming the undercurrent of Japanese foreign policy, it was not yet decisively manifest. On the surface policy drifted, inconsistent in the context of isolation. In January 1933 the U.S. resolved on a course of independence for the Philippines (to take effect by 1944); it looked as if the U.S. were withdrawing from Asia, and pro-Americanism revived. In February 1934 Foreign Minister Hirota sent a message to Secretary of State Hull asserting that there were no fundamentally insoluble problems outstanding between the two countries; Hull made an amicable response, and for another moment expectations of improved relations rose.

However Kiyosawa, who had earlier warned against pessimism, now warned that improved relations were a false hope.[45] First, it was superficial to see Philippine independence as an American withdrawal; Kiyosawa saw it as American extrication from an Asian quagmire, a preparation for the future which actually strengthened her position vis-a-vis Japan, along with the restoration of diplomatic relations with the Soviet Union in November 1933.[46] Second, despite Foreign Minister Hirota's statement that "I fear that terms like 'Asian Monroeism' are going to be misunderstood by foreign countries and therefore I will be cautious about using them," Kiyosawa saw the Monroeist reality of Japanese foreign policy. He saw through Hirota's policy: superficially soft toward America, at heart the hard line revealed in the Amo Statement. He did not share the current abstract pro-American sentiment, which needed to be brought down to earth with concrete proposals for, *inter al.*, the security of the Philippines and for a halt in the Japan-U.S. race in warship construction. Kiyosawa was apprehensive of Hirota's diplomacy, which lacked this concreteness.[47]

What Kiyosawa especially feared was renewed U.S.-Japan competition in shipbuilding. The Washington and London naval treaties were to expire in 1936, and arguments originating in the military began to circulate that the ensuing fluidity would lead to crisis. Therefore the nation had to put all its energies into an arms buildup. There were proponents of these views, such as Army Minister Araki Sadao, in the Saito Cabinet. With Asian Monroeism (and its expansionism vis-a-vis China), the "1935-36 crisis" argument (and its stress on naval arms buildup), and the trend toward warmer relations with America all current at once it is unsurprising how unstable the Saito Cabinet's foreign policy was.

Also unsurprisingly, Kiyosawa rejected the "crisis argument." In the first place, expiration of the treaties did not necessarily imply a crisis: Japan had left the League with impunity and, Germany having also withdrawn, a more weakened League was unlikely to take firm steps now. Second, Kiyosawa noted that those espousing the "1935-36 crisis argument" were the same people who--contradictorily or disingenuously--had advocated withdrawal from the League and abolition of the treaties. Third, he asked, if there might be a crisis, why not launch a "peace offensive" in order to avert it?[48]

Nevertheless, at the end of 1934 Japan announced the abrogation of the naval arms limitation treaties, effective in 1936. From about the middle of 1935 the notion of concert with Germany began to grow, indicative of the acuteness of the insecurity attendant upon Japan's growing isolation. In October 1936 this notion took shape in the German-Japanese Anti-Comintern Pact.

Kiyosawa was opposed to this sort of balance of power strategy from the beginning. When diplomacy was not based on universal understandings, intimacy with one country might threaten others--indeed, it could open the road to war with them.[49] He saw concert with Germany as especially dangerous: since Germany had neither interests nor military forces in Asia it was in no position to offer much help to Japan, and at the same time there was danger that Japan would be drawn into the intense ideological dispute between Germany and Russia. Japan would also be saddled with the world's hostility to Nazi Germany (which Kiyosawa shared). Finally, he pointed out that Hitler expressed open disdain for "colored" peoples and that therefore the respect which alone could make the Pact credible did not exist on the German side.[50] Such sensitivity to racial problems was only natural in one who had experienced discrimination himself.

Kiyosawa had welcomed Hirota Koki as successor to Foreign Minister Uchida. He was soon disillusioned, however, describing Hirota's foreign policy as "seaweed drifting with the waves."[51] Hirota became Prime Minister in 1936, and by 1937 Kiyosawa could see that all the Hirota Cabinet had left behind was a rapidly growing military budget and the Anti-Comintern Pact.[52] In this way Japanese foreign policy wandered aimlessly toward its fateful battlefield encounter with China.

The Sino-Japanese War and U.S.-Japanese Relations
1. The New Order in East Asia and America
When war with China broke out in July 1937 Japanese foreign policy initially became even more erratic. At first, one element in the army opposed widening the conflict and sought a localized resolution, but it did not enjoy the active support of Premier Konoye or Foreign Minister Hirota and was eclipsed by the "punitive faction," which wanted to push on until China surrendered. Peace talks began in November through the intermediation of Germany's ambassador in China, Trautmann, with the General Staff's blessings, but amid the surge of public enthusiasm following the capture of the Chinese capital, Nanking, the cabinet's peace terms became far harsher and in January 1938 it overrode the General Staff, terminated the Trautmann initiative, and issued the famous First Konoye Declaration: "Henceforth we shall have no dealings with the Nationalist government." The Sino-Japanese War was thus not only a military quagmire, but a diplomatic one as well. The pathologies of the "sycophants of public opinion" were becoming ever more acute.

In May 1938 Konoye appointed Ugaki Kazushige as Foreign Minister, in the hope that he could break the developing deadlock in the China War. "At long last Japan has a foreign policy," said Kiyosawa hopefully: Ugaki was not in thrall to abstract ideologies like Asianism; he was inclined not toward counterproductive pronouncements but toward the businesslike resolution of accumulated problems one by one. He achieved a degree of improvement in Japanese-British relations through talks with Ambassador Robert Craigie, and acted swiftly in response to the Changkufeng Incident (July-August 1938) in order to prevent worsening of Soviet-Japanese relations.[53] His negotiations with the British were especially important, since he hoped through British mediation to resolve the Sino-Japanese War. But before they bore any real fruit Ugaki resigned, in September 1938. Kiyosawa noted with regret that the resignation "showed clearly the incongruence of domestic conditions with the implementation of policies such as Ugaki's."[54]

Then, in the immediate aftermath of Ugaki's resignation, on 6

October the U.S. launched a rhetorical attack on Japan for violating the Open Door principle and discriminating unfairly against American citizens in China. Since the outbreak of the Sino-Japanese War U.S.-Japanese relations had deteriorated--in October 1937 Roosevelt had branded Japan and Germany as aggressors in his Quarantine Speech, and in December the U.S. gunboat Panay was sunk by Japanese forces in Chinese waters. But America's overall attitude had been restrained; thus the October 1938 broadside struck with great impact.

The government at first equivocated. As they did so Wuhan and Canton were attacked and the Chinese Nationalist government withdrew to Chungking. At first this looked like a signal victory, but in fact it meant that it would be impossible for Japan to bring the war to an early end. The Second Konoye Statement, of 3 November, which proposed a New Order in East Asia through Sino-Manchurian-Japanese concert, grew out of this reality, as did Japan's 18 November answer to the American protest, which rebutted each American point, adding that "theories and principles appropriate to conditions before the Manchurian Incident" were inapplicable to the present or future. Thus Japan explicitly repudiated the principle of the Open Door set forth in the Nine Power Pact, and set for herself the goal of a New Order in East Asia. Asianism was thus now unfurled as the basic principle of Japanese foreign policy. America's response was swift and predictable: no country had any right to plan a "New Order" in regions not under its own sovereignty. Japan dismissed the protest without reply.

Kiyosawa's own response to the notion of a New Order in East Asia followed these lines: first, the idea was so abstract as to be unintelligible, even to the government. Its one clear message was that the fundamental principles of the U.S. and Japan were in conflict. In Kiyosawa's harsh words, "There is no way in the world that I can accept our country's current bad taste in intoxication with abstract language, in which infantile levels of abstraction extend even into our foreign policy.... If Japan flatly repudiates established treaties, it is perfectly clear that other parties will not recognize our position." There was nothing to win in a quarrel over vacuous principles; doing so would only intensify the hostility.[55]

Second, Kiyosawa thought that the New Order policy was especially inappropriate vis-a-vis America. In his view, the most striking characteristic of American foreign policy was that no single structure possessed supreme authority. The president was sharply restricted by the Senate, and the Senate's power was not absolute either: "The core of American foreign policy is public opinion."[56] This public understood general principles but not concrete details; thus it would be very difficult for Japan to make meaningful concessions, since Konoye and Arita preferred confrontation over principles--empty though they might be--followed by concessions on the sorts of details of little interest to the American public.

2. Will America Enter the War?

It was about this time that American participation in the Sino-Japanese War became a subject of serious debate. What distinguished Kiyosawa's judgment in this regard was that he saw a variety of steps between the alternatives of belligerence and neutrality. He knew that during World War I America, on the basis of its strong affinity for England, had aided France and England in a variety of ways which overstepped the classic limits of neutrality before formally entering the war.[57] Therefore Kiyosawa paid particular attention to the movement of American public opinion, and noted that even in the first stages of the Sino-Japanese War pro-Chinese sentiments wholly overwhelmed pro-Japanese, but that those considering the use of force to maintain the Open Door in Asia were a small minority also. Kiyosawa concluded that the U.S. was already a non-neutral and that the question was not whether she would intervene or not but the extent and scope of that intervention. Of particular significance to him was the American extension to China in December 1938 of a 25 million dollar commercial credit. This was in reality a loan, and in violation of the 1937 Neutrality Act. Thus the announcement of the New Order in East Asia had already led to an ideological collision and, given public opinion, America was likely to embark on a course of support for China with everything short of force of arms. One month later England, following America's example, offered China a *de facto* loan. The fact that England, which had evinced a conciliatory attitude toward Japan during 1938, was now offering China aid in concert with America made America's December policy shift even more significant.[58]

Consequently, when America abrogated the U.S.-Japan Treaty of Commerce and Navigation in July 1939, Kiyosawa--unlike the majority of observers, who were stunned--took the news with relative equanimity. He pointed out that Japan had unilaterally repudiated the Nine Power Pact and other accords and was in no position to criticize the U.S., which had at least followed internationally accepted procedures.

The American abrogation was to take effect after six months. In the interim a number of efforts to reverse the situation were made. One was the opening in December 1939 of the Yangtze River, previously closed for military reasons, which did have a slightly ameliorative effect on U.S.-Japan relations. However, Kiyosawa warned that Sino-U.S. trade was negligible and there was practically no shipping on the Yangtze, and there was thus no reason to expect that opening the Yangtze would be seen as a major concession by American opinion. He predicted that, given the state of public opinion--and the attitude of the Senate which reflected it--without compromise in the areas of ideology and principle, improved relations would be difficult to achieve. And indeed, the Treaty lapsed right on schedule.[59]

And yet, Kiyosawa did not think that war with the U.S. was inevitable; the major focus of American opinion was Europe, and the China issue alone would not provoke war. For this reason it was important that Japan not become entangled in European issues. But in the same way that concert with Germany became attractive as a solution to the international isolation following the Manchurian Incident, so now, with a developing deadlock in the Sino-Japanese War, did arguments for strengthening the Anti-Comintern Pact grow.

Kiyosawa, as noted, opposed the whole matter. Relations with the U.S. had become even more strained since late 1938, and in a climate of worsening American opinion of Germany this option was absolutely to be avoided.[60] Thus when the German-Soviet Non-Aggression Pact was enacted in August 1939 Kiyosawa welcomed the disappearance of the issue, and urged an even-handed policy without further alliances.[61] And when war broke out in Europe in September Kiyosawa threw his efforts into clarifying its character for his Japanese audience, arguing that America's sympathies lay with England and France and that if England in particular were endangered America would unquestionably enter the war.[62] One need hardly add that he opposed Japanese involvement in that war.

However, with the German drive to the West in May 1940 and the fall of France in June the situation changed. For Japan, now intensely worried about natural resources after the lapse of the Commercial Treaty with America, cooperation with Germany and Italy had the new appeal of enabling an advance into French Indochina and the Dutch East Indies and thus strengthening Japan's position vis-a-vis the U.S. It was on these assumptions that the Konoye Cabinet signed the Axis Pact on 27 September and, simultaneously, occupied northern Indochina.

For Kiyosawa, the danger of threatening a country like the U.S., which was governed by public opinion, was clearly shown by the landslide victory of Roosevelt in the presidential election held only 40 days after the conclusion of the Axis Pact. Moreover, the Pact unified American policy. America had thus far had differing policies toward Europe, the Americas, and Asia, and Japan could exploit the gaps between them. For example, she could once have taken advantage of American preoccupation with Europe to resolve the China problem, moderate Pacific tensions, and deflect American hostility toward Germany, but no longer. Kiyosawa asserted emphatically that

> The Axis Pact, making Asia and Europe one, is an epoch-making international event. Sino-Japanese affairs and the European War, hitherto separate, have by this Pact become inextricably interwoven. Oddly enough, Japan left the League of Nations over the Manchurian Incident and set out to reconstruct Asia, but the ramifications of this Asia policy include intimate and unprecedentedly strong organic links to Europe, albeit different in both form and content from those which existed before.[63]

He also foresaw that the Axis Pact would neutralize Russia and precipitate Japanese movement toward Southeast Asia. One week after Germany invaded Denmark and Norway, amid predictions that Holland would be next, Foreign Minister Arita declared in April 1940 that Japan had a strong interest in the security of the East Indies, since they were part of East Asia. Kiyosawa criticized the government's careless use of the concept of East Asia but at the same time predicted that Russia would respond positively to the declaration in order to turn aside Japan's movement toward the north. Ever since the Manchurian Incident Kiyosawa had urged a Soviet-Japanese non-aggression treaty but at this juncture, since it would stimulate further movement southward, he was most apprehensive of Soviet-Japanese amity.[64]

Kiyosawa's anxieties materialized the following April with the signing of the Soviet-Japanese Neutrality Pact. In July southern Indochina was occupied; thus the Axis Pact fulfilled its role as a counter to the U.S., but it also played the extremely risky role of threatening the U.S. Kiyosawa thought that war with the U.S. was avoidable as long as only China was at issue. However, with the Axis Pact and the southern advance Japan had taken two steps beyond the China issue. Indeed, in response to the occupation of southern Indochina the U.S. froze Japanese assets in America and embargoed oil exports, and in the negotiations which continued until just before the outbreak of war placed primary emphasis on the Axis Pact together with withdrawal of troops from China. Thus did Asianist and balance-of-power policies, which Kiyosawa had criticized ever since the Manchurian Incident, become entwined to seal Japan's fate.

In February 1941 the Cabinet Information Bureau issued to all magazine editors a list of proscribed writers, and Kiyosawa's name was on it.[65] However, even had this measure not been taken it would probably have been impossible for Kiyosawa to continue his critical activities. He had been able to continue his criticism thus far by progressively limiting it to regions with which Japan's links were weak. However, the Axis Pact gave Japanese policy worldwide application, and slipping through the policy crevices became impossible. With the complete crystallization of Japanese policy through the Soviet-Japanese Non-Aggression Pact criticism became impossible.

Conclusion

The road from the Manchurian Incident to Pearl Harbor was an exceedingly complex one. Even when measured by the standards of contemporary diplomatic history, Kiyosawa's analyses of that decade are striking for their accuracy and insight. It is hardly an exaggeration to say that he noted the importance and implications of essentially every turning point in Japan-U.S. relations. Let us in conclusion take one more look at the reasons for the accuracy of his arguments, and at the ways he differed from other observers.

The most important source of Kiyosawa's perspicacity was his conviction that economic power was the basis of international relations, and political power a derivative factor. For example, even at the time of the fall of Saipan Kiyosawa urged neither withdrawal nor suicide by Japanese forces and residents but that they remain there in order to maintain Japan's economic position[66]--he was looking ahead, beyond the politico-military apocalypse of war and defeat, to the survival of a more fundamental economic presence. His emphases on relationships with China as a whole rather than just Manchuria, and with the U.S. rather than China (which set him apart from most other intellectuals of his day), were also based on this economic realism.

A country's economic power, in turn, was determined by the productive efforts of its people. Neither political nor diplomatic power could substitute for this. The reason Kiyosawa was pessimistic about the future of Manchuria under Japanese control but optimistic about the future of China, and the reason why he foresaw the recovery of America from the Depression, lay in the people. That his own emigrant experiences lay behind this appreciation of the limited role of politics has already been noted.

These experiences also set Kiyosawa apart from most Japanese intellectuals, who had intimate ties to the state. Even the internationalist pro-Americans were unable to analyze either international relations or the national economy from a standpoint independent of that of the state. Matsuoka Yosuke had gone to the U.S. at the age of 13 and lived there for 9 years, and was hardly Kiyosawa's inferior when it came to knowledge of America but his policy toward America differed totally from Kiyosawa's: scion of a politically-connected business family, he was a diplomat and director, vice-president, and president of the South Manchurian Railway Company, and was too thoroughly integrated into the government and its Manchurian policies for his views to be otherwise. Indeed, even Kiyosawa was not free of this danger: when he attended the 1937 PEN Club meeting in Europe and found himself the target of universal condemnation for the Sino-Japanese War he tried to defend Japan's position as well as he could.[67]

From the above perspective it followed that diplomacy plays an even more limited role than does politics. Its function is to pursue worldwide goals which are compatible with the long run needs of the national economy. The fundamental cause of the failure of Japanese foreign policy in the 1930s was the placing of undue expectations in diplomacy. To argue thus was neither to disregard foreign policy nor to see diplomats as simply mouthpieces for public opinion. On the contrary, Kiyosawa advocated an elitist diplomacy which, within policy limits, allowed for the skills of specialists and on occasion for action taken in the face of contrary public opinion.

Apart from his youthful experiences, what were the bases of Kiyosawa's expertise? First was the prompt and thorough analysis of public information. The speed with which quotations from foreign newspapers and journals such as *Foreign Affairs* appeared in his writings was exceptional for his day. Second, he was proud of the extent of his reading in the central works of politics, economics, history, and philosophy.[68] He seldom relied on unsubstantiated information from miscellaneous sources or on what he alone was able to see and hear. For example, on his return to Japan in 1930 after 15 months' absence he asserted that the notion that travel makes one wise was a myth and that he feared rather the tendency to absolutize narrow experiences and admitted that he felt that, having missed a lot of reading time, he had in fact become out of touch with the times.[69] It was due to both of these skills that, for example, he was able immediately to understand the significance of Roosevelt's Good Neighbor Policy within the historical context of Monroeism. Most U.S. specialists of his day seem to have had weaknesses in either one or both of these areas, and few understood the ways in which America had changed since the days of Woodrow Wilson.

Underlying Kiyosawa's insights as a specialist one must not overlook his strong idealism. One of the decisive elements in his pro-American position was his sympathy for those values of freedom, equality, and the dignity of the individual which he saw embodied in America--despite deviations and disorders--ever since its independence. His economic view, that gain was the yardstick of international relations, was not unrelated to this idealism: relations between nations should be on the basis of equality and should benefit each, just as commercial dealings equally profited both buyer and seller.[70] He insisted that peace is both economically beneficial and intrinsically desirable, and that it is pointless to ask which is more important. His stress on the importance of the industriousness of peoples was indivisible from his love and respect for the working man. And all of these were ideas nurtured by the years spent as an anonymous young emigrant.

In general a realistic perception of and response to the world can grow only out of some value system. A "realism" which lacks such a basis risks becoming a cynical, *ad hoc* reaction to changes in the real world and, as political scientists have pointed out, this is the decisive difference between Machiavelli and many "Machiavellians." The primary condition which supported and contributed to the perspicacity of Kiyosawa's realism during the 1930s was, paradoxically, his idealism.

But realism alone could not influence Japanese policy in the 1930s. On the other hand, insofar as the productive energies of the Japanese people have blossomed, foreign relations are supported by a wide range of activities on the private level and not just by the government, and liberal democracy and international cooperation have materialized as the basis of these, one may say that the requisite conditions for amicable relations with America stipulated by the then-unhonored Kiyosawa have been achieved in the 40 years since the war.

NOTES

1. (Tokyo, 1979).
2. (Tokyo, 1941).
3. 2 vols. (Tokyo, 1942).
4. Kiyosawa, *Nikki*, 8 December 1942.
5. Ito Kazuo, *Zoku Hokubei hyakunen sakura* (Tokyo, 1984), vol. 4, p. 260.
6. The major works dealing with Kiyosawa include Miyata Masanori, "Gaiko hyoronka no teiko," Doshisha daigaku jinbun kagaku kenkyo sho, ed., *Senji-ka teiko no kenkyu* (Tokyo, 1969), vol. 2; Ito, *Zoku Hokubei*; Hashikawa Bunso, "Introduction," in Kiyosawa, *Nikki*; Sakai Mari, "Kiyosawa Kiyoshi no gaiko shiso," *Misuzu* (July 1977); Yamada Ken, "Kiyosawa Kiyoshi no jiyushugi to han-fashizumu shiso," in Nihon shi kokyu kai, ed., *Kumagai Kojiro sensei koki kinen ronshu* (Tokyo, 1981); and Yamamoto Yoshihiko, "Senji-ka jiyushugi no sobo," *Shizuoka daigaku hokei ronshu*, vol. 31, no. 1 (July 1982). These are written largely from an intellectual history perspective; there is almost nothing written from that of diplomatic history. For biographical material I have drawn on Miyata, Ito, and Hashikawa. For more on Kiyosawa's commentaries and ideas regarding domestic politics see Kitaoki Shin'ichi, "Kiyosawa Kiyoshi," in Uchida Kenso, ed., *Genron wa Nihon wo ugokasu* (Tokyo, 1985), vol. 8.
7. Minami Azumi kyoiku kai, ed., *Iguchi Kigenji to Kensei Gijuku* (Nagano, 1981), p. 549.
8. Minami Azumi, ed., *Iguchi Kigenji*, p. 511.
9. Kiyosawa Kiyoshi, *Jiyu Nihon wo asaru* (Tokyo, 1929), pp. 4-5.
10. Minami Azumi, ed., *Iguchi Kigenji*, pp. 594-97, 628-30, 663-65.
11. Ogata, Sadako, "The Role of Liberal Organizations in Japan," in Dorothy Borg and Shumpei Okamoto, eds., *Pearl Harbor as History* (New York, 1973), p. 465.
12. Kakegawa, Tomiko, "The Press and Public Opinion in Japan, 1931-1941," in Borg and Okamoto, *Pearl Harbor*, pp. 536-42; Mitani, Taichiro, "Japanese Studies of Japan's Foreign Relations," in Borg and Okamoto, *Pearl Harbor*, pp. 576-85.
13. Ogata in Borg and Okamoto, *Pearl Harbor*, pp. 467-68.
14. Konoye Fumimaro, "Ei-Bei hon'i no heiwashugi wo haisu," *Nihon oyobi nihonjin* (15 December 1918).
15. (Tokyo, 1925).
16. Kiyosawa Kiyoshi, *Fodo* (Tokyo, 1931).
17. Kiyosawa, *Beikoku no kenkyu*, pp. 54-55.
18. See, e.g., Kiyosawa Kiyoshi, *Kuroshio ni kiku* (Tokyo, 1928), pp. 300-04.
19. Nakami Mari, "Taiheiyo mondai chosa kai to Nihon no chishikijin," *Shiso* (February 1985), pp. 106, 110.
20. Kiyoshi, "Manshu ni okeru tokushu chii to Nihon no iku beki michi," *Gaiko jiho* (15 January 1926).
21. *Chugai shogyo shimpo* (22 August 1924).
22. Kiyosawa Kiyoshi, *Tenkan-ki no Nihon* (Tokyo, 1929), pp. 362-74.
23. Kiyosawa, *Kuroshio*, p. 437.
24. Kiyosawa, *Kuroshio*, p. 440.
25. *Chugai shogyo shimpo* (26 August 1924); Kitaoka Shin'ichi, "Washinton taisei to kokusai kyocho no seishin," *Rikkyo hogaku*, no. 23 (1984).
26. Among those who shared Kiyosawa's economic realism, put similar stress on trade with China, and agreed that the special interests in Manchuria should be relinquished was Ishibashi Tanzan, who became Kiyosawa's close friend during the 1930s. There were noteworthy parallels between his background and Kiyosawa's: a religious upbringing (in this case Nichiren Buddhism), a fondness for English and American books, employment by an economic journal, and almost no ties to the government.
27. On this trip Kiyosawa met again with friends from his emigrant days, and saw how they had fared in the interim: "Isn't it fascinating how they have prospered so remarkably since they ceased to be supported by their homeland...? As we can see also in Korea, Manchuria, and Taiwan, vociferous demonstrations of sovereignty and government backing hurt the overseas Japanese more than they help them." His

longstanding faith in economic success based on hard work, with no political handouts, was confirmed (Kiyosawa Kiyoshi, *Amerika wo ratai ni su* [Tokyo, 1930], pp. 259-61). Kiyosawa's analysis of the American economy is summed up in his *Kakumei no Amerika keizai* (Tokyo, 1933).
28. Kiyosawa Kiyoshi, "Shakaishugika no Beikoku," *Chuo koron* (November 1930), pp. 277-85.
29. Kiyosawa, *Tenkan-ki*, pp. 304-16.
30. Kiyosawa Kiyoshi, *Jidai, seikatsu, shiso* (Tokyo, 1936), pp. 3-29.
31. Kiyosawa, *Gaiko shi*, p. 443.
32. *Amerika wa Nihon to tatakawazu* (Tokyo, 1932).
33. Kiyosawa, *Gaiko shi*, p. 478.
34. "Uchida gaisho ni tou," *Chuo koron* (March 1933).
35. "Matsuoka zenken ni atau," *Chuo koron* (May 1933).
36. Kiyosawa, *Gaiko shi*, p. 490.
37. Kiyosawa, *Gaiko shi*, pp. 5, 574.
38. *New York Times* (28 March 1933).
39. Gaimusho, ed., *Nihon gaiko nempyo narabini shuyo bunsho* (Tokyo, 1966), vol. 2, pp. 275-76.
40. Gaimusho, ed., *Gaiko nempyo*, vol. 2, pp. 284-86.
41. Kiyosawa Kiyoshi, "Man-Mo ni taisuru Nichi-Bei no soi ten," *Gaiko jiho* (1 July 1928).
42. Kiyosawa Kiyoshi, "Gaiko ni suro-moshon wo nozomu," *Tokyo keizai shimpo* (5 May 1934), p. 46.
43. Kiyosawa, *Kuroshio*, pp. 211-12.
44. Kiyosawa Kiyoshi, *Gekido-ki ni iku* (Tokyo, 1934), pp. 264-67.
45. Kiyosawa, *Gekido-ki*, pp. 249-51.
46. Kiyosawa Kiyoshi, "Nichi-Bei kankei wo ikani suru," *Gaiko jiho* (1 August 1933), p. 42; "Sovieto no tai-Nichi sen," *Gaiko jiho* (1 March 1934), pp. 78-79. Kiyosawa took note of the outpouring of anti-Japanese criticism from the USSR after October 1933. In his view, the restoration in 1933 of Soviet-U.S. relations-- given Russia's previous efforts to enter into non-aggression treaties and similar agreements with all its neighboring countrties--was critically significant in the strengthening of Russia's diplomatic position vis-a-vis Japan (Kiyosawa, "Sovieto," pp. 65-66). On the change in the Soviet-Japanese balance of military power between the Manchurian Incident and 1935, and in concomitant Japanese perceptions and policies, see Kitaoka Shin'ichi, "Rikugun habatsu tairitsu no sai-kento," in Kindai Nihon kenkyu kai, ed., *Showa-ki no gunbu* (Tokyo, 1979).
47. Kiyosawa, *Gekido-ki*, pp. 258-61; "Sovieto," p. 66.
48. Kiyosawa, *Gekido-ki*, pp. 185-99.
49. Kiyosawa, *Gekido-ki*, p. 255.
50. Kiyosawa Kiyoshi, "Kensetsuteki gaiko no shian," *Gaiko jiho* (15 May 1936), pp. 81-82.
51. Kiyosawa, *Jidai*, p. 241.
52. Kiyosawa Kiyoshi, "Itsu, ikani jishoku subeki ka," *Nihon hyoron* (February 1937), p.88.
53. Kiyosawa Kiyoshi, "Ugaki gaisho ron," *Kaizo* (September 1938), pp. 71-80.
54. Kiyosawa, *Gaiko shi*, p. 541.
55. Kiyosawa Kiyoshi, "Beikoku tai-Nichi seisaku no shin kyokumen," *Kokusai chishiki oyobi hyoron* (March 1939), pp. 19-20.
56. Kiyosawa Kiyoshi, "Bei-Ei tai-Nichi appaku no teido to gendo," *Chuo koron* (February 1939), p. 97.
57. Kiyosawa Kiyoshi, *Dai-niji Oshu taisen no kenkyu* (Tokyo, 1940), pp. 324-28.
58. Kiyosawa, "Bei-Ei tai-Nichi," pp. 89-94.
59. Kiyosawa Kiyoshi, "Nichi-Bei tsusho joyaku shikko no eikyo," *Kaizo* (February 1940 special issue), pp. 19-20.
60. Kiyosawa Kiyoshi, "Nichi-Doku-I ni taisuru Beikoku no jindate," *Nihon hyoron* (March 1939), pp. 52-53.
61. Kiyosawa Kiyoshi, "Gaiko tenkan ni atatte," *Toyo keizai shimpo* (2 September 1939), pp. 44-45.

62. Kiyosawa Kiyoshi, "Beikoku no tai-sen doko," *Nihon hyoron* (October 1939), p. 193.
63. Kiyosawa Kiyoshi, "San-sen Rozuberuto no hara," *Kaizo* (December 1940), pp. 135-36.
64. Kiyosawa Kiyoshi, "Arita seimei no zehi," *Toyo keizai shimpo* (27 April 1940), p. 23.
65. Hatanaka Shigeo, *Oboegaki showa shuppan dan'atsu sho shi* (Tokyo, 1965), p. 56.
66. Kiyosawa, *Nikki* (29 July 1944).
67. Kiyosawa, *Nikki*, appendix, p. 900.
68. Yamamoto, "Senji-ka jiyushugi," pp. 311-12.
69. Kiyosawa, *Amerika wo ratai ni su*, p. 1.
70. Kiyosawa, *Kuroshio*, p. 440.

8
FRIEND OR FOE: THE AMBIVALENT IMAGES OF THE U.S. AND CHINA IN WARTIME JAPAN

Ben-Ami Shillony

Introduction

The U.S. and China figure today as the two most popular foreign countries in Japan. Indeed, no other country has had such a deep and lasting impact on Japan as these two. Yet, in the early 1940s Japan was at war with both of them.

This war, in which Japan first gained and then lost its immense empire, was the culmination of a fifty-year long period of expansion which had started with the First Sino-Japanese War in 1894. But these five decades of warfare and expansion were an exception in Japanese history. Unlike the international scene in Europe, which was most of the time in a state of endemic warfare, there were hardly any wars between Japan and its neighboring countries in the millennium and a half preceding the First Sino-Japanese War. The abortive Mongol invasions of Japan in the thirteenth century and Hideyoshi's abortive invasions of Korea in the late sixteenth century were traumatic events for the victims of those assaults, but these were exceptions in a very long period of peace in which Japan did not engage in international conflicts, except for the activities of sea pirates prior to the seventeenth century.

As a result of that, and unlike most other countries, Japan lacked a clear image of a national enemy throughout most of its history. Japan was thus one of the very few countries in the world which did not regard its neighbors as enemies.

The purpose of this chapter is to examine the public images of the U.S. and China at the time that Japan was at war with both of them, mainly through the Japanese newspapers and magazines of that time.

I would like to thank the Hebrew University of Jerusalem's Harry S. Truman Research Institute for the Advancement of Peace, as well as the Center for Japanese Studies at the University of California, Berkeley for the help they provided me in writing this essay.

Unrequited Love

Since its forceful opening by Commodore Perry in 1854, Japan harbored a special sentiment toward the United States. America represented all that was new, progressive and fascinating in Western culture. It symbolized the dynamism, optimism and pragmatism of the West that many Japanese wished to emulate and adopt. Most of the Japanese students who studied abroad went to the U.S.

America was the Prince Charming whose kiss had awakened the Sleeping Beauty of Japan from her long slumber. The logic of this tale demanded that they should live happily ever after. Indeed the initial fascination of both countries with each other indicated that this would be the case.

Japan's basic attitude toward the U.S. could perhaps be characterized by Doi Takeo's term *amae*, or deep emotional dependence, and the assumption that no matter what Japan did, the U.S. would understand and condone. Thus, when Japan's high-handed actions in China or Korea provoked protest in the U.S., many Japanese were profoundly shocked. Their cordial relationship with the U.S. was supposed to allow for a wide range of discretion. The assumption was that as the Japanese did not protest American policies in Latin America or the Philippines, the Americans should not interfere in Japanese actions in Northeast Asia, trusting Japan to respect American interests there.[1]

When American opposition mounted, Japanese could only conclude that it derived from a misunderstanding. The Americans were motivated by a peculiar system of values, it was argued, and were therefore apt to misjudge the realities of Asia. Hence, if Japan only explained well its true intentions, the Americans would understand and condone.

Here lay the great asymmetry. America was in many ways a model for Japan, but Japan until the 1970s was never a model for America. The Americans might be fond of Japan, especially when it was weak and exotic, but they suspected and feared that country when it became strong and assertive.

The failure of the U.S. to reciprocate what the Japanese regarded as friendly attitudes was frustrating. The critic Tokutomi Soho, writing in 1920, complained that whereas the Japanese admired the U.S. as "a country based on the principles of Washington and Lincoln," the Americans regarded Japan as a "militarist country, an enemy of freedom and morality ... the Germany of the East ... an armed monster." His conclusion was that "our people have historically overestimated the U.S. At first we regarded it as a country to be feared, then as a country to be loved, and recently as a country to be venerated."[2]

These frustrations by Tokutomi and others arose from the post World War I frictions between Japan and the U.S. which reached their climax in the U.S. Immigration Law of 1924 that excluded Japanese immigrants.[3] But the overall image of the U.S. until the late 1930s remained favorable. Most of the right-wing organizations regarded Britain and the Soviet Union as Japan's main enemies,[4] and one of the ideological leaders of these groups, Kita Ikki, even favored an alliance with the U.S. against British and Russian imperialism in Asia.[5]

When relations between the two countries were strained, as at the time of the immigration issue in the 1920s or the controversy over Japan's aggression in China in the 1930s, many Japanese refused to believe that there was a basic ill-will toward their country in the U.S. They preferred to regard such disputes as temporary quarrels, stemming from the Americans' peculiar tendency to base their foreign policy on morality. When the two countries could not agree on what constituted proper action on the part of one country vis-a-vis the other, the Japanese still hoped that pragmatic calculations if not sentiments would preserve the bond between the two countries.

In 1937, following the outbreak of the Sino-Japanese War, Takaishi Shingoro, one of the top editors of the Tokyo *Nichi nichi* newspaper, toured the U.S. on a semi-official mission to explain Japan's position. On his return, he published an article in the magazine *Kaizo*, in which he said:

> Americans are realistic and pragmatic; therefore, if Japan explains its position clearly, they will certainly understand it.... The Americans sympathize with China because China is the underdog, in the same way that they sympathized with Ethiopia when that country was invaded by Italy. But they are not anti-Japanese and they do not hate us. Japanese residents in the U.S. were not maltreated during the China affair....

Takaishi's conclusion was that Japan should not do anything that might alienate the U.S.: "We should make every effort to improve our relations with the U.S. and refrain from antagonizing its moral sentiments."[6]

Nonetheless, in July 1939 the United States served notice of its intended divorce. Following Japan's seizure of Hainan Island in February of that year, the U.S. announced the abrogation of the 1911 Treaty of Commerce and Navigation, which had been the basis for trade between the two countries. But many Japanese still refused to believe that the marriage was broken. The reaction of the Japanese press to the abrogation was mild and the *Asahi* even expressed the hope that the abrogation of the treaty might actually provide an opportunity for improving American-Japanese relations.[7] An article by Tamura Kosaku in the magazine *Bungei shunju* in January 1940 said:

> The Japanese are America-philes (*shinbeironsha*) and there has never been an anti-American movement in Japan. Japan has never tried to challenge the U.S.... If the U.S. cares about China and wants peace in East Asia, it should support Japan.... On the other hand, the Japanese government should keep its promise to the world that its ambitions in China are indeed limited.[8]

It is significant that both Takaishi and Tamura stressed that Japan, no less than the U.S., was responsible for preserving friendly relations between the two countries, and both warned their country against steps that might alienate the other side.

These pro-American expressions were by no means the opinion of a marginal group of non-conformist intellectuals. The English-language magazine *Contemporary Japan*, which usually reflected the opinion of the Foreign Ministry, in February 1940 carried an article by Hasegawa Satoru who explained that throughout the 1930s relations between Japan and America had been "just a trifle short of cordial." He lamented that the relations between these two powers, "whose past associations have been so warm, exemplary and mutually beneficial, are now at the most delicate and unsatisfactory stage of their eighty-year history. Worse, there seems to be no break in the dark clouds as this article goes to press."[9]

In the following month the same magazine carried an even more emotional article in which the author, Debuchi Katsuji, expressed affection for the U.S. and lamented the tension between the two countries. Like an offended marriage partner still in love with the estranged spouse, the article started by reminiscing about the romantic past, describing the often-troubled period from Perry's arrival to the Manchurian Incident as one long honeymoon. It then went on to praise the naval limitation conferences of Washington and London, which had curtailed Japan's naval strength, as landmarks of friendship. Even the abrogation of the Anglo-Japanese Alliance in 1922 due to American pressure was described as a friendly gesture, while the anti-Japanese immigration law was not mentioned at all.[10]

In analyzing the American-Japanese confrontation following the Manchurian Incident, Debuchi tried to be fair to both sides, citing in full the American accusations against Japan. Explaining American reactions to the war in China, he said:

> In the first place it must be observed that idealism plays an important part in the molding of American public opinion.... In the second place, sentimentalism is also an important factor in the formation of public opinion in America. American sentimentalists denounce Japan's military activities in China which, according to them, have been accompanied by indiscriminate bombings and have reduced the Chinese masses to an extremely pitiful plight.[11]

The last hope of the deserted partner is that the straying spouse will return home for economic reasons if not for love. Thus, in his conclusion Debuchi expressed the hope that "although the Americans are a people who are apt to dash ahead, swayed by sentiment or idealism," because of the strong economic bonds between the two countries, the Americans would "stop short at the right moment and look realities squarely in the face."[12]

In September 1940 Japan joined the Axis, but this did not imply that Japan should join the war in Europe or go to war against the U.S. The editorial of the *Asahi* which supported the pact, expressed hope that despite the demands of "some frantic anti-Japanese advocates" in the U.S., both countries should reestablish their harmonious relations.[13]

The public seemed to share the view that despite all the frictions with the U.S., the old friendship between the two countries would prevail. In December 1940 *Bungei shunju* conducted a nationwide poll to find out what the public thought about the international situation. The poll revealed that most Japanese believed that a war with the U.S. could be avoided.[14]

One of the strongholds of pro-American feelings in Japan was the Christian community. Kagawa Toyohiko, the social worker and Christian preacher who had studied at Princeton during World War I and visited the U.S. several times afterward, toured the U.S. once again in 1941. One month before the attack on Pearl Harbor he published an article in *Chuo koron* in which he described the Americans as a peace-loving nation and stressed the fact that all the

Christian churches in the U.S. were opposed to America entering the war. "Only the Jews are advocating war and this has already created strong anti-Semitic feelings even among those who previously had no prejudices against them."[15]

The scientific community too harbored friendly feelings toward the U.S., partly because many of Japan's scientists had studied in American universities and were in contact with American colleagues. On 8 December 1941, the day of the attack on Pearl Harbor, the newspaper of Tokyo Imperial University carried an article by the physicist Iimori Takeo about his visit to American universities during the previous year. Iimori described the friendly way in which he had been received in the U.S. When he visited the Radiation Laboratory of Professor Ernest O. Lawrence at Berkeley, Lawrence confided to him that nuclear energy might some day be put to military use.[16] Little could they guess at the time that within five years Professor Lawrence would be a member of the Advisory Panel of Scientists which would recommend dropping atomic bombs on Japan.

The Barbarian Foe?

After the attack on Pearl Harbor, the image of the straying partner quickly changed into that of the sinister barbarian. Official pronouncements no longer referred to the United States and Great Britain, but used instead the less formal names of America (*Beikoku*) and England (*Eikoku*). Semiofficial organs such as the daily press went even further: they used derogatory ideographs when spelling the names of these countries, and often referred to them as "American and English devils" (*kichiku Bei-Ei*).

In newspaper articles the U.S. was described as an artificial nation made up of races and groups antagonistic to one another, and as a country weakened by corruption, egoism and materialism. The Tokugawa image of the Westerner as a barbarian was revived. At the time that the American press was describing the Japanese as savages with only a thin veneer of civilization, the Japanese press was portraying Americans in exactly the same terms: savage, brutal, childish, and devoid of morality. A May 1943 editorial of the *Mainichi*, entitled "Those Americans," stated:

> Although there are about one hundred thirty million Americans, they do not constitute a real nation.... They are just a mixture of different races that happen to live in one place.... Believing in the erroneous notion that sovereignty lies with the people, they established a state where the masses rule supreme.... Thus they have become totally uncontrollable, an easily excitable mob that even panics over

such fantastic dangers as an invasion from Mars.[17]

Two weeks later, in an editorial on the sinking of a Japanese hospital ship, the same newspaper averred:

> For a long time we have suspected that the so-called humanitarianism of America and England was just a thin cover to conceal their basic barbarity. Now, in this war against us, they have proved that our suspicions were correct.[18]

America was an evil empire. Its barbarism, it was pointed out, was aimed not only against Japan, but also against its own racial minorities, such as Orientals, Blacks and Indians. American racism at home and designs against Japan in Asia were described as part and parcel of the same plot. In September 1942 the *Yomiuri hochi* accused the U.S. of mistreating the Japanese residents on the West Coast. The editorial's conclusion was that the Americans had lost all sense of shame.[19]

In April 1944, the *Mainichi*'s editorial, entitled "America Wages War by Sacrificing Other Races," charged that the Americans, who had once imported the Blacks as slaves, were now sending black soldiers to the battlefront to serve as coolies and to be slaughtered. This was also the way in which America behaved in Asia, using Chinese troops as its proxies in the India campaign.[20]

Wartime American accusations that the Japanese were barbarians touched a sensitive nerve. In a January 1943 editorial, the *Tokyo shimbun* rhetorically asked: "Aren't the Americans themselves barbarian?... In their veins runs the savage blood of those who slaughtered the innocent Indians and robbed them of their land."[21] A year later the same newspaper returned to this topic in an editorial:

> Contrary to their formal profession of Christianity, the Americans lack the basic virtues of humanity. This is evident in their persecution of blacks at home as well as in the savage way in which they prosecute the war overseas.... They attack hospital ships, force Japanese internees to work and rape Japanese women in America.[22]

Not all Japanese could accept the idea that the Americans were barbarians. The intellectual magazines like *Chuo koron* or *Bungei shunju* that had once admired the U.S. adopted a different line. Instead of describing America as a savage country, they accused the U.S. of having forfeited the lofty American ideals for which it had stood in the past.

In March 1943, Professor Koyama Iwao, a philosopher from Kyoto Imperial University, wrote in *Chuo koron* that America had abandoned the democratic ideals of which it had once been proud. He explained that after the outbreak of hostilities, American institutions had been reorganized on a wartime basis. The Americans were mistaken if they believed that freedom and democracy would return to their land after the war. The trend of that country, he argued, had definitely taken the opposite direction.[23]

During the 1920s and 1930s Japanese intellectuals had discussed the concept of "Americanism," pointing out its positive and negative aspects.[24] During the war this concept continued to puzzle the Japanese. Although "Americanism" was denounced, expressions of sympathy were sometimes allowed to appear. Thus on the occasion of America's Independence Day, on 4 July 1943, the editorial of the *Tokyo shimbun* praised the original virtues of the American way of life, but lamented that these virtues had been trampled by the capitalists. The editorial said:

> Today is America's Independence Day.... One hundred sixty-seven years ago a new nation was born.... At that time its spirit was similar to that on which our empire was founded. It was the spirit of independence, freedom, equality and justice. These values were also manifested when the Civil War was fought to liberate the blacks. The ideals of President Lincoln, who fought for justice, impressed Japan. But as America came under the hegemony of the capitalists and embarked on an imperialistic policy of world conquest, its spirit of justice has all but vanished. On this Independence Day, the people of America should bow low before the tomb of George Washington and reflect deeply on the founding principles of their nation.[25]

The monthlies were not afraid to praise basic American aspirations as long as they could accuse the U.S. of having forfeited them. In the April 1943 issue of *Chuo koron*, Professor Namba Monkichi of Doshisha University in Kyoto, who had studied economics at Columbia University, published an essay which described favorably the basic ideals of the U.S. and expressed regret for their wartime disappearance. According to Namba, there were different definitions of Americanism:

> What is Americanism or the American way of life? There have been various answers to this question. Some say it is

> Judaism and the rule of the dollar, others say it is greed, hedonism and the dominance of machines.... But the basic element of the American way of life is democracy, an ideal which has provided the driving force behind the fast growth of the American continent.... But with this growth, the original spirit of self-governing agrarian communities has been replaced by the spirit of capitalism and imperialism.... When America entered the war, the powers of the President were largely increased so that today he resembles the European dictators.[26]

Thus the most famous Japanese magazine accused President Roosevelt of violating the rules of democracy and of assuming the powers of a European dictator.

The same issue of *Chuo koron* carried also an article by Professor Shimizu Ikutaro of Gakushuin University, which described favorably the American frontier spirit. The magazine's editor at that time, Hatanaka Shigeo, reveals in his memoirs that the authorities reprimanded him for publishing these two pro-American articles. But the issue was not banned.[27]

Contemporary Japan, ostensibly a mouthpiece of the government for anti-American propaganda to other nations in Asia, occasionally published articles favorable to the American way of life. In the September 1943 issue Professor Matsumoto Takizo of Meiji University, who had studied at Harvard, wrote in praise of American individualism and creativity:

> It is a fact that individual initiative and originality are fondly cherished in the U.S..... This is the main reason why the American people have been able to create and invent many new scientific things and objects. They claim that their country accounts for fifteen out of the thirty-four major inventions in the world in modern times, and point out that of the rest Germany accounts for six, France five, Britain three and other countries five. The blessing of individual initiative and originality is at the back of America's creative faculty and the ability to display the highest standard of efficiency....

Matsumoto criticized American worship of money, but he was full of praise for American ingenuity. He stressed that:

> America is the youngest country, the latest product of modern civilization.... Receiving the concentrated assistance

of the best of Western culture, it shortly evaginated [sic] a culture of its own, and then started exercising its creative faculty and initiative to the maximum limit.[28]

In December 1943 the magazine carried an article by Professor Takagi Yasaka of Tokyo Imperial University, a scholar of the American constitution who had received his LL.D. at Harvard. After presenting the war aims of the U.S., Takagi urged his readers to take seriously America's claim that it was fighting to preserve democracy:

> American emphasis on idealism, with all its faults ... is not a mere smoke-screen, as is often alleged, to cover its selfish, realistic designs. It is a mistake to call it a hypocrisy or even a more opportunism.... It is an undeniable historical fact that the American people has fought, more than once, long hard wars in defence of democracy.[29]

Although writing in a semi-official magazine, Takagi was not afraid to assign equal weight to the claims of both belligerents. He explained that both Japan and the U.S. were determined to fight the war out to complete victory. Each nation was absolutely convinced of the justness of its own cause, blaming the other for resorting to force. He emphasized that "my intention is not to single out America, as if the brunt of responsibility were to be laid solely upon her shoulders ... Japan, too, has learned much through the severe and chastening disciplines of war. It is now increasingly clear to her leaders that armed force alone is hardly enough to win the war and also the peace."[30]

Even when American bombers were sowing destruction on Japanese cities, it was still possible to find some expressions of sympathy toward the U.S. In March 1945 the associate editor of *Contemporary Japan*, Kakehi Mitsuaki, wrote that the citizens of Tokyo bore no grudge against the Americans. In fact, the author noted, Tokyoites were referring to the American bombers as "American guests" (*Amerika no okyaku-san*) or "Mr. Enemy" (*teki-san*). This absence of enmity, he claimed, stood in sharp contrast to the hatred toward Japan demonstrated by the American public:

> Americans, even their prominent leaders and officials, call us "Japs," but our armed forces simply call them "Mr. Enemy." What a contrast! It shows distinctly the fundamental difference in the Japanese and American national traits.[31]

Kakehi deliberately ignored the grim realities of that time which were less rosy. Captured American airmen were often lynched by angry mobs or summarily executed by the military. Yet, the fact that he wished to project an image of his people respecting the American enemy may mean that such behavior was still considered praiseworthy at that time.

Despite the fierce hostilities and the vehement propaganda war, the U.S. and Japan shared several ideals. As Akira Iriye has pointed out, both countries believed in the historical inevitability of decolonization in Asia and both wanted to hasten this process and achieve a post-colonial order on the continent.[32]

Chastising an Ignorant Brother

If Japan's prewar attitude toward the U.S. could be compared to that of a frustrated lover, its attitude toward China might be termed that of an annoyed brother. The Japanese could not deny their ethnic and cultural affinities with the Chinese, but China's decay and disintegration at the very time that Japan was prospering and forging ahead caused the Japanese embarrassment. The notion of dissociation from China, propagated by Fukuzawa Yukichi in his 1885 article "Datsu-A ron" ("In Favor of Separation from Asia") was the line followed by official Japan for most of the Meiji and Taisho periods. Successful Japan did not want to appear in public with its poor and ignorant Chinese brother; but once the two were left alone, as happened during World War I, Japan was quick to assert its family right to manage the affairs of this retarded relative. Even those romantic, pan-Asianist Japanese who wanted their country to side with China against the West manifested a patronizing attitude toward the Chinese, treating them as impoverished and needy relatives. As Marius Jansen has shown, the greatest Sinophiles were sometimes the most extreme nationalists.[33]

Japan's seizure of Manchuria in 1931 produced a nationalist excitement that engulfed the media. Although some scholars, like Yoshino Sakuzo, Yokota Kisaburo, and Yanaihara Tadao, all of them of Tokyo Imperial University, publicly opposed Japan's actions on the continent, their voices were drowned by those who supported the creation of the puppet state of Manchukuo.[34] Manchukuo became the model for future relations with China: a Japanese-controlled, nominally-independent part of the continent, where all races were supposed to co-exist in harmony under Japanese tutelage.

The outbreak of the China War in 1937 did not produce a worse image of that country. On the contrary, in order to justify the war, the authorities described it as a mission to save China from Anglo-

Saxon imperialism and Soviet bolshevism. In November 1938 Prime Minister Prince Konoye Fumimaro proclaimed a New Order in East Asia (*To-A shinchitsujo*), according to which Japan was fighting the war in China in order to establish a new community of East Asian nations under its leadership. In June 1940 the New Order was expanded into the Greater East Asia Co-Prosperity Sphere (*Dai To-A kyoei ken*), which included Southeast Asia as well.

The wartime glorification of China went together with denunciation of the U.S. America stood for materialism, greed and brutality, while China represented spirituality, culture and morality.[35] Fukuzawa's ideal had been fully reversed: Japan was now trying to dissociate itself from the West and rejoin Asia.

The argument that Japan was fighting China to save it from even greater evils was accepted not only by ignorant chauvinists but also by some of the outstanding intellectuals of that time. Former Marxists like the philosopher Miki Kiyoshi, the historian Shinobu Seizaburo, and the sinologists Ozaki Hotsumi and Hosokawa Karoku argued that the "China Incident" was a just war against Western imperialism and its Chinese stooges.[36]

The outbreak of the Pacific War was explained by these intellectuals as the logical culmination of the China War, the expansion of the New Order in East Asia into the Greater East Asia Co-Prosperity Sphere. The Western powers that had been supporting Chungking against Japan were now being challenged directly, and were soon to be expelled from Asia. The name "Great East Asia War" (Dai to-A senso) announced by the Information Bureau on 12 December 1941, was to be applied to the war in China as well as the one in the Pacific and Southeast Asia.[37]

In his March 1943 essay in *Chuo koron* the philosopher Koyama Iwao explained that although the two are referred to by different names, the China Incident and the Great East Asia War were fundamentally one and the same. The aid that America and England had extended to China, and the hostility of these two nations toward Japan had aggravated the situation to the point that Japan felt it necessary to extricate itself from the economic bond to these hostile powers and to construct a New Order in East Asia.[38]

The press echoed the government's expectations that China would carry its share in the war against the common enemy. After the Nanking puppet government's declaration of war on the U.S. and Britain, the *Tokyo shimbun* commented that the efforts and sacrifices of Sun Yat-sen for the sake of China were still vivid in Japan's memory. The newspaper expressed the expectation that the young people of China would follow Sun's example by rallying to the battle cry of puppet leader Wang Ching-wei in order to liberate their country from the traitors.[39]

As Japan saw it, China was divided into the "patriots" in Nanking and the "traitors" in Chungking. As the *Mainichi shimbun* put it on the sixth anniversary of the China War:

> In striking contrast to the daily progress of the National Government in promoting the well-being of the people under its rule, the Chungking government, subservient to the interests of America and England, is in total disarray. Its people are disenchanted and its military men try to desert.... They are suffering, cursing and breaking out in riots.[40]

Before the Pacific War, Chiang's cardinal crime was his alliance with the Chinese communists, who were considered to be agents of Japan's arch-enemy, the Soviet Union. But now that Japan was fighting the Atlantic powers and strictly observing the neutrality pact with the Soviet Union, Chiang's main crime was his cooperation with the U.S. and Britain. The communists were seldom denounced, as the Soviet Union was a power whose goodwill Japan was eager to court. Japanese newspapers sometimes even quoted Mao to substantiate their attacks on Chiang Kai-shek. The *Yomiuri hochi* in September 1943 pointed to Mao Tse-tung's essay on the new democracy to prove Japan's claim that the purpose of Chiang Kai-shek's so-called democracy and constitutional government was not the welfare of the people, but rather his own aggrandizement.[41]

In an effort to incite the people of Chungking to revolt against Chiang and his American supporters, the Japanese authorities appealed to Chinese national pride. Thus, in December 1943, the *Tokyo shimbun* devoted an editorial to the issue of American pilots' behavior in China. The American pilots in Chungking, it wrote, wore the finest clothes, occupied the best houses, drank the highest-quality whiskey and smoked the most expensive cigars, while the Chinese masses around them lingered in total misery. "The Chungking authorities, servile to their foreign masters, close their eyes while the American pilots help themselves to China's women, treasures, and land."[42]

When Chinese students at Yunnan University clashed with American pilots at a nearby air base, the *Tokyo shimbun* praised the students: "Although these students had for a long time been educated in the wrong way, they manifested real patriotism by revolting against the arrogant Americans."[43]

The Japanese press kept stressing that Japan was not fighting the Chinese people, but only their traitorous government. In June 1944, one month after a major Japanese offensive started, the *Mainichi* editorialized that the military operations in China were not directed against innocent Chinese, but only against the Anglo-Americans and their Chinese lackeys. It concluded that the "Chungking hordes will soon collapse under the blows of the Imperial Japanese Army fighting for justice."[44]

Yet, as the military situation in the Pacific worsened, the official attitude toward Chiang Kai-shek changed. By 1944 Japan was ready to make peace even with this detested enemy if he would join the Co-Prosperity Sphere or at least remain neutral. In September of that year the government decided to despatch secretly a high-ranking emissary to Chiang to offer a peace treaty which would include a restoration of the island of Hong Kong to China, but nothing came out of this plan.[45]

In July 1944 the *Yomiuri hochi* explained that Chiang Kai-shek was not regarded any more as an enemy:

> Although we are fighting against the Chungking army, we know that Chiang Kai-shek has been dragged into this war by America and England. Our real enemy is neither the Chungking army nor the Chinese communists, but the Americans and the British who stand behind them.[46]

In October, the *Asahi* openly invited Chiang to join Japan in the struggle against Western imperialism. By changing its policy and joining the fight for Asia's liberation, Chungking would show its true Asian spirit. "We have been enemies, but enemies can become friends when they face a common foe."[47]

But Chiang Kai-shek had no incentive to bail the Japanese out. As the war situation deteriorated, the long-chastized brother had only to wait a short while until his arrogant sibling was completely defeated.

Why Do They Still Hate Us?

Although the Japanese tried to persuade the world that they were fighting to save their Chinese brethren, the Chinese themselves remained unimpressed by this form of forceful salvation. China's failure to reciprocate the professed brotherhood upset the Japanese and obliged them to look for explanations.

One week after the outbreak of the China war, the August 1937 issue of *Chuo koron* went on sale carrying articles on the tense situation on the continent. In one of them, Fujieda Takeo admitted that hatred of Japan was universal in China:

> It is not an exaggeration to say that at present all the Chinese, young and old, men and women, high and low, are

participating in the anti-Japanese movement.... This movement is extremely popular and attracts all segments of the population.[48]

The Japanese authorities as well as much of the public believed that the establishment of the Nanking regime in 1940 and the outbreak of the Pacific War in the following year would convince Chungking to stop its futile resistance to Japan. Chiang Kai-shek's continued opposition to Japan seemed senseless and absurd. An *Asahi* editorial on 23 December 1941 stated: "It is impossible for us to comprehend the stubbornness of the Chungking regime in continuing its pointless resistance."[49] The following month the *Nichi nichi* pondered: "We wonder whether the Chungking leaders have enough vision to understand the lofty ideals of Japan."[50] Chiang seemed to be betraying the best interests of his people by pinning his hopes on a Western victory. As the *Tokyo shimbun* claimed in December 1942: "In their total blindness, the Chungking leaders believe that final victory in this war lies with America and England. But they do not grasp that, even if America and England do win, China would still be a colony of these two powers."[51]

To their great chagrin the Japanese discovered that even the Wang Ching-wei regime was not overwhelmingly friendly toward them. Although a formal ally, the Nanking government declared war on the U.S. and Britain only in 1943, and even then its efforts were far from wholehearted. Thus, while praising Wang Ching-wei, the Japanese press occasionally hinted that Nanking could be doing more for the common war effort.[52] The Chinese were urged to emulate the positive example of Manchuria, where initial hostilities were short, resistance against Japan minimal, and collaboration smooth.[53] Yet this was of little avail.

Nowhere was this asymmetry of attitudes more striking than among the intellectuals. In Japan, the intellectuals were the most enthusiastic about a Sino-Japanese alliance, praising the common heritage of the two nations and advocating the idea of *dobun doshu* ("same script, same race"--also translated as "common culture"). Many of them went to China in an attempt to foster ties with their counterparts on the continent. But they quickly realized that in China the intellectuals were at the forefront of the anti-Japanese movement and most were extremely hostile to Japan.

Some Japanese commentators openly admitted this asymmetry. In April 1943, Kanesaki Ken observed in the *Nippon Times* that while Japanese intellectuals were studying Chinese classics "with great avidity," very few people in China were interested in the Japanese classics.[54]

Hayashi Fusao, a proletarian writer who had turned nationalist in the 1930s, admitted in the *Nihon hyoron* in 1943:

> The Japanese government is well aware that for the realization of a lasting understanding between Japan and China, the cooperation of Chinese intellectuals is essential. However ... up to the middle of last year, the majority of the Chinese remained apathetic toward the friendly approaches of Japan and stubbornly turned their backs to projects of mutual understanding.... The Chinese intellectuals residing in territories under Japanese control practiced a sort of tacit disengagement from the cultural policies of Japan.[55]

The cultural asymmetry was also acknowledged by a Chinese intellectual who collaborated with Japan. T'ao K'ang-te, editor of the journal *Jih-hua jih-pao,* who had attended the 1944 Great East Asia Literary Conference in Tokyo, wrote in *Chuo koron* that while strolling in Kanda he was surprised to see how many books on China had been published in Japan. Nothing of this sort, he noted, had happened in China, where interest in Japanese culture remained small.[56]

The failure of China to respond to Japan's "brotherly hug" convinced many Japanese that there was something fundamentally wrong with the Chinese national character. The Chinese were too stupid or too arrogant to know what was good for them. This view was shared by prominent intellectuals, such as the philosopher Kosaka Masaaki of Kyoto Imperial University who wrote that the trouble with the Chinese was that throughout their history they regarded themselves as the most important people on earth. This inflated self-esteem had made them act in an arrogant way and had prevented them from forming equal partnerships with other peoples. This was the main reason for their poor performance in modern times.[57]

The strange behavior of the Chinese struck Japanese observers as being part of the old, inscrutable Oriental tradition which they themselves had discarded long ago. In an article on China, Kosaka Masaaki called on the Chinese to shed the "dregs" of their "Oriental culture" in order to be able to take part in constructing the Co-Prosperity Sphere.[58]

A major defect in the Chinese national character seemed to be the exasperating slowness with which they reacted to changing world circumstances, in contrast to the swiftness characterizing Japan's moves. As the retired diplomat Yonayama Tsuneo explained, speed was the keynote of Japanese life, but in China speedlessness was still strikingly prominent. To illustrate this, he pointed to the fact that while in Japan the September number of a magazine made its appearance in August, in China it often happened that a journal scheduled to appear at a definite time was published six months later. According to Yonayama, the reason for that was the Chinese natural inclination to act slowly. All of China's accomplishments in the past had been achieved in gradual slow stages, and the same slowness still prevailed in that country.[59]

The Chinese were arrogant and cunning; as the *Mainichi* put it: "The outstanding feature of the Chungking regime is its craftiness. The traditional arrogance of the Chinese has been reinforced by a self-righteous revolutionary ideology."[60]

Another Chinese defect was their oversensitivity. The Japanese found it difficult to understand why the Chinese felt insulted when their country was referred to by the Western term *Shina*, instead of the traditional *Chugoku* or the official *Chuka Minkoku*. Kanesaki Ken explained in the March 1943 issue of *Contemporary Japan* that in the Japanese mind the official term Chuka Minkoku did not register the same degree of friendliness as conveyed by the familiar expression Shina. "Some Chinese people do not like to have their country called Shina, but on our part we find it difficult to abandon this historical term of endearment."[61]

Thus the Japanese continued to use the term Shina (or its abbreviated form *Shi*), despite the fact that many Chinese detested it. An expression of the resentment that the Chinese felt when referred to as *Shinajin* (Chinaman) is found in the writings of Kuo Mo-jo, one of the leading Chinese intellectuals of that time. Kuo, who had studied in Japan for more than a decade, wrote while he was a student there:

> Japanese! Japanese! Ungrateful Japanese! What have we done to you that you must despise us so? Your extreme ill-will is manifest even when you utter the word 'Shina-jin.' When pronouncing 'Shi' you deliberately shift to the front of the nose, and when you say 'na' you draw it out into a long nasal sound.[62]

According to some observers, China's problems derived from its women wielding an inordinate amount of power. A writer by the name of Mogi Kyuhei explained:

> With the Chinese women there is much that taxes our understanding. They insist upon their rights, demanding men to respect them. When a Chinese woman becomes ill,

it is a matter of course for her to ask her husband to take that day off to attend to her. This is one Chinese characteristic which, despite its difficulty for the Japanese to understand, must be grasped if Japan is to assume her mission of leadership.[63]

An opposing view, held by Chinese women residing in Japan, was that China's backwardness was due to the low status and oppression of its women. Madame Wu Wen-chi, a graduate of Nippon Toyo University and wife of Professor Yu Ping-tse of Peking University, wrote in the *Nippon Times* that half of Japan's amazing strength was due to the solid backing of Japanese women, while half of China's decline was due to the weakness of Chinese women. In China such customs as foot binding and arranged marriages made the women into mere toys of men and machines for breeding children. In past years, she wrote, many Chinese women had led idle, luxuriant lives, leaving the household tasks in the servants' hands. The wartime circumstances changed all of this. Thanks to the war, the Chinese women could see "the happy lives the diligent and sound Japanese women are leading in their homes," which made them reflect upon their own mistaken lives.[64]

Not all Japanese writers, however, subscribed to the simplistic theory that China's hostility toward Japan proved that there was something wrong with China. There were writers who were not afraid to state publicly that the blame lay with Japan's cultural arrogance and imperialistic designs. The wartime authorities did not suppress such critical views as long as they referred to general attitudes toward China and did not criticize the military actions there.

Among those who raised their voices against Japanese actions in China were the philosopher Miki Kiyoshi and the statesman Sato Naotake. Miki, who had initially supported the war in China, was shocked by the misbehavior of Japanese nationals there, and blamed his countrymen for alienating the Chinese people. Those who visited China, he wrote in *Chuo koron*, realized that the behavior of Japanese nationals there was deplorable. This had already harmed Japan's relations with the people of China and had caused the Japanese great shame. As long as this state of affairs continued there was no chance that the Chinese would stop hating Japan and despising it. Miki remarked that it had often been said that the reason for the unfortunate situation was that the wrong people were sent to China, and that if only better people were sent there everything would work out well. But the problem was more complicated than that: "Quite often the people who go to China are no worse than the ordinary folk who stay at home. The tragedy is that the same Japanese whose behavior at home is beyond reproach start behaving in a manner which shocks even their own countrymen once they set foot in China."[65]

Miki claimed that the only way to enlist the cooperation of the Chinese was to treat them as equals. He urged his readers not to regard the Chinese as "Chinks" (*chankoro*), because those who were contemptuous of others would in the end be themselves despised. He reminded his readers that China was the oldest civilization on earth, and in the same way that the Japanese were proud of their national traits, they should respect the national traits of others. "Those who think that their own nation is superior to all others and who look down upon other nations as inferior are imperialists." The Japanese government, he wrote, claimed that it had no imperialistic designs on China, "but after what I have seen there I must admit that Japan does not show proper respect for China's tradition, and instead tries to impose its own institutions and norms."[66]

Miki rejected the chauvinist notion that Japan was basically different from and superior to China. In his view, the only meaningful difference between the two nations was that one was an earlier and the other was a later modernizer: "When we read descriptions of Japanese in the Meiji era, we are astonished to realize how much they resembled the Chinese of today."[67]

Sato Naotake, a former foreign minister who was Japan's ambassador to Moscow in the last stages of the war, was also critical of Japanese policy in China. Writing in *Contemporary Japan* he warned:

> Japan must not lay all the blame at the doors of Chiang Kai-shek.... We must not overlook the shock which the Manchurian Incident may have given to the Chinese people, as well as the extension of Japanese influence into North China, which no doubt served to stimulate further Chinese sentiment.... The means employed by the Chinese in their anti-Japanese movement were often improper ... but even in these cases Japan should reflect upon her own attitude. Japan ... has to assume partial responsibility for the Chinese boycott against her, if her high handed way of dealing with the Chinese government needlessly stimulated Chinese sentiments.[68]

Sato's conclusion, like that of Miki, was that the only way to solve the problem in China was by discarding the attitude of superiority. Peace with China could not be established as long as Japan possessed a superiority complex. "The writer therefore counsels the Japanese nation to discard all its prejudices ... and fraternize with them upon an equal footing."[69]

Sato contested the logic of those who claimed that Japan was entitled to special rights in China because of its own sacrifices in the "liberation" of that country. This kind of reasoning was, according to Sato, self defeating. The case of Germany after World War I showed that an inconsiderate attitude toward a defeated and proud people only planted the seeds for future conflict. Japan could not afford to seek "a patched-up, short sighted peace with China," as the chauvinists wanted, but had to listen to the wishes and aspirations of the Chinese people.[70]

Tokiwa Daijo, professor emeritus of Tokyo Imperial University and expert on Buddhist philosophy, writing in *Chuo koron* in 1944, warned against treating the Chinese contemptuously:

> Until the outbreak of the China Incident, we used to admire everything that came from the West and reject everything that arrived from China. We did not treat the Chinese as our friends.... The old relationship between the two countries, by which China had once been the teacher and Japan its student, was reversed.... But we should not forget that the Chinese are a proud people and there are many learned men among them.... Our relations with China should be based on mutual respect.[71]

There were also businessmen who protested the wrongdoings of their countrymen in China, warning that such actions could only breed hatred and boycotts. Takagi Rikuro, president of the South Manchurian Mining Company and an influential business leader in Japan, writing in the foreign-affairs magazine *Gaiko hyoron*, blamed Japan's high-handed policies for alienating the Chinese:

> During World War I, when the attention of the world was concentrated on Europe, Japan should have allied with China and declared the independence of Asia.... Instead it used its military superiority to present the Chinese with Twenty-One Demands. This act made the Chinese suspect our motives and produced an anti-Japanese movement in China.... Later, the Manchurian Incident impressed the Chinese that Japan was ready to do everything to fulfill its ambitions. As a result, the anti-Japanese movement spread all over China and the ground was prepared for the Marco Polo Bridge Incident.[72]

There were also right-wing intellectuals who thought favorably of

Chiang Kai-shek, defended his personality and blamed the Japanese government for having turned him into an enemy. Tsukui Tatsuo, an ultra-nationalist writer who had been involved in the Shimpeitai Affair of 1933, wrote in 1944:

> It must be admitted that Japan before the War of Great East Asia was not entirely above reproach. It will not do to blame China alone. Remember, Chiang Kai-shek was once a staunch anti-Communist. Even now he is in all probability anti-Communist at heart.... It can hardly be denied that part of the blame for his recourse to anti-Japanese lies at the door of the Japanese statesmen.[73]

Thus, by the end of the war many knowledgeable Japanese had reached the conclusion that Japan's policies toward China had been a colossal mistake. These people were allowed to express their disenchantment publicly, in line with the government's last-minute efforts to strike a deal with Chiang Kai-shek. Yet, this change of heart came too late to have any immediate results.

Conclusion

For eighty-three years, from the opening of Japan in 1854 to the Marco Polo Bridge Incident in 1937, the Japanese admired the West as their major source of inspiration and denigrated Asia which reminded them of their obscurant past. The United States, the Western country which first opened Japan and then helped it in many ways, enjoyed a special position in the hearts of the Japanese. Admiration for the U.S. lingered on even when relations between the two countries were often strained. On the other hand, China, which had served as a cultural model for a millennium and a half but was now in the throes of revolution and anarchy, elicited little respect. The only good that Japan seemed to be able to do for China was to lead it and shape it in its own image.

With the outbreak of the China War in 1937 and the Pacific War in 1941 the public attitudes toward these two countries changed dramatically. The Japanese justified these wars as being part of a great holy war to liberate Asia from Western imperialism and Communist subversion, and to construct a new and indigenous international order in East Asia. As a result of this new ideology, the U.S. ceased to be the model of culture and progress, turning instead into a materialist and blood-thirsty monster that was trying to strangle Japan. "Liberated" China ceased being a synonym for anarchy and backwardness and became again the cultural jewel in a new East.

But this official shift in roles was too quick and short-lived to strike deep roots. More than eighty years of admiration for the U.S. could not be erased by one stroke, and friendly expressions toward the U.S. kept cropping up during the war despite the official barrage of hostile propaganda. Similarly, long-ingrained feelings of contempt for China continued to be expressed in various ways. These ambivalent attitudes were reflected in the wartime newspapers and magazines.

The propaganda war with the U.S. and China was fierce, but the themes that both sides used were often similar. Thus, when the Americans were accusing Japan of inhuman brutality, the Japanese were hurling the same accusations at the U.S.[74] At the time when the Chinese were blaming Japan for having forfeited its duty as a sister nation by attacking China, the Japanese were accusing Chiang Kai-shek of betraying the East Asian community by allying himself with the imperialist powers.

Still, there was a basic difference in the images of these two countries. America was a foe to be expelled. The Japanese did not try to conquer the American mainland, nor did they wish to reform the U.S. China, however, was a country to be saved and reformed. Therefore it was conquered on the one hand, but also extolled on the other.

Despite the favorable official image of China, it seems that the Japanese understood the Chinese even less than they understood the Americans. Time and again we find wartime commentators expressing exasperation in their efforts to make sense of China's behavior. The Japanese regarded themselves as modern, rational and highly motivated, while the Chinese appeared to them as backward, inscrutable and untrustworthy. After three generations of modernization, the Japanese had internalized not only the techniques and ideologies of the West, but also its prejudices against Asians. It was ironic that such prejudices should be expressed in the midst of a military campaign, the declared purpose of which was to drive out the West from Asia.

The shallowness of the wartime images was manifest after Japan's defeat in 1945, when traditional admiration for the U.S. once again became the norm, while dissociation from China assumed new forms.

Postwar Japan returned to Fukuzawa's dictum of leaving Asia and embracing the West. But the prewar contempt for China was not revived. The high esteem for China, propagated during the eight years of war with that country, together with the feelings of remorse and culpability that had already appeared during the war, produced a favorable image of post-war China, as that country was going through the throes of civil war, revolution and reforms.

As a result, post-war Japan has until recently entertained favorable images of both the U.S. and China, two countries with which it had been locked in a most traumatic war.

NOTES

1. For Japanese attitudes toward the U.S. see Marius B. Jansen, "Modernization and Foreign Policy in Meiji Japan," in Robert E. Ward, ed., *Political Development in Modern Japan* (Princeton, 1968); Akira Iriye, *Pacific Estrangement, 1897-1911* (Cambridge, 1972).
2. Tokutomi Iichiro (Soho), *Taisengo no sekai to Nihon* (Tokyo, 1920), pp. 677-679.
3. Asada Sadao, "Nichibei kankei no imeji (senzen)," in *Nihon no shakai bunka shi*, vol. 7: *Sekai no naka no Nihon* (Tokyo, 1974), pp. 307-359.
4. Takashi Ito, "The Role of Right-Wing Organizations in Japan," in Dorothy Borg and Shumpei Okamoto, eds., *Pearl Harbor as History, Japanese American Relations 1931-1941* (New York, 1973), pp. 507-508.
5. George M. Wilson, *Radical Nationalist in Japan: Kita Ikki, 1883-1937* (Cambridge, 1969), pp. 82-83, 185 n. 34.
6. Takaishi Shingoro, "Nichibei shinzen ron," *Kaizo*, vol. XX, no. 5 (May 1938), pp. 65-67.
7. *Asahi shimbun* (29 July 1939). All references to Japanese newspapers hereafter are to the morning editions.
8. Tamura Kosaku, "Nichi-Bei kokko chosei no kompon kosatsu," *Bungei shunju*, vol. XVIII, no. 1 (January 1940), p. 90.
9. Satoru Hasegawa, "Estranged Relations between Japan and America," *Contemporary Japan*, vol. IX, no. 2 (February 1940), p. 149.
10. Katsuji Debuchi, "Readjustment of American-Japanese Relations," *Contemporary Japan*, vol. IX, no. 3 (March 1940), pp. 237-38.
11. Debuchi, "Readjustment," pp. 239-41.
12. Debuchi, "Readjustment," p. 246.
13. Quoted in Tomiko Kakegawa, "The Press and Public Opinion in Japan, 1931-1941," in Borg and Okamoto, *Pearl Harbor as History*, p. 547; *Asahi shimbun* (12 October 1940).
14. "Kokumin wa ko omou, yoron chosa," *Bungei shunju*, vol. XIX, no. 7 (January 1941), p. 239.
15. Kagawa Toyohiko, "Amerika no kanjo," *Chuo koron*, vol. LVI, no. 11 (November 1941), pp. 128-129.
16. *Teikoku daigaku shimbun* (8 December 1941).
17. *Mainichi shimbun* (5 May 1943).
18. *Mainichi shimbun* (21 May 1943).
19. *Yomiuri hochi shimbun* (22 September 1942).
20. *Mainichi shimbun* (7 April 1944).
21. *Tokyo shimbun* (18 January 1943).
22. *Tokyo shimbun* (12 February 1944).
23. Koyama Iwao, "Soryoku-sen to shiso-sen," *Chuo koron*, vol. LVIII, no. 3 (March 1943), p. 4.
24. Henry D. Smith, "From Wilsonian Democracy to Modan Life: Changing Japanese Conceptions of Americanism, 1916-1931." A paper submitted to the Bi-National Conference on Japanese-American Relations from World War I to the Manchurian Incident (Kauai, Hawaii, 1976).
25. *Tokyo shimbun* (4 July 1943).
26. Namba Monkichi, "Amerikanizumu no hatan," *Chuo koron*, vol. LVIII, no. 4 (April 1943), pp. 70-71.
27. Shimizu Ikutaro, "Teki to shite no amerikanizumu," *Chuo koron*, vol. LVIII, no. 4 (April 1943), pp. 81-88; Hatanaka Shigeo, *Showa shuppan dan'atsu shoshi* (Tokyo, 1965), pp. 79-82.
28. Takizo Matsumoto, "Monasticism of America," *Contemporary Japan*, vol. XII, no. 9 (September 1943), pp. 1140-46.
29. Yasaka Takagi, "War Aims of America," *Contemporary Japan*, vol. XII, no. 12 (December 1943), p. 1572.
30. Takagi, "War Aims," pp. 1579, 1581.
31. Mitsuaki Kakehi, "Tokyoites under Air Raids," *Contemporary Japan*, vol. XIV, no. 1-3 (January-March 1945), pp. 75-84.

32. Akira Iriye, *Power and Culture: The Japanese American War, 1941-1945* (Cambridge, 1981).
33. For Japanese attitudes toward China see Marius B. Jansen, *The Japanese and Sun Yat-sen* (Cambridge, 1954); *Japan and China: From War to Peace* (Chicago, 1975); "Konoe Atsumaro," in Akira Iriye, ed., *The Chinese and the Japanese* (Princeton, 1980), pp. 107-123; and, tr. with Shinkichi Eto, *My Thirty-Three Years' Dream* (Princeton, 1982).
34. Taichiro Mitani, "Changes in Japan's International Position and the Response of Japanese Intellectuals: Trends in Japanese Studies of Japan's Foreign Relations, 1931-1941," in Borg and Okamoto, eds., *Pearl Harbor as History*, pp. 575-594.
35. For an analysis of the cultural dichotomy during the war see Ben-Ami Shillony, *Politics and Culture in Wartime Japan* (Oxford, 1981), ch. VI.
36. Miki, Ozaki and Hosokawa were members of Konoye's brain trust, the Showa Kenkyu Kai. Ozaki was arrested in October 1941 when the police discovered that he was a member of the Sorge spy ring. He and Sorge were sentenced to death and were executed in November 1944. Miki was arrested in March 1945, when the police found a fugitive communist hiding in his house, and died in prison in September of that year. See Chalmers Johnson, *An Instance of Treason* (Berkeley, 1974). For the views of Miki, see William M. Fletcher, *The Search for a New Order* (Chapel Hill, 1982); Mitani, "Changes in Japan's International Positions," pp. 588, 592.
37. *Japan Times and Advertiser* (13 December 1941).
38. Koyama, "Soryoku-sen," pp. 5-6.
39. *Tokyo shimbun* (4 March 1943).
40. *Mainichi shimbun* (7 July 1943).
41. *Yomiuri hochi* (15 September 1943).
42. *Tokyo shimbun* (22 December 1943).
43. *Tokyo shimbun* (5 June 1944).
44. *Mainichi shimbun* (18 June 1944).
45. For details of these efforts see John H. Boyle, *China and Japan at War, 1937-1945* (Stanford, 1972), pp. 313-14.
46. *Yomiuri hochi* (6 July 1944).
47. *Asahi shimbun* (19 October 1944).
48. Fujieda Takeo, "Konichi undo no gendankai," *Chuo koron*, vol. LII, no. 8 (August 1937), pp. 52-53.
49. *Asahi shimbun* (23 December 1941).
50. *Nichi nichi shimbun* (26 January 1942).
51. *Tokyo shimbun* (1 December 1942).
52. As for instance the editorial in *Asahi shimbun* (2 February 1944).
53. *Miyako shimbun* (15 September 1942).
54. *Nippon Times* (29 April 1943).
55. Hayashi Fusao, "Chugoku bunka undo gukan," *Nihon hyoron*, vol. XVIII, no. 9 (September 1943), p. 81.
56. T'ao K'ang-te, "Nisshi teikei no hoto," *Chuo koron*, vol. LIX, no. 2 (February 1944), pp. 65-66.
57. Kosaka Masaaki, "Dai To-A kyoei ken e no michi," *Kaizo*, vol. XXIV, no. 1 (January 1942), p. 34.
58. *Nippon Times* (30 October 1944).
59. Tsuneo Yonayama, "The Chinese Way of Life," *Contemporary Japan*, vol. XI, no. 8 (August 1942), pp. 1211-1215.
60. *Mainichi shimbun* (24 November 1944).
61. Ken Kanesaki, "Our Classical Spirit and China," *Contemporary Japan*, vol. XII, no. 3 (March 1943), pp. 297-298.
62. Quoted from Nagai Michio, *Higher Education in Japan* (Tokyo, 1971), p. 114. This passage is part of Kuo Mo-jo's article "Hsing-lu nan," which was written in 1924 and published in the collection *Kan-lan* in 1932. See also David T. Roy, *Kuo Mo-jo, The Early Years* (Cambridge, 1971).
63. This passage, which appeared in the magazine *Keikoku*, is quoted in *Japan Times and Advertiser* (21 December 1942).
64. *Nippon Times* (5 January 1943).

65. Miki Kiyoshi, "Kokuminsei no kaizo," *Chuo koron*, vol. LV, no. 6 (June 1940), 412-418.
66. *Loc. cit.*
67. Miki, "Kokuminsei," pp. 418-419.
68. Naotake Sato, "Future Relations Between Japan and China," *Contemporary Japan*, vol. IX, no. 1 (January 1940), pp. 7-10.
69. *Loc. cit.*
70. Sato, "Future Relations," pp. 12-13.
71. Tokiwa Daijo, "Tai-Shi bunka kosaku no hansei," *Chuo koron*, vol. LIX, no. 2 (February 1944), pp. 52-60.
72. Takagi Rikuro, "Waga tai-Ka seisaku no ikkosatsu," *Gaiko hyoron*, vol. XXIV, no. 10 (October 1944), pp. 52-60.
73. Tatsuo Tsukui, "Dr. Sun's Three Principles and the Imperial Way," *Nippon Times* (19 June 1944).
74. John Dower, *War Without Mercy* (New York, 1986).

9
A MATTER OF TRANSCENDENCE: WAR EXPERIENCES AND THE TRANSFORMATION OF JAPANESE AND AMERICAN FIGHTER PILOTS

F. G. Notehelfer

Introduction

Images have always performed an important role in the cultural and political assessment of one nation by another. The part that such images play in major conflicts between nations is also well established. Indeed, wars have generally heightened the need to reduce the other side, or if we use the more value laden term, the enemy, to stereotypical depictions. Moreover, international conflicts, particularly those pitting one race against another, have tended to utilize overt or latent racism to denigrate the enemy while shoring up domestic confidence.[1]

The stereotyping of opponents, the need to reduce the other side to an inferior, and sometimes subhuman, status may well represent a common psychology of the nation-state at war. Americans have hardly avoided this general trend. Even a cursory glance at *Time*, *Life*, or *Newsweek* for the years 1941-1945, or a screening of one of Frank Capra's films, is sufficient to confirm such an impression. Wars, as any one living in the twentieth-century is only too conscious, bring out the best and the worst in man. Acts of self-sacrifice, heroism, and humanity are easily juxtaposed to those of senseless violence, cowardice, and inhumanity that all too often are justified in terms of the "nature" of the opposing side.

But while most nation-states have gone to war utilizing images of the enemy camp that are decidedly less than flattering, it should also be noted that wars serve as powerful forces in altering and shaping images. In fact, one of the least studied aspects of modern wars is the manner in which combat experiences have transformed and altered the mental perceptions with which combatants entered the field. World War II in the Pacific was no exception to this rule.

The average American and Japanese went to war knowing little about the other side. What they knew had been derived from the images to which they had been exposed by their education and the national media. While Japanese viewed Americans as hedonistic, materialistic, and racist, Americans saw the Japanese as aggressive, cruel, and untrustworthy. If, in addition, Japanese were convinced that Americans were fully bent on depriving them of their rightful "place in the sun," Americans were equally certain that Japan was preoccupied with a course of militaristic expansion at the expense of her neighbors. Such views were directly linked to the images most widely disseminated in both countries.[2]

But it is equally clear that many men who entered the war with hatred for one another, and who were dedicated to killing as many of the enemy as possible, emerged from the war with more respect than hatred, tired of the killing, and with a new perception of themselves as well as the enemy. Nowhere was this more obvious than in the battle-hardened veterans who entered Japan as part of the Army of Occupation in 1945. The majority of these men made every effort to substitute a genuine humanitarian affection and desire to help for their earlier hatred and xenophobia. On the other hand many of those who received their help could do so graciously because they had made their own breakthroughs of perception. In short, what had happened to both sides allowed the War to come to an end, both on the personal and national levels.

And yet, while it is clear that the experiences of World War II transformed Japanese conceptions of Americans and American conceptions of Japanese in such a way that both nations were able to build closer peaceful ties in the postwar era, we know relatively little of the way in which this process worked at the micro level among specific individuals.

The object of this essay is to explore in greater detail what the war meant to a select group of participants. In the process we are particularly concerned with the way that war experiences served to alter, or reinforce, prior conceptions, or images, on the part of combatants. The fact that the typical soldier, sailor, and airman brought to the battlefield his own set of images which were largely stereotypical and based on little personal contact or exposure is hardly surprising. Nor is it surprising that such images served as initial sources of action. After all, what the war basically did was pull thousands of Kansas farm boys, New York clerks, and Washington state apple pickers, Tohoku farmers, Tokyo railway station attendants, and Shikoku fishermen into the far reaches of the Pacific. Taking men, who for all intents and purposes had neither mentally nor physically travelled many miles beyond the limits of their childhood environments, the war set these same individuals down in distant places that possessed neither the luxury nor the security of their homes, and in the process provided the wedges that were to split through the hardened grains of their traditional conceptions.

To argue that men are transformed by their war experiences is hardly new or startling. War literature dating to the times of Homer has attempted to explore the experiences of men who have left their homes, and the known world of their cultures and civilizations, to do battle with enemies, and in the process have found themselves forced to reevaluate not only the enemy but themselves. The very nature of war, its confinement to "no man's land," to borrow Eric Leed's phrase, a sphere that lies outside of generally known and experienced cultural contexts, the traumatic aspects of combat, the tearing apart of established conventions and ethical patterns, have all served to affect men's conceptions of themselves and the world in which they live. In the "no man's land" of war men often find themselves forced to deal with that which lies outside, above, or below the norms to which they are accustomed. As Leed wrote of World War I, it was precisely beyond the outer boundaries of social life, caught between the known and the unknown, that combatants found themselves challenged, if not forced, to construct a new world for themselves.[3]

Dealing with the war experiences of modern armies is no simple task. Confronted in sheer numbers by literally millions of combatants who played a part in the Pacific War, the scholar who hopes to deal with the war's effect on individual attitudes is faced with a number of significant problems. While he can reach for the sampling methods of the social scientist, such sampling--or its counterpart, interviewing--at a distance of nearly four decades from the event is fraught with the danger of an inverted past in which present attitudes are imposed on earlier experiences. While such a methodology can identify changes in values and the degree to which past images have been transformed, it can tell us little about the process of change itself. In order to explore this process one has to return to the micro level, to look at individuals and personal experiences. It is at this level, as Leed has demonstrated for World War I, that one can determine what a particular war meant to a particular generation of combatants and how it transformed their conceptions of themselves and their societies.

The group that I have chosen to write about in this essay consists of Japanese and American pilots. While this is a limited sample of participants in the war, and the specific cases I have chosen to concentrate on represent a further selection from this group, I have adopted this approach largely because of the nature of the documentation available. What I propose to explore inevitably necessitates a solid body of material, and, more importantly, writings that are of some comparative value. Here the experiences of fighter pilots become particularly important.

World War II fighter pilots, like the samurai or knights of an earlier age, were not only the last of a disappearing breed of single combatants, but they tended to be better educated and more articulate than their footsoldier counterparts. Air warfare, which Gregory Boyington, one of our subjects, once observed, consists of "hours and hours of dull monotony sprinkled with a few moments of stark horror,"[4] seems to have provided not only long periods of quiet inaction--time for thought and reflection--but also moments of intense concentration, of mental and emotional stimulation that few other combatants were exposed to. Fighter pilots were beset by a compulsion to record and evaluate their experiences, which were highly transitory, extremely personal in nature, and largely unobserved by others. This produced not only a considerable body of autobiographical literature, but more importantly, because the motivation behind that literature was often as much a personal quest for self-discovery and understanding as an effort to impress the reading public, such writings proved to be particularly useful for our purposes.

What these writings tend to show is a growing consciousness on the part of individuals about themselves as well as the enemy. Writing about World War I, scholars such as Eric Leed have used the tools of cultural anthropology and psychology to conclude that modern wars incorporate elements that are strikingly similar to the rites of passage common to primitive societies. In these, individuals are deliberately forced into the unknown and unfamiliar. Only after traversing this realm, a strange and uncanny world of danger, are they ritually "brought to the other side," a symbolic end to their journey that provides them with a more profound understanding of themselves and their society, and one which primitive man associated with maturation and adulthood. Leed argues that some wars, particularly World War I, took modern man into the same uncanny world of the unfamiliar, a world of liminality, as he describes it, that lay beyond the rules of social existence. But unlike primitive rites of passage this war did not allow him to achieve a final resolution, or an "arriving on the other side." For such individuals the psychological impact of the war never came to an end. And Leed sees clear ties between this dilemma and the outbreak of World War II.

While I find such arguments provocative and share the view that war forces man beyond the known and accepted, the following study indicates that combatants in World War II could, and in many cases did, break through to a position of "transcendence," as I have termed it, from which they were able to see themselves and the enemy in a new way. This position of transcendence allowed them to "arrive on the other side," and in the process to prepare the way for the termination of both the internal and external war.

American Pilots and the War: Robert L. Scott and Gregory Boyington

It is worth noting that two of America's bestsellers to appear out of World War II were fighter pilot autobiographies that dealt with the air war over China and the Pacific: Colonel Robert L. Scott's book, *God is My Co-Pilot* and Gregory "Pappy" Boyington's *Baa Baa Black Sheep*.[5]

While Scott and Boyington were among the most widely read American pilots who recorded their experiences of the war, they were certainly not the only Americans to do so. Claire L. Chennault's *Way of a Fighter* and various accounts by David McCampbell, Cecil E. Harris, and Joseph J. Foss, who ranked among America's leading aces in the war, also helped to shed light on the American pilot's response to the war and the Japanese. While the following concentrates on Scott and Boyington, I have tried to explore their experiences against the backdrop of their fellow pilots.

Robert L. Scott, Jr. was born in Georgia in 1908. Hardly past the age of ten he catapulted himself from the roof a colonial mansion in Macon in a homemade glider--his first lesson in flight which quickly terminated in a rose bush below. At thirteen he made his first solo flight in a surplus World War I Jenny he had bought and assembled with the help of a friend.[6]

Scott's interest in military flying led him to West Point from which he graduated in 1932. While his autobiography reveals no concern for the outside world, let alone Japan, in the section devoted to his youth, there was one incident at West Point which gives us some insight into his attitudes towards the Japanese. As part of the normal course on military history all cadets were required to write on the strategy used in one of the world's great battles. Scott, whose class standing was not high, was ordered to write on a battle in the Russo-Japanese War. Regarding the war and battle as of no consequence, Scott created an entirely fictitious battle with an elaborate battle plan.[7]

Scott's fabricated battle nearly resulted in his expulsion from West Point in 1930. And yet the reasons for this were not so much his refusal to take a major Japanese victory seriously--the review board was willing to share his light hearted, flippant approach to the Japanese--but because he had tied his paper in a broad red ribbon, and when asked the reason readily answered that it stood for military red tape.[8]

In 1939 Scott was assigned as Assistant District Supervisor to the Army Air Corps' West Coast Training Center. Here he was in charge of selecting future pilots. By this point, as he viewed it, war with Japan seemed imminent and he "tried to 'figure out' every cadet" who came to him to see if he had "the urge for combat."[9]

As we shall see Scott's urge for combat involved a certain blood lust which needs to be explored in greater detail. What is of interest here is that by the late 1930s Scott's earlier flippant and amused treatment of the Japanese--a refusal to take them seriously or to treat them as equals--had been further transformed into seeing them as "enemies." Unfortunately Scott's new position does not appear to have involved any greater effort to understand the Japanese, even as "enemies." In the back of Scott's mind remained the simple notion that American boys with the proper urge for combat would easily dispense with the new Japanese enemy.

Such sentiments were hardly unique to Scott. John Goette, one of the rare American war correspondents who actually flew with the Japanese Army in China in the late 1930s, reflected similar sentiments. Goette saw Japanese pilots as humorless, grim, and unsmiling men. He pictured them as "mechanically skillful" but lacking in imagination. Initially he was convinced that Soviet pilots (flying for the Chinese) "would fly rings around the Japanese," because as Westerners they had the imagination the Japanese lacked. But when the Japanese shot down many of the Russians, he quickly attributed Japanese successes to the fact that Russian pilots were "mercenaries" who did not "have their hearts in the business." Americans, Goette insisted, would be different. As he wrote, "the Japanese air arm would be no match for our own." Once again it was the "imagination and quick thinking" which would tip the scales in America's favor. "I never saw Japanese pilots stunting over China," he added, "there was none of the effervescent trick flying such as I associated with Americans in the air...."[10]

The unwillingness to see the world clearly, the naivete and ignorance which many Americans shared with Scott and Goette, extended itself into the field of their expertise--airpower. Scott demonstrated this only too clearly in the initial hours following the Japanese attack on Pearl Harbor. Hearing of the attack he instinctively rushed back to his base, "expecting any minute to be told to jump in a P-38 or a P-40 and to go up to protect Los Angeles."[11]

But to protect Los Angeles from what? From a Japanese fleet that had seriously overextended itself in reaching the mid-Pacific? From Japanese planes that could not range more than five hundred miles from that fleet? In fact, the West Coast panic, of which Scott's response was a part, demonstrated only too precisely the degree to which irrational images penetrated far beyond the realm of hard logistical reality. Fear and bravado were different faces of the same coin. Unwilling to treat the Japanese as part of a known, and knowable, human community, Americans such as Scott inevitably found themselves in a dual dilemma. On the one hand, they gained satisfaction in reducing the Japanese to subhuman, "monkey," or "animal" status--terms Scott frequently used--and on the other, they were forced to admit that these same "monkey-men" were capable of superhuman feats such as the attack on Pearl Harbor. Unprepared to be limited by the rules of reason in the first instance, men such as Scott were no more willing to submit to the voice of logic in the latter. In the curious image world of Americans such as Scott, subhumans quite readily became capable of superhuman feats. The mirror image of the inferior and unknowable became the demonic.

Unlike Scott, Gregory Boyington does not dwell on his family background and early experiences in his autobiography. Other than telling us that he was raised on an "apple ranch" near Okanogan, Washington, Boyington does not discuss his upbringing and early education before becoming a Marine Corps pilot. In fact, besides the observations that he was constantly in debt, and that he was a "whiz at a cocktail party"--a problem with alcoholism that constituted an ongoing struggle--we know little about his life before his recruitment to fly for the American Volunteer Group which Claire Chennault had organized in China.[12]

Boyington's motivation for going to China in the summer of 1941 was less Scott's "urge for combat" than a need to bail out his financial indiscretions. To one in need of cash the Army Air Corps recruiter's promise of $675 a month plus a $500 bonus for every Japanese plane shot down seemed particularly appealing. Moreover, as he recalled, the recruiter was quick to reinforce his preconceptions. "The Japs are flying antiquated junk over China," he added reassuringly, "many of your kills will be unarmed transports."[13] The recruiter's final line incorporated the epitome of American prejudices about Japanese flyers: "I suppose you know," he added, "that the Japanese are renowned for their inability to fly. And they all wear corrective glasses."[14]

If Scott knew little about Asia and the Japanese, Boyington was not far behind. As he freely admitted, "I didn't know anything about the Orient ... and I didn't believe that the United States would ever be at war."[15] Indeed, he described the curious nonchalance with which he and his fellow pilots headed into the Pacific with "golf sticks, tennis rackets, and dress clothes" in their footlockers.[16]

Sailing to Southeast Asia on a Dutch ship, Boyington received his first inkling that things might not turn out as anticipated. Travelling with him was another pilot, Bob Heising, who questioned the low pay the Chinese were offering, given the fact that the Dutch were paying pilots $2000 a month. When Boyington mentioned "easy bonuses," Heising concluded that he must have "rocks in his head."[17] "All Japs don't wear thick glasses, if any glasses at all," Heising told him, "hell, they wear clear goggles, the same as you do, dope."[18] "Right then," Boyington tells us, "I commenced dividing my financial future by denominators of various sizes."[19]

While Scott was about to go up to protect Los Angeles from an imagined Japanese attack, Boyington found himself in Rangoon, Burma, confronted with the very real Japanese push into Southeast Asia. It was here, flying out of Mingaladon Field for the American Volunteer Group, the "Flying Tigers," that he encountered his first combat with the Japanese. Like other American pilots he found these initial encounters highly instructive. Moreover, unlike many of his American counterparts, he was lucky enough to survive.

Boyington's initial battle involved a tangle with forty to fifty Japanese I-97s, a highly maneuverable fixed gear airplane. It seemed odd to him that the American group was constantly climbing "into the sun," and from a position that put them directly under the Japanese planes. He hoped the squadron leader knew what he was doing, but later discovered that this "was also his first fight."[20]

Boyington's concerns were soon interrupted by the waiting Japanese who turned into a half roll on their backs and started down for the Americans. As he remembered it he saw a P-40 above him writhing in agony just like a fish out of water as Japanese tracers were everywhere. Like the rest who survived he decided that the only thing to do was to dive away. No Japanese plane could catch a P-40 breaking away in a dive.

But the battle was far from over. Embarrassed by his first response Boyington decided to rejoin the action. Soon he spotted two Japanese planes to one side which he thought represented better odds and started to stalk them. The pair lured him into a trap which required all his flying skill to escape. After trying every flying trick he knew, he seemed always to be "looking back down someone's gun barrels" with tracers closing in around him. Boyington's blunt response was, "'Frig this racket,' I thought, and dove away."[21]

And yet, like many American pilots (as Sakai Saburo, one of our Japanese subjects, observed), Boyington was blessed with persistence.

Forced to dive away a second time he was still not ready to give in. Realizing that the close formation tactics he had been taught were worthless, he decided to try once again, this time alone. Making a much faster pass from a thousand feet above he approached one of the Japanese fighters. The Japanese plane allowed him to get close enough to where his tracers were sailing about the enemy plane. "Then," Boyington wrote, "I witnessed this little plane perform one of the most delightful split S's I have ever seen, and then I discovered that I was turning again with some of his playmates."[22] In frustration Boyington recorded: "Who the hell said: 'These little bastards can't fly'? To hell with this routine! I thought, and dove out. Bonus money of the fantastic variety fluttered to the ground like so many handbills, and with them the last of my illusions."[23]

With his illusions shattered, Boyington was prepared to face what he called a "grim picture." In Singapore the Brewster fighters had been rapidly wiped out by the Japanese. Even the famous Spitfire was no competition for the Japanese Zero. Suddenly, he noted, "I knew only too well that this was going to be a struggle for survival--not for money."[24]

By the early months of 1942, as Boyington faced the "grim picture" of Japan's relentless push into Southeast Asia, Scott's urge for combat was pulling him toward the Far East as well. Volunteering to fly twelve B-17 bombers to Asia by way of South America and Africa, he headed for what he thought would be a bombing run on Japan from China. Having reached the Assam, Burma, China theater on his "road to Tokyo," Scott was distinctly aware that he had left his own known world behind. Also left behind, although not as quickly, were numerous naive preconceptions that he shared with the highest military planners. From the steaming jungle airfields of Burma and the dusty airstrips of West China the vastness of Asia was to do irreparable damage to the simple notion that a dozen American bombers would promptly knock Japan out of the war. Moreover, soon trading his bomber, and later a Burma to China transport, for a fighter--the lone escort plane for a group of transports--his urge for combat was about to get its first realistic testing. On the verge of putting his life on the line, he was still not prepared to take the Japanese seriously. Indeed, while Goette recorded that American officers in the Pacific now presented Japanese pilots as "capable and dangerous,"[25] and insisted that there was absolutely no basis for American scorn of Japanese airmen, Scott retained his earlier views. It was only later that he realized how lucky he had been. For many another American pilot in the early days of the war macho over-confidence and an unwillingness to accept Japanese equipment and manpower as equal to that of the Americans--when both were often superior to those of the Americans--led to instant unmarked graves at the end of flaming smoke trails.

Scott, who was convinced that he had "a date with destiny" which he saw as sliding in behind one of the enemy bombers or fighters that was driving Stilwell out of Burma and "shoot it down," was later only too thankful that the "Great Flying Boss in the Sky" had not yet decided to put him to the test. "Lord! the ego that I possessed!" he exclaimed in a flash of rare introspection, "I honestly believe I thought I could shoot down any number of Japs with my single fighter."[26]

As the months of 1942 passed, and he survived his first direct encounter with the Japanese, Scott's images of the Japanese as incompetent flyers, and of their equipment as technologically inferior, came under increasing pressures. No doubt he felt much like George Paxton, who had gotten him his first flight with the American Volunteer Group, and to whom he ascribed the following incident. Paxton had been fighting with a group of Zeroes over Mingaladon. His plane had been literally shot to pieces, and there were huge holes in the tail, wings and fuselage. In the end Paxton had been forced to crash land his plane on the field without the aid of his landing gear. Those racing out to the plane expected to find little more than a body. "Instead," Scott tells us, "they found George Paxton standing by the side of his ship ... the instrument panel was just about shot away, the rudder pedals were partly shot to pieces, the armor of the pilot's seat was badly bent--but Paxton was out there yelling: 'I still say those little bastards can't shoot'!"[27]

One need hardly belabor the logic of Paxton's statement. What it clearly contained was the anger and frustration of an unwilling admission. "Those little bastards" *could* fly and shoot. Moreover, they could fly and shoot as well as Scott and Paxton. The pain of that admission was in every way as intense as that instilled by the doctor who had to spend the afternoon extracting rivets from Paxton's back where they had been imbedded by exploding Japanese shells. Scott was soon destined for a similar encounter.

Forced out of the necessity of survival to regard the Japanese as equals, Scott had reached the point at which other air combatants often made a significant breakthrough in their conceptions of themselves and the enemy. In a world of equals victory often hung by a thread. Position, timing, visibility--all these heavily influenced the odds that determined success or failure. In the process luck or fate could influence the outcome of a battle as much as skill. Pilots on both sides who daily confronted this reality often developed a philosophical perspective on themselves and their opponents. In doing this they came to see themselves as part of a general human dilemma and not only in the throes of a national confrontation. By transcending the particular and national they were able to see each other not merely as opponents and enemies, but as human beings, whose skills, fortunes and tragedies could be mutually comprehended and were often determined by forces beyond their control. For such individuals, as we shall see in the case of Boyington, Sakai, and Kuroe, war, which had begun in defense of the particular, led to a new comprehension of the universal.

Scott, too, found himself under circumstances which had caused other pilots to grasp the subjective and objective qualities of their acts, and in the process to come to grips with the fact that the fate of another pilot might very well be their own. His first experience of this kind took place in the skies over southern China:

> At Nanchang, on August 11, 1942, I shot down my fourth enemy plane that was confirmed. Though I hate the Japs with a passion, I felt sorry for that pilot, for he never saw me at all. But as I left his burning ship north of the runway he had taken off from, I thought of the boys in the Philippines and Java, and I wasn't so sorry.[28]

On the edge of a deeper understanding, Scott decided to back off in favor of the simple explanation that he was righting the score for other American victims. But as the passage suggests, Scott was not totally comfortable with his explanation. His initial, and more genuinely human, response of feeling sorry was almost instantly vitiated by the rationalization of revenge. The situation in which Scott found himself was a complex one. Forced to accept the Japanese as equals, his previously distorted sense of superiority could easily turn to fear. And yet, fear undermined the "urge for combat" with which his identity had been so closely associated, and which he regarded as the most important trait in the younger pilots he had trained for service in the war.

In Scott's case the "urge for combat" was in many instances only one step removed from a love of killing. That this peculiarity inhibited the type of existential breakthrough experienced by other pilots is a distinct possibility. A persistent volunteer for punitive expeditions--strafing and bombing missions--Scott liked to have the odds clearly in his favor. While in Burma he enjoyed strafing everything in sight. On one occasion he even tried to unload his guns into the top of Mt. Everest.[29]

It was around this time that Scott decided to call his plane "Old Exterminator." As he wrote, "as I listened to the roar of the Allison engine and patted the gun-sight affectionately, 'Old Exterminator' was more than ever a character to me--it was an institution. I knew right then that the ship was almost a human being." And clearly it was, in the sense that Scott's plane became an extension of his personality. That the poor figures running from the pagoda might not have been the enemy, but harmless Buddhist priests; that the men he enjoyed strafing in the water desperately trying to flee from the barges he was shooting up might be hapless Burmese workers impressed into service by the Japanese; that on another occasion, when he shot up the Peninsula Hotel in Hong Kong, the victims that he strafed who were trying to hurry down the fire escapes were not all Japanese officers but many of the same Chinese for whom America and the American Volunteer Group was fighting, never seems to have entered his consciousness. Moreover, if as a result there was blood on his hands, as there increasingly was, any qualms of conscience were quickly dispensed with. As Scott wrote, "I never knew a pilot who thought about it."[30]

And yet, despite his denials one senses that Scott thought more about the Japanese than he cared to reveal. Unable to deal with his fears directly--a result of his unwillingness to admit openly what his war experiences had forced him to accept, i.e., Japanese equality--Scott found his only alternative in constantly bolstering his ego by denigrating the Japanese. No longer simply "monkey-men," who were basically imitative and inferior to Westerners, the Japanese were now pictured as a "race of fanatics, who had been repressed for so long in their warped minds that they were barbaric madmen."[31] Such fanatics were not just out to defeat Americans, they were out to "EXTERMINATE" them.[32] In the end the Japanese were no longer seen as part of the human sphere at all, but as dangerous animals.[33] The function of "Old Exterminator" was clearly to exterminate them first!

To counter his own fear Scott felt compelled to dwell on that of the Japanese. "Don't think they're supermen," he told the young flyers of his group, "for I assure you they're not. They're little, warped brained savage animals ... they have fear ... their fear is worse, for there's that phobia of having nothing to live for--the inferiority complex they try to overcome."[34]

Scott's approach differed considerably from that of John W. Mitchell whose group of pilots later shot down Admiral Yamamoto Isoroku's plane over Bougainville, but whose morale was initially affected by survivors of a squadron that had been mauled by Japanese carrier pilots in the Solomons and spread stories of "enemy supermen in super-planes." Mitchell countered the tales of Japanese invincibility not by denigrating the Japanese, but by building his men up, telling them: "you're hot and getting hotter. You can handle anything that flies, if you stick to our team work. You're great pilots, and don't forget it."³⁵

Indeed, in reading Scott carefully one soon discovers a hollow ring to his mounting efforts. The extreme pressures under which he found himself were illustrated by an incident that he saw as confirming Japanese fear, but which may well tell us more about Scott than his opponent. Scott had been flying over Southwest China when he encountered a lone Japanese pilot flying an I-97. He was able to move in close to the plane and at a hundred yards to put a burst of machinegun fire into it at the usually fatal spot where the wing joined the fuselage. As he swerved out from behind the plane he expected it to stream fire and perhaps explode. But when it did not burn, he went back to take another look. For the first time he confronted another pilot directly:

> I saw into the cockpit. The canopy had been shot away and I could see the Jap's face--and on it was a look of terror such as I had never seen before.... Then I savagely held a long burst from less than fifty yards while I shot the ship to pieces. Even after the enemy plane had fallen and I had flown through the debris, I found that I was continuing to fire at the empty heavens, for I had learned to hate also.³⁶

One may well question whether the real issue in the above passage was the fear of the Japanese pilot. It seems more convincing to argue that what we have here is one direction in which image transformation could move. Scott was unable or unwilling to break through to a position of transcendence, in which the realistic evaluation of the enemy required for combat survival corresponds to a similar destruction of stereotypical images. We may have instead a situation where an unwilling, but forced, realistic evaluation of the enemy is countered by a desperate effort to deny such an admission by the creation of an extended realm of reinforced images in which one's failing sense of security can be maintained. In such a world one is literally firing at the empty heavens, not in order to bring down the enemy, but to assure oneself.

A comparison of Scott's encounter with that of Sakai Saburo and an American pilot over Guadalcanal on 8 August 1942 is revealing in that it shows decidedly different possibilities.

In the mad melee in the skies over Guadalcanal, where half of Mitchell's "hot" pilots were to be killed, Sakai observed an American Wildcat chasing three Zeroes. Never had he seen an enemy plane move so quickly and so gracefully. Moreover, the American pilot was using his own favorite tactic of coming up from below to stalk him. In the intense battle that followed neither pilot could gain the advantage. Sakai who had already shot down more than fifty American planes felt he had met his match. "There was a terrific man behind that stick," he admitted to himself. But the American pilot finally made a fatal error. Taking his Wildcat into a series of loops, Sakai was able to use his Zero's superior maneuverability to close the distance between the two planes. At fifty yards he pumped 200 rounds into the Grumman's cockpit, "watching the bullets chewing up the thin metal skin and shattering the glass." And yet the American fighter would not go down. He could not believe what he saw. "The Wildcat continued flying almost as if nothing had happened ... I could not understand it ... the entire situation was unbelievable." Sakai dropped his speed until both planes were flying next to each other in wing-to-wing formation. He opened his cockpit and stared out:

> The Wildcat's cockpit canopy was already back, and I could see the pilot clearly. He was a big man, with a round face. He wore a light khaki uniform. He appeared to be middle-aged, not as young as I had expected.

For several seconds Sakai flew alongside the American pilot in this "bizarre formation" with their eyes "meeting across the narrow space between the two planes."

> The Wildcat was a shambles. Bullet holes had cut the fuselage and wings up from one end to the other. The skin of the rudder was gone, and the metal ribs stuck out like a skeleton ... [I also realized] why the pilot had not fired. Blood stained his right shoulder, and I saw the dark patch moving downward over his chest.

Badly wounded, flying a crippled plane, the American pilot was a sitting duck. And yet something within Sakai rebelled against killing this brave man:

> But this was no way to kill a man! Not with him flying helplessly, wounded, his plane a wreck. I raised my left hand and shook my fist at him, shouting, uselessly, I knew, for him to fight instead of just flying along like a clay pigeon. The American looked startled; he raised his right hand weakly and waved.

The wounded man's efforts proved even more disconcerting:

> I had never felt so strange before. I had killed many Americans in the air, but this was the first time a man had weakened in such a fashion directly before my eyes, and from wounds I had inflicted upon him. I honestly didn't know whether or not I should try to finish him off. Such thoughts were stupid, of course. Wounded or not, he was an enemy, and he had almost taken three of my own men a few minutes before. However, there was no reason to aim for the pilot again. I wanted the airplane, not the man.

A few seconds later Sakai poured a short cannon burst into the Wildcat's engine. The plane streamed fire and the wounded pilot managed to bail out. Sakai last saw him drifting towards the Guadalcanal beaches.[37]

As we shall see, Sakai Saburo's encounter with this American pilot over Guadalcanal was part of the process through which his own views of the enemy were being transformed. It is worth noting that despite the anonymity of air combat a surprisingly large number of pilots recalled such experiences. What is of further interest is the fact that these experiences bear a marked similarity to those of World War I ground troops, who were also rarely in direct contact with each other and about whom Eric Leed has written:

> To encounter, face to face, that which had been made strange by propaganda and countless frustrated attacks, and to realize they were "like us" was an uncanny experience. It revealed to many what they had forgotten [or in the case of the Pacific War what they had perhaps never accepted]-- the intrinsic similarity of men. The penetration of the wall that separated the known from the unknown provoked a shudder of recognition in the few who accomplished it.[38]

Moreover, it was precisely this shudder of recognition, this transcendence of the "accepted" and "known," on the part of Japanese and American pilots that forced them to reconsider their views of each other and the war.

The process can be followed more precisely in the case of Gregory Boyington. Unlike Scott, Boyington's destroyed illusions did not result in a need to exaggerate stereotypical images as a means of bolstering his "urge for combat." Quite the opposite, Boyington was to move gradually towards a more transcendent position. While Scott was reiterating the "need to hate," and attempted to juxtapose "good Chinese" with "evil Japanese," Boyington was soon to conclude there was "no such thing as bad people."[39]

While Boyington's business was also "killing Japs," and he once described his war years as "sitting behind a single engine killing people," he rejected the blood lust that one finds in Scott.[40] In fact, by the end of 1943 and the early months of 1944, as Boyington left China for the United States and a new tour of duty as a Marine pilot in the mid-Pacific, battle experiences were to transform his attitudes.

Combat flying, as Boyington was well aware, tended to be a highly impersonal experience. Machines, rather than men, encountered one another in the skies above Espiritu Santo, Guadalcanal, and Rabaul. Action was often a matter of seconds. One engagement, during which he shot down three Japanese fighters, and which struck him as "lengthy," was timed by a fellow pilot at a total of thirty seconds. Occasionally, as we have seen in Scott and Sakai's cases, the human reality of war could tear its way through the protective metal facade. Boyington, too, was confronted with experiences of this type. One he described as follows:

> On this occasion I had sent a burst into this little fellow. He had an open-cockpit fighter. The plane didn't burst into flames, and it didn't fall apart, but was definitely going down, out of control. As I flew right beside him, I could see his arm dangling out of the cockpit, flapping in the slipstream like the arm of a rag doll, and I knew definitely he was dead. For no other reason, or maybe because we were supposed to bring a claim back in our teeth to get credit, I sent another long burst into his ship and literally tore it up. That was the only time I ever felt squeamish about the entire affair.[41]

The response of Boyington and Scott to comparable circumstances is worth noting. While it is clear that Boyington was strongly affected by the experience, he did not counter his "squeamishness" by an effort to ascribe fear to his Japanese opponent. Killing was a reality of war; it was also a reality of survival, but for Boyington it was not an end in itself. Indeed, as Boyington pushed through to a broader perspective on himself and the enemy other attitudes changed as well. Revenge, which remained a dominating motive for Scott and other American pilots such as Alexander Vraciu, who vowed to shoot down ten Japanese planes for the death of a friend,[42] soon provided little more than empty victories for Boyington. Arriving too late to aid a fellow Marine pilot whose plane plowed into the Pacific near the Shortland Islands with a Zero on its tail, Boyington went after the enemy pilot. "Revenge is truly a hollow quantity," he remembered himself thinking, as he "sent the Zero into the drink" not far from his American victim.[43]

Occasionally, as on Christmas Day, 1943, Boyington could not avoid pondering the paradoxical qualities of war. As he wrote:

> and on Christmas, the peace-on-earth-good-will-to-all-men day, I went around the skies slaughtering people. Don't ask me why it had to be on a Christmas Day, for he who can answer such a question can also answer why there have to be wars, and who starts them, and why men in machines kill other men in machines. I had not started this war, and if it were possible to write a different sort of Christmas Story I would prefer to record it, or at least to have had it occur on a different day.[44]

Boyington's Christmas Day present was four Japanese planes. But in his description of the day one senses a growing pathos--a willingness to see what was happening from the other side. This was particularly true as the day's battle progressed.

The first Japanese fighter he encountered was not even aware of his presence. "The little Nip," Boyington wrote, "was a doomed man even before I fired. I knew it and could feel it, and it was I who condemned him from ever reaching home--and it was Christmas."[45] The next two fared little better. The first of what was a pair of Zeroes quickly flamed. Boyington remembered the scene only too distinctly:

> from a new position I watched the pilot from the burning plane drift slowly down to the water, the same as the other had done. This time his flying mate slowly circled him as he descended, possibly as a needless protection.
>
> I remember the whole picture with a harsh distinction--and on Christmas--one Japanese pilot descending while his pal kept circling him. And then, after the pilot landed in the water, I went after the circling pal. I closed in on him from the sun side and nailed him about a hundred feet over the water.[46]

The human pathos of one man trying to protect a friend and in the process losing his own life, the universality or, as some might argue, the humanity of such an act which transcended national and racial boundaries was not lost upon Boyington. The consciousness that your own luck might soon run out and that you had "finally gotten it," as Boyington was to concede in his own flaming plane a few days later,[47] tended to create a sense of dimension which, while it did not relieve the fact that both sides were in the air to eliminate each other, created the basis for a subtle bond of respect between combatants. Trapped in the inevitability of the war process which was governed by the dictum "kill or be killed," Boyington still found himself voicing an inner protest that this was a "hell of a thing for one guy to do to another guy on Christmas."[48]

A few days later, after shooting down two more Japanese planes and breaking Eddie Rickenbacker's World War I record, Boyington found himself on the other end of his Christmas Day experiences. Trying to protect his crippled wingmate, he left himself open to a group of pursuing Zeroes. A hundred feet above the ocean his gas tank blew up, and in the split second between the explosion and the time his plane plowed into the water he managed--miraculously--to bail out. A few hours later, drifting in the Pacific with multiple wounds, he was taken captive aboard a Japanese submarine.

Life as a prisoner was to continue the process of image transformation that had begun in the air. Gradually, Boyington noted, his opinions of the Japanese people "gathered from propaganda, stories, and my own imagination" began to change.[49] Making his way across the Pacific towards a Japanese prisoner of war camp he ran into a series of Japanese who were willing to take risks on his behalf. One was the interpreter to whom he was assigned and who constantly attempted to shield his prisoners. On Saipan he met a warrant officer and his wife who provided him with his "first civilized meal" since being taken prisoner. Telling him that the "majority of Japanese are ashamed of the way you are being treated," he urged Boyington to "have faith," and assured him that the war would soon be over and "we shall all be friends again."[50] On Iwo Jima the Japanese guards generously shared their food and cigarettes with the prisoners, and it was only after arriving in Japan that Boyington and the others realized what true generosity such acts entailed.

At the Ofuna prisoner of war camp Boyington ran into "Auntie," a little old lady who worked in the camp's kitchen, "didn't know a word of English," and had "never been outside of Japan."[51] Auntie helped him to survive in a multiplicity of ways. "To Auntie," he wrote, "I was just a starving boy. The fact that I was from America ... had nothing to do with it." Moreover, Auntie's kindnesses were matched by those of a young college trained guard who refused to beat the American prisoners, and who was in turn beaten by his fellow guards. "It was a strange thing," Boyington wrote, "that when I used to talk with him I never thought of him as a Jap, as I thought of the other guards. He was one of the sweetest and nicest fellows I ever have known."[52] Finally there was Mr. Kono, who Boyington described as "one of the greatest men I ever met." Kono had been a wealthy importer, who had offered his services as an interpreter for the prison authorities. A Christian, he despaired at the brutality of his fellow Japanese and at the same time completely understood the suffering of the prisoners. "But my admiration," Boyington wrote,

> came not from the way he felt, especially, but from the manner in which he handled himself with no outward fear of consequences--not even death.... This man's courage in saving lives and preventing hardship will apparently go unrewarded in the ordinary sense--like medals from either Japan or the United States. But I can assure you that he will stay in the hearts of many men--for here was a far braver man than I.[53]

The interpreter, the warrant officer on Saipan, "Auntie," the young college-trained guard, and Mr. Kono were all individuals who helped Boyington to break through his preconceptions and allowed him to see the Japanese as individuals who shared the bonds of a common humanity. The process which had begun in the air above China and the South Pacific had come to completion in Japan. Moreover it is worth noting that the very process in which he was personally involved was one he observed at work among the Japanese. This was true even of the guards:

> Contrary to what people would think, the guards who gave us the most trouble on the whole were the young ones who never had left the mainland. Those who had been out to different parts of the world and had seen action, and even some of those who had been terribly wounded, seemed to be of much better nature than the young ones who had stayed in Japan. These were the fellows who administered most of the beatings.[54]

Boyington, too, was now prepared to deal with the Japanese in a more objective manner. "The years have taught me something I should have known in the beginning," he wrote, "never to generalize authoritatively about races or peoples." For Boyington the idea that "all Japanese are..." no more applied than "all Frenchmen are...," or "all Englishmen are...." "Whenever people ask me about the Japanese," he wrote, "I rather suppose I am expected to hate them ... but we can find right here in the United States, almost in any city block ... people who at heart are as primitive and brutal and as stupid as those [Japanese] guards with their baseball bats."[55]

In his final resolution Boyington had come to see the Japanese as no different from Americans in their basic human qualities and human potential. On both sides there were good and evil men, on both sides there were individuals who enjoyed killing or inflicting pain, on both sides there were men who were willing to sacrifice themselves in an effort to save their brothers, and on both sides there were those who were willing to sacrifice themselves to save the enemy. Having broken through to a position of transcendence Boyington found himself past the barriers of stereotypical images and ill founded preconceptions. In the process he had discovered not only his own humanity, but that of the Japanese. His final understanding was perhaps best summed up by a paragraph in his autobiography in which he wrote:

> As the years go on, we are going to learn more and more from the Japanese, the same as they are going to learn from us--and want to learn from us. With the bars of hate and suspicion no longer existing we can regard ourselves not as nations but as people.[56]

Japanese Pilots and War: Sakai Saburo and Kuroe Yasuhiko

The writings of Robert Scott and Gregory Boyington have allowed us to explore the effects of combat on the transformation and expansion of images that American pilots brought with them into the Pacific War. As the foregoing suggests, the war forced American pilots into the "no man's land" of combat, an environment that pressured them to reevaluate the enemy as well as themselves. The writings of Sakai Saburo, Kuroe Yasuhiko, and fellow Japanese pilots will help us to examine the way in which this process could work among the Japanese.

Like Scott and Boyington, Sakai and Kuroe wrote extensive autobiographies. Sakai's book, *Samurai*, made its debut in English in 1958. The Japanese edition, titled *Ozora no samurai* (*Samurai of the Sky*), was not published until 1967. Kuroe's autobiography, *Aa hayabusa sento tai: kaerazaru gekitsui-o* (*Alas! The Hayabusa Squadron: An Ace Who Never Returned*), was published posthumously in 1969.[57] In addition to the writings of Sakai and Kuroe there are a number of Japanese pilot accounts that have been published since the late 1960s.[58] As in the case of Scott and Boyington, I have tried to explore the experiences of Sakai and Kuroe from within the context of their fellow pilots' writings.

Sakai Saburo was born in Saga on the island of Kyushu in 1916. The product of an impoverished farm family that claimed samurai descent, he experienced a turbulent childhood. An early adoption into the home of a Tokyo uncle, and a brief period of study at Aoyama gakuin, a Methodist preparatory school, ended in failure and disgrace. Sent home, he enlisted in the Japanese navy in 1933, where he started as a seaman recruit, but soon advanced through study and hard work. In 1935 Sakai was given the "great honor" of being admitted to the Navy's elite flying school at Tsuchiura. After two years of rigorous training that reduced his original class of seventy to twenty-five, Sakai graduated in 1937 with the distinction of being awarded the "Emperor's silver watch" as the outstanding student pilot of his class.

The year that Sakai graduated from Tsuchiura was also the year that Japan went to war with China. As a result, he was soon introduced to combat flying over the continent. By the time the Pacific War broke out he had chalked up over four years of combat experience, indeed, his years as a pilot in China and in the early days of the Pacific War, flying out of Lae and Rabaul, turned Sakai into something of a living legend in wartime Japan. The story of his effort to bring back his crippled Zero from Guadalcanal to Rabaul in August 1942, paralyzed on the left side, blinded permanently in the right eye, and filled with shrapnel, remains one of the great air epics of the Pacific War. That Sakai was able to return to flying with only one eye, an unbelievable feat for a fighter pilot, and that he was not only able to survive, but actually shot down four more American planes in the final days of the war--bringing his combat victories to sixty-four--bears tribute not only to his greatness as a pilot, but to a deep inner strength and determination.

Trained as professional soldiers, Sakai and Kuroe revealed little if any initial consciousness of the outside world. In their accounts of their early years one finds few impressions of Americans, Chinese, or even Russians. Other than the fact that Sakai briefly attended a school established by missionaries, we see virtually no contacts, or concerns, with foreigners. Sakai regarded himself as a professional warrior, a modern "samurai," whose duty was to fight the enemies of his country. "In the Imperial Japanese Navy," he wrote, "I learned only one trade--how to man a fighter plane and how to kill enemies of my country."[59] In this view he was joined by Kuroe and other Japanese pilots. For the Japanese pilot, doing one's duty appears to have superseded the need to reduce one's opponents to stereotypical formulas. If Japanese pilots such as Sakai and Kuroe possessed images of the enemy, they tended to see their opponents in coldly abstract and mechanical terms. For Sakai and Kuroe the term *teki*, or enemy, first denoted the Chinese (and in a few cases Russians) against whom they flew in China and Manchuria in the late thirties, and later the American and Allied pilots they encountered in the South Pacific and Southeast Asia. In the majority of cases opponents were reduced to impersonal machines, technically respectable, but not part of the known human continuum.

Sakai and Kuroe's initial combat experiences took place in China and Manchuria. In these Sakai, like Scott, was only too happy that the "Great Flying Boss of the Sky" was on his side. In his first sortie, Sakai recalled, "two sleek enemy fighters raced in against my plane." They were Russian-made E-16s and Sakai froze. Failing to charge his guns, and unable to act, he was suddenly in deadly peril. As he observed, he should have met his end at this point, but suddenly the Russian planes moved away. Sakai saw this as "miraculous," but the reason had little to do with miracles. Worried about their inexperienced pilot Sakai's wingmates had flown cover for him and one of them was in the process of attacking the Russian fighters when they turned away. Sakai was soon to rectify his errors, and subsequently shot down one of the enemy planes. But back on the ground he was assured by his commanding officer that he was a "damned fool," and that he was lucky to be alive. Not exactly an auspicious beginning for one of Japan's greatest pilots of the Pacific War.[60]

On the other hand, Sakai possessed an unusual ability to see himself and air combat directly without the need to conceal its tensions in a false buildup or denigration of the enemy. "To me," he wrote, "a dogfight has always been a difficult, grueling task, with almost unbearable tension. Even after my first combats were behind me and I had several enemy planes to my credit, I never emerged from the wild aerial melee without being soaked in perspiration. There was always the chance of committing that one slight error which meant flaming death."[61]

Sakai's seriousness contrasted distinctly with the nonchalance with which Kuroe went to war in China. In fact, Kuroe's feelings remind us a little of Scott's initial "valor of ignorance." As Kuroe wrote he "headed into the blue skies over China without anxiety, untroubled by ill omens, and unobstructed." He "ate well, drank well, and slept well," and in his heart he could "hear the song of victory."[62] In describing his initial battles he often used sporting terms. "The feeling that overcame me," he wrote in recording his encounter with a Russian plane at Nomonhan, "was not unlike that of a hunter who has caught sight of the pheasant he has been stalking and is about to raise his gun to bring it down."[63]

But the "song of victory," like Scott's "valor of ignorance," was soon to sound distinctly hollow. As many of his friends were shot down by the Russians, the once rosy optimism with which he had soared into the tempting skies over Manchuria turned to anxiety. The sky now became a "terribly dangerous bridge that had to be crossed daily."[64]

Kuroe's experiences further illustrated the peculiar tensions to which Japanese pilots were subject as a result of the close personal obligation structure of the Japanese social system. As members of the group were killed, those left behind often felt a heavy burden of responsibility for the death of their compatriots. The guilt (or in the Japanese case shame) of survivorship, which was not restricted to Japanese combatants, nevertheless posed particular problems for Japanese flyers. In some instances such a sense of responsibility could become self destructive. Kuroe writes poignantly about a fellow pilot who noted in his diary that he felt deeply "ashamed" to be left alive when all his senior officers had been killed. "It is a shame, it is a shame," he wrote again and again. The diary ended with the entry: "This shame can be rectified only by death."[65] The same day its author flew out on a mission and never returned.

Kuroe felt similar pangs when he lost most of his group over Burma some years later. Conscious that his two wingmates had heroically given their lives to save his, he was filled with remorse. "Now I was in the sky all by myself," he wrote, and "a heartwrenching desolation overcame me." "Tear after tear ran down my cheeks. Making no effort to stop the flood of tears I finally grasped firmly onto the instrument panel and issuing a loud cry wept bitterly."[66]

By this time Kuroe's war experiences had come to transform the once happy-go-lucky flyer into a far more contemplative and philosophical individual who was well on his way to a position of transcendence that lay beyond the boundaries of his known world. At the same time, Kuroe, Sakai, and other Japanese pilots often sensed a fundamental contradiction between the experiences of aerial combat and the nature of the Japanese social system and value structure. What survival in the air required was neither the automaton mentality that the Japanese Army and Navy tried to instill in their recruits, nor the group mentality and particularistic relationships that were common to Japanese society.

Aerial warfare required a high degree of independent action, of self reliance, and the ability to make personal, split-second decisions. Flying created a fraternity of equals. Hierarchy, if it existed at all in such a world, existed on the basis of ability or talent, and not on the basis of birth, age, schooling, or social position. The very nature of flying, therefore, pushed Japanese pilots away from traditional Japanese values. The demands of survival forced Japanese flyers from the known and familiar into a realm that lay beyond their established mores. In this they were no different from their American counterparts. But for the Japanese the process was more complex.

Being forced to move beyond the known and established conditions of their upbringing could not only be liberating and lead to a position of transcendence from which new values could be used to criticize the former order, it could also lead to a profound sense of inner tension--a situation in which there was a direct clash between the well-established values of one's past self and the new self that emerged out of combat. For those who judged their new selves from the perspective of the old values there was always the potential for extreme guilt. For the Japanese pilot, therefore, the very independence that modern aerial combat required, the fact that flying forced them to become free, also retained a destructive potential. In a world in which individualism was all too frequently seen as selfishness, and personal choice as egoism, the type of independence that flying required could also be seen as a kind of *tsumi*, or sin, that could be rectified only by death. As Kuroe wrote, "those with a strong sense of responsibility felt more and more trapped by such feelings."[67] For such individuals death provided the ultimate escape from an unbearable dilemma. Indeed, here may well lie one of the previously unexplored clues that can help us to understand why so many Japanese pilots were willing to volunteer for hopeless, or outright suicide missions in the final days of the war.[68]

Kuroe's experiences confirmed the general process through which combat brought pilots to a deeper understanding of themselves and the enemy. Like Scott, Boyington, and Sakai, Kuroe too experienced a direct confrontation with an enemy pilot that caused him to see himself and his victim from a more detached perspective. For Kuroe the moment of truth came over China. Flying out of Hankow in central China, Kuroe went up after ten Russian made SB bombers that had wrought death and destruction at his airbase. Too late to catch the bombers, he observed that one of the bombers appeared to have crashed, for he could see fire below, and in the same instant he caught sight of a "parachute with a man dangling beneath." At first Kuroe thought the man might be a Japanese naval flyer, but square parachutes were not issued to Japanese airmen. Then he recalled that he had seen similar parachutes used by the Russians at Nomonhan. Now he concluded that "It's got to be one of them.... But if it is the enemy, what should I do?" Kuroe was well aware of the international rules of war that "outlawed attacks on combatants who possessed no power of resistance." At the same time, he was filled with doubt and uncertainty. Japanese pilots, he remembered, had been terribly mutilated by the Russians at Nomonhan. "And if one side was capable of such crazy and cruel acts, wasn't it fair for the other to do the same?"[69]

And yet, he could not bring himself to act. Again and again he circled the descending pilot until he finally landed in a dirt field, his parachute softly folding up like an umbrella. Now that the pilot was on land, Kuroe decided to test his identity by making a firing pass at him. Deliberately aiming his guns some distance from the downed flyer, he looked back and observed the pilot nimbly running from the spot where he had landed to a small woods about a hundred yards away. Kuroe concluded, "there was absolutely no question about it, he was instinctively trying to escape." Although he could no longer see the man, Kuroe pumped several hundred rounds of machinegun fire into the woods before returning to his base.

A week later he learned that the body of a young Russian officer had been discovered. Those who found him were not certain whether he had bailed out of an SB bomber and had subsequently committed suicide or had been killed by local partisans. "Hearing this I was overcome by something akin to a bitter sense of remorse," Kuroe wrote. "The only person who really knows whether I was the offender responsible for the death of this young Soviet officer was the dead man himself." And while it was possible to console himself with the argument that this man deserved to die, Kuroe too found vengeance a hollow answer. The more he thought about it, the more he came to see the Russian flier as "one of many 'young men who fought in the air,' who suddenly found themselves suspended at the first stage of their lives from a parachute, descending to earth only to be suddenly attacked on the ground by an unforgiving fighter plane. For him that fighter was no doubt a monster without feelings or mercy."

Suddenly Kuroe began to see himself in the enemy pilot. Were the two of them really that different? "The question 'was he a friend,' or 'was he an enemy,' registered close to home and hinted at my own possible future fate. Indeed, it struck me that although he seemed to have been destined to die ... he was also a hero of his motherland, a fine, bright, and purely motivated youth who had dared to cross into enemy territory alone and by himself."

From this vantage point Kuroe broke through to a new perspective. "As I thought about these things," he wrote, "I came to see my opponent from the perspective of one man's struggle against another, and I was struck by how terribly vulnerable a flyer becomes when he throws off the protective armor of his plane. As I did, I became overwhelmed by an inexpressibly deep sense of sympathy towards this airman. Unable to clear up my contradictory feelings by arguing that war is cruel and filled with tragedy, I regularly offered up prayers on his behalf."[70]

The more he flew in combat the more Kuroe became a fatalist who saw himself and the enemy as facing the same dilemma: "A person who a few moments earlier started out on his flight with laughter, suddenly falls from the sky and disappears without leaving so much as a trace or shadow." Faced with the immediacy of life and death, his experiences in the air pushed him to a deeper and more profound view of himself and those around him. Sometimes his experiences bordered on the religious. Flying over a forest fire on a night flight in Southeast Asia he wrote of one such experience:

> The magic flames of that forest fire far down below a sky that was continuously filled with the dark clouds of brutal sentiments, aroused a sense of self that I was not even aware had been asleep within me. Indeed, I had the feeling that this sense of being transcended my own physical birth. This was the I of the far off past, long before I was born--the self of the progenitors of the human race. And suddenly I was overwhelmed by a strong pang of nostalgia for that world.
>
> In the bright flames of that fire amidst the dark clouds of smoke that covered the heart of the mountain range over which we were flying at four thousand meters, I thought I could see the "eyes of god" staring with indifference at the conditions of frail men who angered by the purity of science have invaded the great realm of nature to battle with and consume each other.

And the frailty of men was not restricted to one side:

> An airplane is after all a machine that is not possessed of the providence that an omnipotent god has bestowed upon the perfect objects of nature. Struggling firmly against the laws of the universe, it is able to maintain only a brief momentary existence in the sky. If even a single bullet penetrates its body it is quite likely to sever a pipe or screw, and in the process, this complicated machine will run amuck. If one is lucky the damage may not be fatal, but if luck is not with one, the plane's engine may simply stop running without the least ceremony or concern for the pilot's wishes. Faced with such a cruel and heartless fate, man has no choice but to submit.
>
> How puny, weak, and pathetic human beings really are!
>
> As I thought along these lines, I once again felt a sense of nostalgia welling up in me for the flames of that forest fire below which bound us together eternally as human beings and caused me to want to offer up a prayer for all of us.[71]

From his own new position of transcendence, from the desire to say a prayer for all of us, it was only a step further to see the other side from a new perspective. As Kuroe put it, the battle had to be won, but this did not mean that one had to "suppress one's feelings for the other side that were close to feelings of friendliness." It was precisely the willingness of all pilots to accept their mutual fate and to do so with good will and gallantry, that "has united all pilots friend and foe alike." "As great as their hatreds and the causes of resentment may have been," he wrote, "I think it is not surprising that for men caught up in such dreadful and deadly fighting there should exist at least some breathing space of humble human feelings to be shared by both sides."[72]

Finally, Kuroe was not ashamed to express the contradictory feelings to which he was subject. While he had learned to see the enemy in a new light, he also admitted that "it is equally strange that every time I encountered an enemy plane in the sky I found a fierce sense of hostility boiling within me."[73] But even under such circumstances he was prepared to respect the other side:

> In contrast to those on the ground, deadly battles in the air are filled with excitement. At times the action is fierce, but as a pilot gradually regains his composure, the sense of superiority he feels as he cries "I've got you!" when the enemy plane he is shooting at bursts into flame and falls away, may well be replaced by feelings of sympathy for the unlucky opponent, or by a sense of respect for the brave enemy pilot who is about to meet his end.[74]

Such experiences confirmed the common humanity of Japanese pilots as well as those flying for the other side. "In the final analysis," he wrote,

> it is clear that it is those elements that human beings hold in common in their environment, their work, their interests, and their research, that unites them with ties that transcend the concepts of race and ideology.[75]

What we see here is a transformed "urge for combat" that is a long way from the need to denigrate the other side or to reduce it to subhuman categories.

While the outbreak of the Pacific War pulled Kuroe into Southeast Asia, the attack on Pearl Harbor sent Sakai south against the Philippines. On December 8th Sakai participated in the attack on Clark Field that wiped out American air power in the Philippines.

About the initial days of the war he recorded, "we were curious, of course, as to the opposition we would encounter from the Americans." Sakai admitted that he and his fellow pilots knew little about American planes or the performance of their pilots, except that they anticipated "that they would possess even greater flying ability than the pilots against whom we had fought in China."[76]

In reference to the war itself he wrote: "not a man questioned the wisdom of launching the war. We were, after all, noncommissioned officers who had been trained--painfully--to respond immediately to orders. When we were told fly and fight, we did so unquestionably [sic]."[77]

As a professional soldier, who constantly tried to evaluate his own and the enemy's position realistically, Sakai was surprised by the American unwillingness to deal with the reality of what was happening in the Japanese push south. Distrustful of all rash pilot claims in aerial battles, he found it difficult to comprehend why Americans daily claimed air victories that far exceeded all reasonable possibility--in some instances even exceeding the total number of Japanese planes assigned to a sector. By the later years of the war, as the tide turned against Japan, he was able to understand this phenomenon better, but even then he was bitterly opposed to the type of delusion that such reports generated.[78]

Flying out of Lae, on the eastern coast of New Guinea, Sakai was to engage in some of his most important air battles. It was also at Lae that he developed a new respect for the Allied pilots who often flew inferior planes, but who were in no way lacking in courage and persistence:

> The willingness of the Allied pilots to engage us in combat deserves special mention here, for regardless of the odds, their fighters were always screaming in to attack.... The men who fought then were among the bravest I have ever encountered, no less so than our own pilots who, three years later, went out willingly on missions from which there was no hope of return.[79]

With expanded battle experience in the New Guinea theater, Sakai was to develop a growing respect for his American and Australian counterparts. Like other pilots he was struck by the transitoriness of air combat which reinforced the fleeting quality of man's existence and human vulnerability in a world in which matters of life and death were settled in a few split seconds. On a flight out of Lae, Sakai and his wingmates encountered four American P-39s flying in close formation. In the battle that followed Sakai shot down two of the

American planes, while his wingmates got the other two. "It was incredible," he wrote, "that in less than five seconds the fight was over, and four enemy fighters were smashing on the surface far below."[80] A few days later, coming out of a "slump," Sakai shot down three enemy planes in less than fifteen seconds.[81]

As the months of flying turned into years, Sakai's experiences were to lead to a deeper humanistic understanding that began to challenge the mere automaton conception of the fighter pilot with which he had entered the war. Flying daily within a hair's breadth of life and death, more than ever conscious that survival depended not only on skill but on forces beyond the individual's control, Sakai, like Boyington and Kuroe, managed to break through to a new perception of himself and the men who flew against him. Confronted by constant death, he developed a new appreciation for the human spirit, for the values of sacrifice, valor, and striving that were common to all men and were not limited to a particular racial or national group. As if to outline the strength of the human spirit that transcended any particular nationalism, Sakai recorded the story of a bomber pilot who left an indelible mark on his memory.

The Japanese pilot had landed at Lae on a run to Port Moresby. While talking with Sakai and his fellow Zero pilots, he looked wistfully at the fighters and indicated that one of his greatest ambitions had alway been to fly a fighter, "not one of these trucks we go around in." Then he spoke of the increased danger they all faced and the fact that many of his fellow pilots thought they would never see home again. "I feel the same way," he told Sakai. "Yet," he continued, "I would be satisfied if there was one thing I could do." "I'd like to loop that truck I fly," he said grinning. "Can you picture that thing going around in a loop?" One of the Zero pilots quickly warned him not to try. "You'd never come out of a loop in one piece, even if you could get up and around into one," he told him. "I suppose so," the pilot replied, and Sakai watched him walk across the field, climb into one of the fighters and study the controls. "At the time," Sakai wrote, "we didn't know that all of us would remember this pilot for the rest of our lives."[82]

A few days later, escorting a group of bombers on a run to Port Moresby, Sakai witnessed a lone P-39 plunge with tremendous speed into the bomber formation, spit shells into the last bomber in the flight, and dive away. The bomber streamed flames, and as Sakai closed in to watch he noticed that it was the same Mitsubishi Betty that had landed at Lae, the plane with whose pilot he and his friends had talked. Sakai recorded the pilot's final moments:

The flames increased in fury as the bomber nosed down and

skidded wildly. It lost altitude quickly, and seemed on the verge of going out of control. At 6,000 feet it was only a matter of seconds; the flames were engulfing the wings and fuselage.

Suddenly, still blazing fiercely, the nose lifted and the bomber went into a climb. I gaped at the plane in astonishment as its pilot started to draw a loop--an impossible maneuver for a Betty. The pilot--the same one who had told us he wished to loop in a fighter--hauled her back and up. The bomber went up, hung on its nose in a half loop, and then burst into a seething ball of flame which blotted it out entirely.

The flaming mass fell. Just before it struck the ground a violent explosion shook the air as the fuel tanks went off.[83]

The effort of a doomed man to fulfill his life through a last human achievement, by trying to accomplish that which he had always hoped, but never dared, to explore, was not lost upon Sakai. The pilot's final act--which had nothing to do with the war or with the enemy, but with an inner personal quest--made a deep impression on Sakai precisely because he was himself moving towards a more transcendent position. The bomber pilot's final act also underscored what Kuroe had observed on death in the air. "There is no one," Kuroe had written of doomed pilots on both sides, "whose heart is not moved by the desire to live. But to turn that fear and desire to avoid death into a dauntless courage, radical as such an act may seem, is a kind of incalculable performance that among the brave is called pride."[84]

For Sakai the impact of the war was coming home in different ways. Not long after the loss of the Mitsubishi pilot Sakai shot down an American B-26 and "gagged" as he watched its four man crew devoured by sharks after they had successfully parachuted to the water below.[85]

Nor were the tragedies of combat limited to the American side. Sakai soon witnessed with dramatic clarity the effects of a fighter's guns on another plane and its crew. Once more returning with a flight of bombers from Port Moresby, he noticed that one of the planes was flying erratically. A closer look showed that the bomber was a shambles. There were gaping holes everywhere which gave the bomber the appearance of a sieve. As he flew closer he could see blood on the instrument panel and the seats. The pilot and copilot lay sprawled in a pool of blood. The plane was, in fact, being flown by the flight engineer. All the plane's turrets were smashed and the men who manned them either dead or seriously wounded. Somehow the flight engineer, who had no pilot's training, was able to bring the plane towards the Lae air strip, and then, miraculously, the badly injured pilot managed to crash land the crippled plane. Witnessing the carnage inside Sakai wrote:

> It was the first time we had ever seen with such intimacy the terrible power of a fighter's weapons. Death in the air had never been close. Even those men who died in burning planes were remote and distant. A man either came home or he didn't. But now we saw it for what it really was.[86]

Not long thereafter Sakai was to experience his direct encounter with the American pilot over Guadalcanal discussed earlier which further served to break through the impersonal quality of air combat. A half hour later, by another strange twist of events, Sakai found himself in the same position as the American pilot. Caught by a group of American Avengers he was badly shot up, desperately wounded, and virtually blind. Now it was his turn to be a "sitting duck." That he managed to bring his crippled plane back to Rabaul remains, as I indicated, one of the great sagas of the war.

If Sakai's battle experiences transformed him from a mere automaton into a thinking and feeling human being, who came to regard the enemy on a new level from which the "we" and "they" distances were considerably reduced, he also demonstrated that in the case of the Japanese pilot the breaking through to a more universal perspective also affected his attitude towards what was Japanese. In this respect, it was from the perspective of the value of human life, and the importance of individual choice, that Sakai became most critical of what was happening on the Japanese side in the final days of the war.

Returning to air combat in the skies over Iwo Jima after recovering from his wounds in Japan, Sakai was struck by the sloganeering that he now found everywhere. From a flag at the end of the Iwo field there fluttered a banner reading *Namu hachiman daibosatsu*, calling on the Shinto god of war to help in the struggle with the Americans. "When we were at Lae," Sakai recalled, "our fliers had never resorted to such psychological crutches as moral boosters." To Sakai such "theatrical displays" were a "sign of weakness" and nothing more--a kind of modern "witchcraft."[87]

Sakai wondered why it was so difficult for the Japanese to face the truth--that their once vaunted planes could now be outflown and outgunned by a vast array of American aircraft and that a far superior

American armada relentlessly pushed on towards the Japanese islands. Sakai rejected the irrational appeal to ultranationalism and its strange corollary that a sufficient expression of sincere self sacrifice could still turn the tide of what was otherwise a hopeless conflict.[88] In an effort to secure the necessary leverage to deal with the demands of an all encompassing Japanese loyalty structure he began to support his war-honed humanistic values with a reinterpretation of the Japanese tradition:

> I loved my country dearly, and never would I hesitate a moment to defend Japan with my life. But there is a vast gulf between defending one's land even to the last and wantonly wasting one's life.... I was willing to die for my country, but, only in my faith, in the tradition of the Samurai, as I had been taught all my life, as a man, as a warrior![89]

As Sakai saw it there was a world of difference between the samurai who "lives in such a way that he is always prepared to die," and the man who wantonly throws his life away in the name of modern "witchcraft." "The Samurai code," Sakai wrote, "never demanded that a man be constantly prepared to *kill himself*." As he saw it:

> There is a great gulf between deliberately taking one's life and entering battle with a willingness to accept all its risks and hazards. In the latter case death is acceptable and there can be no regrets. Man lives with his head held high; he can die in the same fashion. He forfeits neither his personal honor nor that of his country ... but how does one quietly and objectively decide in a few hours to go out and kill oneself?[90]

Having lived on the edge of life and death for so long, Sakai was not ready to simply throw his life away in blind propitiation of forces which he did not accept. Ordered to fly a suicide mission by his commanding officer, Sakai became one of the rare Japanese pilots, who, unable to locate his target because of adverse weather conditions, had the courage to return. Most of his compatriots simply ended their lives by crashing their bomb-laden planes into the Pacific. And yet, even Sakai remembered all too distinctly the apprehension with which he approached the command post to report to the commanding officer that he had returned. Having brought back another brilliant young pilot and discovering that he was weeping openly and could not bring himself to report, Sakai assured the young flyer, Muto, that they would "go in together." In the act of reporting, Sakai noted, something "snapped inside me."

> Suddenly cold anger at everything which had passed this terrible day gripped me. I thought of Muto, brilliant in the air, already an ace, willing to fight at any time, anywhere.... I thought of him weeping abjectly, sorrowful, fearing that he had shown himself a coward when he had been sent out on a fool's mission.
> I swore that, no matter what happened, if any superior officer attempted to vent his wrath on the young pilot by beating him, I would throw all caution to the winds and throw myself on that man and reduce him to pulp.[91]

What had "snapped" for Sakai were the particular ties and obligations that lay at the heart of the Japanese social system. Suddenly, amidst the crisis of Japan's final hours, Sakai managed to break through to a new perspective not only on the outside world, but on Japan. In the name of his new inner values he had at last "broken with the 'unbearable chain' of tradition and order,"[92] as he described it, that had elicited so many sacrifices from all Japanese for the past five years. Despite the pain, the war had at last forced him to be free. Moreover, it was from such a position of "freedom" that new and lasting ties with the outside world could once again be constructed. In such a world, Sakai has written, "I have met men against whom I fought in the air, sat and talked with these men, and found friendship.... This is to me the most impressive fact of all," he wrote, "these same people who, for all I know, came under my guns so long ago, sincerely offered friendship."[93] And more importantly, we might add, it was a friendship that both sides were now prepared to reciprocate.

Conclusion

In his study of World War I, Eric Leed considered the two basic models that have often been used to define the relationship between war experiences and normal social life. The first of these models can be identified as the "drive-discharge" model which has been most commonly encountered in psychoanalytical theories of war. This model argues that organized conflicts, war, revolution, and warlike games, serve to discharge drives which are blocked from expression in normal social life. War in such a model functions as a "safety valve" for aggression.[94]

By contrast to the drive-discharge model, Leed identifies a

second model he calls the "cultural patterning" model. The cultural patterning model basically argues that restraints upon aggression learned in the process of socialization are not purely external rules and inhibitions that can be left behind with one's civilian dress. If restraints upon aggression are truly learned they become constituent elements of the citizen soldier. "The cultural patterning model," Leed writes, "holds that individual aggression in war is a function of the rules and values which have governed aggression in social life. The individual who goes to war--if he is a 'normal' member of his society--fears his own aggression as much as the aggression of the enemy, even though he may be less conscious of the cultural inhibitions that restrain him."[95]

In dealing with World War I, Leed found neither of these models satisfactory in explaining the effects of the war on the men he studied. Both models, he felt, argued that in order to operate effectively in a world of disorder, men must leave their culture behind, or that their culture, through inhibitions and restraints, loses its grip on behavior and ceases to define their identity.[96] Leed argued instead, that what the experiences of World War I did was to take front soldiers beyond the known and previously socially determined sphere of their culture into a world of liminality, a situation in which they found themselves between the known and unknown, between the familiar and the uncanny. As stated at the start of this essay, he argues, moreover, that this situation is fundamentally similar to rites of passage in traditional (or primitive) societies, especially the first two phases of such rites--those of separation and transition.[97] The problem with World War I was that unlike traditional rites of passage there was no final resolution, no arriving on the other side. Instead, it was as if separation and transition, which were to serve as means to a more profound end, became instead the ongoing reality. For many such combatants the war never ended.

What is interesting about the pilots that I have dealt with in this essay is the fact that they too mirror a good deal of the process that Leed found at work among the combatants of World War I. But in a number of cases such as Boyington, Sakai, and Kuroe the "rites of passage" could be completed and could lead to a final resolution. Indeed, the position of transcendence that I have argued for represents that very resolution. Why some combatants in the Pacific War were able to move beyond the liminal position is, of course, an interesting question in itself. Clearly the nature of the war, so different from World War I in its mobility--and this was even more true of pilots--has to be taken into account. Certainly the men I have addressed in this study found no need to continue to fight the war after 1945. Quite the opposite, both sides were prepared to see the war come to an end so that the new era for which the war had prepared them could come to life.

NOTES

1. The author wishes to express his appreciation to the Henry Luce Foundation for the financial assistance that made possible the seminar, "Japan and the United States: 1941-1952," which resulted in this essay.
2. The question of longterm American images of Japan has been studied by Sheila K. Johnson (*American Attitudes Towards Japan, 1941-1975* [Washington, D.C., 1975]), and that of mutual images by Ben-Ami Shillony in this volume. John Dower (*War Without Mercy* [New York, 1986]) has examined wartime images held by both sides.
3. Eric J. Leed, *No Man's Land: Combat and Identity in World War I* (Cambridge, 1979), pp. 12-15.
4. Gregory Boyington, *Baa Baa Black Sheep* (New York, 1958), p. 38. (Hereafter cited as GB.)
5. GB; Robert L. Scott, *God is My Co-Pilot* (New York, 1943). (Hereafter cited as RS.) For a discussion of Scott and Boyington's books within the context of postwar American attitudes towards Japan see Johnson, *American Attitudes*, pp. 12-13.
6. RS, pp. 1-4.
7. RS, p. 8.
8. RS, p. 10.
9. RS, p. 43.
10. John Goette, *Japan Fights for Asia* (New York, 1943), pp. 74-77.
11. RS, p. 45.
12. GB, p. 5. Scott was also later associated with this unit.
13. *Loc. cit.*
14. *Loc. cit.*
15. GB, p. 7.
16. *Loc. cit.*
17. GB, p. 13.
18. *Loc. cit.*
19. *Loc. cit.*
20. GB, p. 47.
21. GB, p. 48.
22. *Loc. cit.*
23. *Loc. cit.*
24. GB, p. 52.
25. Goette, *Japan Fights*, p. 79.
26. RS, p. 131.
27. RS, pp. 140-41.
28. RS, p. 197.
29. RS, p. 98.
30. RS, p. 254.
31. RS, p. 253.
32. *Loc. cit.*
33. RS, p. 256.
34. RS, p. 255.
35. Burke Davis, *Get Yamamoto* (New York, 1969), p. 80.
36. *Loc. cit.*
37. The above incident is recorded in Sakai Saburo, *Ozora no samurai* (Tokyo, 1967), pp. 282-89. The quotations are from the original English edition, *Samurai* (New York, 1957), pp. 150-52, hereafter cited as SS.
38. Leed, *No Man's Land*, p. 20.
39. GB, p. 80.
40. GB, p. 91.
41. GB, p. 64.
42. Edward H. Sims, *Greatest Fighter Missions* (New York, 1962), p. 107.
43. GB, p. 190.
44. GB, p. 203.
45. GB, p. 204.
46. GB, p. 205.

47. GB, p. 221.
48. GB, p. 206.
49. GB, p. 264.
50. GB, p. 259.
51. GB, p. 290.
52. GB, p. 272.
53. GB, p. 322.
54. GB, p. 325.
55. GB, pp. 270-71.
56. GB, p. 296.
57. SS; Kuroe Yasuhiko, *Aa hayabusa sento tai: kaerazaru gekitsui-o* (Tokyo, 1969), hereafter cited as KY.
58. Among these are Hinoki Yohei, *Tsubasa no kessen: kaerazaru hayabusa sento tai* (Tokyo, 1967); Iwai Tsutomu, *Kubo reisen tai: kaigun sentoki soju junen no kiroku* (Tokyo, 1979); Kofukuda Terufumi, *Shikikan kusen ki: aru reisen taisho no ripoto* (Tokyo, 1978); Moji Mitoku, *Sora to umi no hate ni: dai-ichi kokukan tai fukukan no kaiso* (Tokyo, 1978); Odaka Noritsura, *Aa seishun reisen tai: moretsu ni ikita nijusai no seishun* (Tokyo, 1969); Otawa Tatsuya, *Yokaren ichidai: aru kanko pairotto no akusen kuto ki* (Tokyo, 1978). Several Japanese accounts translated into English have also been useful; these include Hagoromo Society of Kamikaze Divine Thunderbolt Corps Survivors, *The Cherry Blossom Squadrons: Born to Die* (Los Angeles, 1973); Rikihei Inoguchi and Tadashi Nakajima, with Roger Pineau, *The Divine Wind: Japan's Kamikaze Force in World War II* (Annapolis, 1958); Yasuo Kuwabara and Gordon Allred, *Kamikaze* (New York, 1957); Ryuji Nagatsuka, *I Was a Kamikaze* (New York, 1972).
59. SS, p. 11.
60. SS, p. 29.
61. SS, p. 26.
62. KY, p. 14.
63. KY, p. 44.
64. KY, p. 37.
65. KY, p. 38. The pilot wrote: "*tsumi, manshi ni atai su.*"
66. KY, p. 238.
67. KY, p. 37.
68. What needs to be noted here is the fact that in many instances pilots flew out on *kamikaze* missions, were unable to locate targets, and refused to return to their home bases. How many pilots simply crashed their planes into the sea is not easy to determine. But as we will see in Sakai's case that number may have been considerable. On the outlook of the pilots themselves see Ivan Morris, *The Nobility of Failure* (New York, 1975); the guilt of survivorship is discussed in Robert Jay Lifton, *Death in Life: Survivors of Hiroshima* (New York, 1967). Lifton also comments on the "collective suicide" of kamikaze pilots in his *Six Lives Six Deaths: Portraits from Japan* (New Haven, 1979), p. 283.
69. KY, p. 62.
70. The incident involving the Russian pilot from which the preceding quotations are taken is related in KY, pp. 60-67.
71. KY, pp. 228-29.
72. KY, p. 250.
73. *Loc. cit.*
74. KY, p. 251.
75. *Loc. cit.*
76. SS, p. 48.
77. *Loc. cit.*
78. SS, p. 68.
79. SS, p. 76.
80. SS, p. 83.
81. SS, p. 93.
82. SS, pp. 108-09.
83. SS, p. 112.

84. KY, p. 226.
85. SS, p. 115.
86. SS, p. 120.
87. SS, p. 219.
88. As indicated earlier, one aspect of the kamikaze phenomenon that needs to be looked at in greater detail, especially among the older pilots, is the problem of survivor guilt. There is, however, a second issue that deserves equal attention, and this involves the question that Sakai raises about the irrationality of sacrifice in the later stages of the war. The idea that if enough sincere Japanese were willing to sacrifice their lives for the good of the state, the gods would once again intervene in history as they were thought to have done against the Mongols in the 13th century, was prevalent among various Japanese leaders in the latter days of the war. The kamikaze were in one sense sacrificial victims, inspired by a primitive belief in divine intervention in history. For such victims, as Sakai became aware, the rational act of hitting one's target was less important than the willingness to selflessly offer up one's life. Under such conditions, crashing one's plane into the ocean was little different from striking an American warship. The degree to which such concepts penetrated even the top administrators of the government can be seen in a statement made by Koiso Kuniaki, who replaced Tojo Hideki as Prime Minister after the fall of Saipan in July 1944. At one of his first press conferences Koiso stated: "Japan is the land of the gods, but unless the country does its utmost we cannot count on their protection. The reason for the ordeal they are putting us through now is that the nation failed to understand the true and fundamental meaning of our national policy.... The enemy raids will certainly come. If we do everything we can and more, only then will the spirits of the gods give us their divine assistance." Quoted in Robert Guillain, *I Saw Tokyo Burning* (New York, 1981), pp. 164-65. See also Morris, *Failure*.
89. SS, p. 220.
90. SS, p. 222.
91. SS, p. 233.
92. SS, p. 234.
93. SS, p. 12.
94. Leed, *No Man's Land*, pp. 6-7.
95. Leed, *No Man's Land*, p. 9.
96. Leed, *No Man's Land*, pp. 11-12.
97. Leed, *No Man's Land*, pp. 15ff.

EPILOGUE: NATIONAL IDENTITY, NATIONAL PAST, NATIONAL ISMS

Michio Umegaki

The chapters in this volume are lenses for focusing on how modern Japan grappled with its unstable identity and its even more unstable relationship with the outside world down to 1945. Japan's prewar path was treacherous partly because it ended in disastrous defeat in World War II. But this consequence tells only part of the story. Japan's mid-19th century opening to the West was abrupt. The international stage onto which Japan was thrust soon turned into the rough terrain of ruthless colonial competition. Both individuals and the nation as a whole confronted a multitude of difficult tasks. The Japanese tried to set aside the past with minimum disruption, transform their society in the mold of those who had coerced Japan into transforming itself, and forge relatively smooth relationships between Japan and the external environment, while simultaneously stabilizing their national identity even as they also attempted to redefine it.

Modernization and industrialization were especially taxing for the Japanese because the established world powers were intolerant of latecomers. Japan's more advanced competitors closely scrutinized each step the country took toward industrial strength and grew increasingly suspicious that Japan was endangering the already unraveling regional balances of colonial empires. Japanese hopes for international acceptance and claims to a rightful place for their rising nation among the powers were met with paltry gains and often ill-disguised attempts to check Japan. These unfulfilled expectations became the basis for national grievances against an intolerant world and the script for Japan's ultimate undoing in World War II.

In a way the chapters in this book are the biographical notes of a nation that constantly tried to make peace with its changing identity and with the world around it, yet often ended up being at war with both. These notes raise several broad questions that deserve examination.

The Dialectic of Identity

Each study in this volume captures a specific facet of Japan's vacillating self-confidence amid rapid modernization. This vacillation goes back to the xenophobic reaction provoked by the forcible opening in 1853 of a nation that had previously been spared from outside intrusion. In this light Aizawa Seishisai's synthesis of the Chinese and American experiences as a way of coping with the outsiders is intriguing, both because of the lack of a discriminating view of the "barbarians" and because of his optimism about how Japan might control them. Thus it is not surprising that Aizawa's xenophobia and optimism could so easily be fused into the fanatical *joi* movement at one moment and into the demand for the almost uncritical importation of things Western soon thereafter.

A more profound vacillation of confidence began with the massive infusion of Western technologies and ideas after the Meiji restoration of 1868. Even the physical appearance of the country began to change, the distance between cities began to shrink, and people began to move more freely from place to place and from one stratum to another. "To have lived through the transition stage of modern Japan makes a man feel preternaturally old," a Westerner observed, "for here he is in modern times, with the air full of talk about bicycles and bacilli and 'spheres of interest,' and yet he can himself distinctly remember the Middle Ages."[1] Along with these changes came another, far more intrinsic to Japan's national confidence: the earlier uncritical (and thus inconsistent and unsystematic) acceptance of things Western gradually gave way after the mid-1880s to the view that things Japanese were capable of existing side-by-side with things Western.

There is a sort of Hegelian dialectic at work in this vacillation. The indiscriminate borrowing from the West may have started because of a lack of confidence in things Japanese and in old Japan. Yet operating the borrowed items in a Japanese context resulted in modifying them and using them selectively. Things Japanese not only survived the influx of Western technologies and ideas but also forced the imports to adapt to the new environment. Consequently people in Japan began to view things Japanese more positively than before. Such a dialectic seemed to operate also within individuals, as William Naff observed in the literary figure Shimazaki Toson. Indeed there were many Tosons, to whom reconciliation with a new Japan meant in some degree the rediscovery of Japan after a long foray into (and often gruelling confrontations with) the unfamiliar West, the unknown and the new.

There was also a down side to the dialectic of national confidence. Japan's initial modern intimacy with its Asian neighbors--"Asia is one"--did not last long. In fact the efforts of neighbors, especially the Chinese, to emulate Japan's encounter with the West left many Japanese unimpressed. Instead the admiration of the early Meiji synthesis by these countries began to fuel the arrogance of many Japanese that was inflamed by victory over Ch'ing China in 1895. As Japan successfully coopted the West, or grew similar to it, Japan grew more and more distant from old Asia. Japanese views of the outside world began to differentiate accordingly--the beginning of what Ben-Ami Shillony calls Japan's peculiar ambivalence: a "frustrated lover" of the United States (and the West) but an "annoyed brother" of China (and Asia).

Unsympathetic to its Asian neighbors, Japan began exhibiting the traits of an aggressive and insecure modern state. It started to see the world in terms of market opportunities, bidding for scarce resources, and hostile competition. For some like Yamagata Aritomo and his proteges, Asia became the key to Japan's economic and political survival--the area of Japan's "special interests."[2] Expressions of cultural affinity with the mainland concealed Japan's more secular interests in a China that, for a time, was receptive to Japan's ambitions and capable of blocking the advance of Russian influence from the north.

This dialectic development of Japan's self-confidence as a modern state was ironically accompanied by a deepening insecurity different from mid-19th century xenophobia. American and European accolades for Japan's campaigns against Ch'ing China and imperial Russia could not mask a new and far more pervasive fear of Japan, embodied in the perverse language of the Yellow Peril. The suspicion deepened in the outside world that industrializing Japan was intruding on the colonial order in East Asia. Thus, fantasies of Pacific rivalry were particularly appealing to the Japanese as they became aware of the increasing costs of protecting their country's new status as a regional power.

Coming out on the winning side in World War I did little to alleviate Japanese insecurity. Instead it gave rise to the notion that the Eurocentric order was extinct, highlighting even more acutely the rising significance of the United States as Japan's Pacific rival. This new conceptual current took time to seep into the minds of academics, journalists, and government and military officials. But when it did, as Kimitada Miwa's chapter shows, Japan emerged as a principal actor in a new polyarchic world order, with all the assertiveness and defensiveness of a newcomer.

In retrospect it seems that Japan may have narrowed the options for its political and economic survival in direct proportion to its rising national self-confidence after World War I. The cost of demanding a predominant role in the polyarchic world order in the 1930s was Japan's isolation, especially when the demand was accompanied by an aggressive policy on the continent and a naval buildup in the western Pacific. The ultimate down side of this dialectic was a Japan facing an increasingly unsympathetic Asia and caught in an ever deeper rivalry with the United States.

Benign views of Asia held by Pan-Asianists at the turn of the century had by now almost evaporated. In their place was the doctrine that Asia should be extricated from colonial competition with the West and made the basis of Japan's new policy of autarky, the "New Order" in East Asia. The earlier economic policy of heavy reliance on the United States as trading partner had little place in the new Japan-centered regional order. As Kitaoka's chapter points out, a similar fate befell the idea of regional stability proposed by Kiyosawa Kiyoshi, who respected self-determination for countries in the region and posited economic interdependence among the principal powers. Even his own associates marginalized Kiyosawa's warnings of impending conflict with the United States, an ominous sign of what awaited Japan. By now self-confidence had been replaced by extreme self-assertion, often called ultranationalism, stemming from Japan's sense of isolation and consequent apotheosizing of its own post-1868 modernization.

At the culmination of the dialectic of Japanese self-confidence, Japan was the only remaining country that admired and relied on Japan. All other countries were lesser entities, susceptible to hysterical stereotyping by many Japanese. In the end, it was the untoward nature of combat that helped free Japanese (and Americans) from these stereotypes. As Fred Notehelfer's sketches of fighter pilots dramatically illustrate, confronting their own mortality freed many men from their initial images of the enemy and helped them form bonds as humans linked by the common experience of facing death.[3]

From National Isms to Nationalism

Notehelfer's observations raise a puzzling question: why was the appeal of nationalism so irresistible that only a brush with death seemed to dispel it? Explicit in certain of the foregoing chapters and latent in others is the process by which national consciousness became nationalism in the lives of most individual Japanese before 1945. What did people seek in prewar Japanese nationalism, and what did nationalism offer them?

The orientations and actions nationalism inspired before World

War II were far from uniform. Nationalism during the last years of the Tokugawa period was hardly worthy of the name--little more than a diffuse sense that intruders from abroad were violating Japan's natural boundaries and political traditions. But after the Restoration nationalism in a more familiar sense unleashed immense energies for changing the country. The means to bring about change seemed to matter little, even when they introduced unfamiliar social norms. Late Meiji nationalism, in turn, sounded a different, more defensive note as the newly industrializing and expansionist Japan gained less international recognition than many Japanese believed was due. A brief interlude followed in the 1910s and 1920s, during which the internationalism of Shidehara Kijuro, Nitobe Inazo, and others temporarily quelled the defensiveness of late Meiji. After 1931 a final phase of Japan's prewar nationalism resurrected the earlier hostility toward outsiders in the form of an aggressive continental policy.

This seeming lack of uniformity in national orientations and actions may represent not so much an absence of consistency as it did the diverse appeals the nation had to citizens in a rapidly changing society. Aizawa Seishisai offers a convenient point of departure. Despite earnest attempts at synthesizing the unsuccessful Chinese and successful American experiences in dealing with intruders, Aizawa's was a nationalism only in a qualified sense: a generalized defense of Japan's "folkways" in the face of Western encroachment. This diffuse nativism did not liberate him from parochial loyalties to the Bakufu, costing him--as Bob T. Wakabayashi observes--a place among the most prominent late Tokugawa nationalists. At the same time, Aizawa's gradual recognition of Western superiority awakened him to the possibility that a Japan capable of surviving the outside encroachment might be different from the existing one. This awakening made him a *realpolitiker* willing to contemplate profound adjustments to the Tokugawa power structure.

At work in Aizawa's embryonic nationalism may be an archetypal relationship between people and their immediate environment: changes in the relationship threatened to discredit long-held values and to demand that new ones be established. Aizawa's changing outlook and behavior suggests the variety of contradictory actions taken by Japanese in later decades as their immediate environment changed even more dramatically.

The defense of nativism was a recurring theme throughout Japan's prewar development. As Eleanor Westney demonstrates, modernization was testimony to Japanese adaptability and innovativeness, but it was essentially a destabilizing process for the Japanese people. New varieties of social, economic, and political life corroded the familiar sources of cohesion without yet forging stable new societal relationships. Moreover, the benefits of modernization were unequally distributed; often they were outweighed by heavy costs such as the tax burden on farmland to finance industrialization. At each step of the modernization process the Japanese asked themselves: What was the point if the result for them was a life that was destabilized and a Japan that was growing less familiar and more like the West?

Actions inspired by such nativist skepticism were predictably anti-modernist and even violent, such as the assassination of Mori Arinori in 1889. Even the government, which was the chief beneficiary of modernization, was not immune to nativist inclinations. Finding itself immersed in new tides of social consciousness carrying socialist and Christian ideals, the government quickly acted to control the new beliefs--especially in the Imperial Rescript on Education of 1890--by reemphasizing traditional values to assure sufficient social cohesiveness for the nation undergoing transition. Four decades later, following the turbulent Taisho democracy of the 1910s and 1920s, Showa Japan was even more ripe for resurrecting nativism because of social malaise. New concentrations of wealth in big businesses, the plight of farm villages ripped by falling grain prices and absentee landlords, and the collusion among corporate, military, party, and bureaucratic elites were the social ills against which deep grievances were registered by nativists of all stripes--from the agrarian ideologue Gondo Seikyo to the rebellious young army and navy officers.

Perhaps nothing better describes the magnetism of nativist orientations for restless modern Japanese than Shimazaki Toson's return to Magome in the Kiso valley in the 1920s. Nationalism with a strong appeal to nativism was symptomatic of a rapidly changing society. It offered values that uprooted Japanese could use to restore some degree of stability within themselves or possibly even to arrest the changes that were causing their psychological and emotional upheaval.

However, expressing grievances against foreign intrusion and radical change was not all that Aizawa foreshadowed. His recognition of the need to change the Tokugawa power structure in order to deal with the West indicates another appeal of nationalism: it frees people from commitment to the existing system. Outgrowing their initial repugnance at things Western, many Meiji modernizers used nationalism to renounce the status quo, and imported technologies to bring about change. This rejection of the existing system was sustained by external pressures as well as domestic needs. The established powers consistently dashed Japan's expectations of winning international acceptance, beginning with treaty renegotiations at the end of the nineteenth century. These unfulfilled hopes fortified Japan's resolve to press for further changes. As many Japanese saw it, their country was "aggrieved" by the Triple Intervention in 1895, anti-Japanese legislation in California, the Yellow Peril hysteria, and other expressions of foreign hostility. The more Japan was slighted, the more the Japanese pressed to become less Asian and more Western. *Datsu-A nyu-O* ("exit Asia, enter the West") now replaced the less focused *fukoku kyohei* ("enrich the country, strengthen the army") as a slogan of national ambitions.

One consequence of this drive was a new bias Japan developed toward China. As Shillony observes, on one level the Japanese never wavered in their admiration of the United States, even during the Pacific War. Yet it was increasingly apparent to many Japanese that China was lacking something--the willingness to "shed the dregs of Oriental Culture," as Kosaka Masaaki puts it in the Miwa chapter above--that prevented its cultural and geographical proximity to Japan from generating a positive relationship with the Japanese. In large part this bias originated in changing Japanese perceptions, not in events on the mainland. To Japan the United States was an inspiration as the Meiji leaders challenged the existing system, whereas China was a reminder of the existing system and of what the failure to pursue change might bring about.

Another consequence was far more international in scope. The attack on the existing system had an immense appeal to Japanese who sought to bring their country into harmony with the outside world. Before 1895 they might have been interested in helping their Asian neighbors to free themselves from old systems.[4] Just as there were Miyazaki Totens, however, there were also Uchida Ryoheis to whom the Triple Intervention starkly revealed that the system in need of change was the Eurocentric colonial order in East Asia. Japan's growing international entanglements after 1900 further confirmed this revelation. The Paris peace conference of 1919 opened Konoye Fumimaro's eyes to the Anglo-American collusion of interests in maintaining the international status quo. In short, the romantic nationalism of bakumatsu and early Meiji may have found industrializing Japan less and less receptive to its appeals on domestic issues; instead, it demanded that Japan become the vehicle of its external expression through expansion in East Asia.

By the early twentieth century Japan had outgrown much of its earlier inferiority complex toward the West. Japan was now a major power, confirmed in the Washington treaties of 1921-1922 that supplanted the Anglo-Japanese alliance forged in 1902. Yet operating at a higher level of self-confidence, the Japanese were blind to an important contradiction as they challenged the established regional and international order: Japan was now a status quo power seeking changes in the very system that assured such a status. Thus Showa Japan had to maintain a difficult balance between realism as an established power (as pursued by Shidehara) and revolutionary romanticism as projected by the Eastern Conference. The breakdown of the balance eventually led to military intrusion into Japan's continental policy.

To be sure, the breakdown in favor of continental adventurism cannot be attributed solely to the growing voice of the military. The 1924 immigration legislation in the United States was equally damaging to Japan's effort to stay within established international norms of behavior. For one thing, as Kitaoka points out, the passage of this law silenced most of the pro-Anglo-American moderates who might have been able to help prevent Japan's eventual quagmire in China. For another, the law discredited the United States in the eyes of many Japanese who hoped for a reliable partner for managing East Asian and western Pacific affairs. Once the delicate diplomatic balance between realism and romanticism tipped in favor of the latter, the ghost of earlier Pan-Asianism reappeared after 1930 in projections of Japanese power in defiance of the existing order in East Asia. Asia was again one--but now an Asia in which the way of the emperor, not national self-determination, was to be supreme.

Aizawa's proto-nationalism inspired at once resistance and commitment to change--and one more important trait: the concept of national sovereignty within an international order. Aizawa was more than a mere nativist defender of Japan; he reconciled national defense with his vision of world order. Japan's seclusion was not simply a Bakufu choice but one sanctioned by the "providential intent of Heaven," an intent extended beyond Japan alone--"Heaven has endowed each thing with its own peculiar character," as Wakabayashi notes. Thus Japan's seclusion was fully compatible with a world order sanctioned by an authority higher than any of its components. Behind this seemingly familiar argument that Japan is unique are the ingredients of a modern nationalist ideal: the concept of a nation as master of its own fate and the assumption that a higher authority instills order in the otherwise anarchic relationships among autonomous nations.

Among the post-Restoration leaders were purveyors of this surprisingly modern concept of nationalism. They actively sought to lend a hand to fellow revolutionaries in nearby Asian countries that were struggling to achieve nationhood. This cosmopolitan nationalist synthesis did not fade out even when Japan gained increasing international stature. Writers such as Miyake Setsurei understood the positive contributions to global welfare that nationalistic competition could make. They argued that competition of national interests could result in an equilibrium among nations and that the refinement of each nation's cultural heritage could redound to the advantage of humankind.

Yet receptivity to German geopolitical thought was equally strong among the Meiji leaders, whose first step toward modernization had been to ward off the foreign threat. Military as well as political leaders soon began to dictate Japan's continental policy. To them East Asia was a gray area of colonialist competition, and competitors' gains meant irreparable losses to Japanese national interests. By the end of the Russo-Japanese War, deference to each nation's autonomy had become routine only among the established powers in the region. An excellent case in point was the Root-Takahira agreement of 1908, which mutually recognized Japan's "special interests" in Korea and southern Manchuria and America's in the Philippines.

Furthermore, the Japanese began to counter the increasing Western intolerance of Tokyo's continental policy by justifying this policy as the prerogative of Asians wronged by the "White Peril" of Americans and Europeans. The seeming resemblance of this claim to the earlier Pan-Asianist sentiment that Asia was one is deceptive. For one thing, the Pan-Asianism of the Showa period presumed (with help from some Japanese sinologists, as Miwa points out) that China might not be capable of nation-building. Japan was now more concerned with China's susceptibility to internal chaos than with China's self-determination. For another, as Sun Yat-sen pointed out in his 1924 Kobe speech, Japan was now suspected of European-style imperialism. By the 1930s Japan was deepening its alienation from both the West and Asia.

Consequently the "New Order in East Asia" was only partly intended to liberate Asians from the "White Peril." The earlier cosmopolitan nationalist synthesis was clearly in decline. The New Order was a hegemonic design, like the Monroe Doctrine in the Western Hemisphere, to establish Japan's claim that its national interests were identical with those of the region as a whole. Its enlarged version, *hakko ichiu*, was a romantic projection of a Japan-centered world order in which the liberation of Asians would take place through "imperial benevolence" and "assimilation." Little room was left for persons like Kiyosawa Kiyoshi or the young Ishibashi Tanzan to assert any influence on official policy. Their idealistic nationalism--tolerant of others' nationalisms and presuming a higher authority regulating the relationships among states--had little chance of survival.

The magnetism of prewar Japanese nationalism thus emanated from its diverse appeals. It responded to people's desire for stability when society was in constant turmoil, but when stability could not be restored, nationalism could all too easily be used to justify denouncing the sources of turmoil. Nationalism also appealed to the desire to perpetuate and direct the changes that began in the mid-nineteenth century, but it could also blind Japanese to the fact that changes could not occur in isolation. Finally, nationalism appealed to Japan's hope to define its rightful place among the same powers that had coerced Japan into giving up seclusion. Yet the same appeal could just as readily justify an insistence on bringing the international order into harmony with Japan's interests.

As extensive and integral as these nationalist appeals were among prewar Japanese, defeat in World War II did not end people's receptivity to them. As a defeated nation, Japan's identity was obscured, its proper place in the world was clouded, and the need for change as well as a certain degree of continuity from the past was even more acute than during the mid-nineteenth century. The sudden disruption of national life brought about by surrender prepared a special place for nationalism in Japan's postwar history.

Postwar Japan: Back to the Future?

Briefly it is worth calling attention to a few characteristics of the Japanese reaction to their defeat in 1945 that have a bearing on postwar Japanese nationalism. The first relates to an outburst of what Marius B. Jansen calls an "exorcism of the irrationality of the recent past."[5] At the end of the war the noted literary critic Ara Masahito likened the surviving Japanese to Dostoyevski at Semyonovsky Square on that cold December day in 1849 when the Russian writer's life was spared at the very last moment. Ara called postwar Japan the second coming of youth (*dai ni no seishun*) for the nation. His sentiment went beyond mere relief at the reprieve after fifteen years of war; it included unmitigated anger at imperial Japan for having unmercifully put Japan's "youth" at risk. In his vastly popular *Darakuron*, Sakaguchi Ango went even further: he preached the primacy of raw human desires instead of wartime self-sacrifice in the name of emperor or empire. It is doubtful whether most Japanese were fully cognizant of Ara's or Sakaguchi's vengefulness against the past. Yet it is fascinating to contemplate how such intolerance of their own past has impinged on the subsequent national debate about the basic characteristics of Japanese modernization.

At the same time it should not be forgotten that during the brief period between August 1945 and the spring of 1946 many prewar Japanese leaders were slow to come to grips with the scope of reforms the Occupation authorities proposed to carry out. The prewar party chieftains openly hailed the imperial system as the foundation for a new Japan as they rushed to resurrect their parties. Constitutional theorists such as Minobe Tatsukichi had little difficulty defending the

Meiji constitution as capable of surviving in the postwar era if it were adjusted somewhat. There was a distinct sense of national liberation from a specific Japan--from the extremes of nationalism during the 1930s and early 1940s. Whereas Ara and Sakaguchi refused to single out 1930-1945 as anomalous, these leaders may have represented a broader national sentiment that the excesses of the 1930s and early 1940s could be corrected without totally discrediting the post-1868 modernization of their country.

Finally there were reactions that owed their formation to the Occupation reforms themselves. The massive purge orders, the war-crimes investigations and trials, the drafting of a new constitution, and the waves of social, economic, and political reforms had a cumulative reinforcing effect on one another. In the midst of this psychological and political upheaval, mixed with relief for those who had feared much harsher punitive measures, Japanese began to realize the ultimate consequence of defeat: postwar Japan was going to be substantially different from prewar Japan.

Yet the end of the Occupation did not fully liberate the Japanese from American constraints. The San Francisco peace conference of 1951 muddled rather than marked the clear end of Japan's status as an occupied nation. Despite signing the peace treaty, Japan remained still at war with two formidable neighbors (China and the U.S.S.R.). Japan was forced to accept a security treaty with the United States containing problematic clauses that threatened Japan's sovereign status, and to accept foreign rule over certain territories the Japanese considered integral to their nation. Not surprisingly, resolving these problems became a principal concern of successive Japanese cabinets, sparking continuing debate about when to date the end of Japan's anomalous status. As a consequence, conflicting assessments of occupied Japan have become as consuming an issue among postwar Japanese intellectuals as were the debates about the nature of Japanese development among intellectuals in the 1920s and early 1930s.

A distinctive feature of Japanese reactions to military defeat was a preoccupation with the past, whether the post-Restoration era, the wartime era, or the Occupation. This preoccupation with the past has forced Japanese at each step of postwar development to question whether a new national identity might be carved out as the possibility of returning to prewar conditions diminishes; or by constructing constitutional and other safeguards against the resurgence of militarism and ultranationalism; or by removing the anomalous legacies of the Occupation.

Preoccupied with their past, postwar Japanese are thus uniquely retrospective. For most of the postwar era Japan has walked through the present with its back to the future. At the same time retrospective Japanese are particularly receptive to one nationalist appeal: to free themselves from their commitment to the existing system. The past offers itself as an opportune frame of reference for seeking change. As long as the Japanese see even the remotest sign of the past--"feudalistic" prewar Japan, "militaristic" Japan of the 1930s and early 1940s, or "occupied" Japan--they cannot make peace with the existing Japan, prompting them to engage in seemingly endless efforts to make their country less a Japan of the past.

Obviously the "past" cannot forever weather the passage of time or the dwindling numbers of Japanese with distinct memories of the war. Already on the horizon are questions about the changing ways people define a new Japan, or its relationship with the outside world, with little reference to this "past." Will Japanese begin to regenerate traditional values and salvage some sort of "Japan" from the past? What might be the form of the Magome of a present-day Shimazaki Toson? What might the "providential intent of Heaven" entail for a new Japan, liberated from the self-imposed burden of the "past?" The Japanese may demand that a new Japan be fully prepared to wield political influence commensurate with its economic might; or the same Japanese, recognizing the diminished value of military power in an interdependent world, may settle for a Japan with the already formidable political leverage that economic prowess has provided.

At the same time, one should not discount the possibility that the Japanese may have already devised ways to preserve the "past" continuously in the present and future. The euphemistic and often indiscriminate use of the prefix *sengo* (postwar)--as in *sengo demokurashii*, or postwar democracy--in nearly every term describing Japan's postwar achievements is a case in point. The use of this prefix reflects an amorphous yet pervasive feeling: the period of the Japanese postwar preoccupation with the "past," starting in 1945 when they began to examine the values and the meaning of the "past" to a present Japan, may not yet have seen its end, even after the death of the Showa Emperor. With the use of the prefix, the Japanese consciously or unconsciously perpetuate the debate over whether a new Japan has finally shed the legacies of the "past." The question--Is the sengo over?--itself is the reminder that Japan has not liberated itself from the "past" or its legacies.

Such self-perpetuating debate and questioning have been further reinforced by what may amount to an annual ritual--the exchanges of views on the characteristics of postwar Japan and its development--every summer since 1945. The major Japanese dailies continue to devote much space each August 15 to reflections on Japan since the defeat in the War and what "went wrong" before it. The regular contributors to the August 15 issues of major monthly journals continue to assess a "new Japan" in terms of its similarities and dissimilarities with an "old Japan" and the likelihood, growing or diminishing, of it assuming political characteristics similar to those of the "old Japan."

The apotheosis of retrospection occurred in January 1989 upon the death of the Showa Emperor. Even as it engulfed the nation in a wave of televised documentary histories of the era, some observers suggested that the sengo period had finally ended in this cathartic event. But one wonders: similar endings of the sengo period have been announced before, and the entire drama of the Emperor's terminal illness, death, and interment--not to mention the coronation of his successor yet to come--was little more than variations on a theme of national consciousness the roots of which penetrate every nook and cranny of the past century.

Perhaps what sustains the summer debates, and drove the drama of Imperial succession, is Japan's uneasiness about not having a stable frame of reference by which to gauge its own new identity, or perhaps even fear of a Japan with only "a kind of formless and free-floating national pride."[6] Rather than outliving the nation's past, the Japanese may have devised ways of defining and redefining Japan perpetually in its relationship with various aspects of the "past," to prevent this historical anchor, or benchmark, from slipping away.

NOTES

1. Basil Hall Chamberlain, *Things Japanese* (London, 1902), p. 1.
2. For a stimulating discussion of the intellectual background, see Banno Junji, *Meiji shiso no jitsuzo* (Tokyo, 1977), ch. 3.
3. For an important statement debating this conclusion see John Dower, *War Without Mercy* (New York, 1986).
4. See, for example, Marius B. Jansen, *Japan and China: From War to Peace, 1894-1972* (Chicago, 1975), chs. 4, 5; "Konoe Atsumaro," in Akira Iriye, ed., *The Chinese and the Japanese: Essays in Political and Cultural Interactions* (Princeton, 1980), pp. 107-23.
5. Marius B. Jansen, ed., *Changing Japanese Attitudes Toward Modernization* (Princeton, 1965), p. 88.
6. Kenneth Pyle, "The Future of Japanese Nationality: An Essay in Contemporary History," *Journal of Japanese Studies*, vol. 8, no. 2 (summer 1982), p. 263.

INDEX

Aizawa Seishisai, 2-3, 12-34, 252, 255, 258
Akamatsu Hiroyasu, 122
American revolution, 13, 19-21
Anti-Comintern Pact, 175
anti-Japanese discrimination in U.S., 158-62, 257, 259
Ara Masahito, 260-61
Axis Alliance, 179-81, 191

Before the Dawn, 5, 79-108
Boyington, Gregory, 216-17, 219-21, 223, 227-32, 236, 246
Broken Commandment, 89-91

Chang Chih-tung, 62-63, 73, 76
Chiang Kai-shek, 141, 198-201, 207
China, Japanese cultural influence and, 61-76; Japanese images of, 7-8, 164-67, 169-78, 197-207; *see also* cultural models
Christianity, 15-16, 17-18, 24, 31, 84-86, 158, 193, 231
cultural models, Chinese, 3, 11-34; Japanese, 4, 61-76; Western, 3, 39-57, 188

Debuchi Katsuji, 190-91
discrimination, *see* anti-Japanese discrimination in U.S.
Dutch, 11-13

education in China, 63-65, 66-70
emperor, 22, 29, 65, 152-54, 263
England, *see* Great Britain

Family, 91-92
Fillmore, Millard, 22-24, 26
France, as organizational model, 42, 46-48, 52
Fujieda Takao, 200-201
Fukunaga Kyosuke, 127

Germany, 146-48; as organizational model, 40, 42, 47-48, 107-108; relations with Japan, 175
Goette, John, 218, 221
Great Britain, 17, 19-21; as organizational model, 41-57
Greater Asia Association, 138-40, 149
Greater East Asia Co-Prosperity Sphere, 6, 133, 137-38, 147, 150-54, 198

Haga Noboru, 98
Harris, Townsend, 26-28, 30-32, 34, 161
Hasegawa Satoru, 190
Hauptmann, Gerhardt, 106
Hayashi Fusao, 202
Heaven's Will, 25-26
Hirata Shinsaku, 122-23, 127
Hirota Koki, 174-76
Holland, 11-13
Hotta Masayoshi, 27, 31

Ii Naosuke, 27-28, 30
Iimori Takeo, 192
Ikezaki Chuko, 123-26, 128
Immigration Exclusion Act (U.S.), 161-62
Institute of Pacific Relations, *see* Japan Institute of Pacific Relations
Ishimaru Tota, 120-22, 127-29

Ishiwara Kanji, 123-24, 129, 138, 145

Jansen, Marius B., 63, 197, 260
Japan Institute of Pacific Relations, 151, 164, 167

Kada Tetsuji, 149-50
Kagawa Toyohiko, 191-92
Kaheki Mitsuaki, 196-97
Kanesaki Ken, 201, 203
Kato Kanji, 126
Kawashima Seijiro, 122
Kimura Takeo, 145
Kiyosawa Kiyoshi, 7, 117, 157-83, 254, 259
Komaki Saneshige, 147-48, 153
Konoye Fumimaro, 6, 133, 138, 140-41, 143-46, 148-49, 162, 176-78, 198, 257
Kosaka Masaaki, 202, 257
Koyama Iwao, 194, 198
Kuo Mo-jo, 203
Kuroe Yasuhiko, 232-39, 242, 246

language reforms in China, 70-76
Lawrenceville School, 145
League of Nations, 160-61, 170-72, 175
Leed, Eric J., 215-16, 245-46

Maejima Hisoka, 41, 43, 45-47, 50-52
Manchuria, 164-67
Manchurian incident, 169-72
Mann, Thomas, 107-108
Matsumoto Takizo, 195-96
Matsuoka Yosuke, 149-51, 170-71, 181
Miki Kiyoshi, 198, 204-205
Mitchell, John W., 224-25
Mito, 26-30, 32
Mizuno Hironori, 118-19
Mogi Kyuhei, 203-204
Mori Arinori, 65
Motoda Eifu, 65

Naito Konan, 136-37
Nakayama Masaru, 138, 140-43, 145-46, 148-49
Namba Monkichi, 194
National Learning, 102-103
nationalism, 2, 6, 9, 251-63
Netherlands, 11-13
New Order in East Asia, 6-7, 133-54, 176-78, 254, 259
New Theses, 14, 17, 33-34
Nitobe Inazo, 7, 161, 164, 255

Oda Man, 136-37
Opium War, 17-18, 22
organizational models, Western, 39-57; *see also* France, Germany, Great Britain
Oto Ryusen, 118

Pacific War, *see* World War II
Pan-Asianism, 6, 134-40, 149, 172-75, 254, 258-59
Paxton, George, 222
Perry, Matthew C., 22-23, 26, 30-31, 34
Phaeton, 13, 17

postal service, 40-57
Princeton, 145
Princeton Theological Seminary, 191
publishing in China, 66

Royama Masamichi, 6-7, 137-38, 140, 145-49, 151-54
Ryu Shintaro, 140

Saito Takao, 133, 143-45, 152
Sakaguchi Ango, 260-61
Sakai Saburo, 220-21, 223, 225-27, 232-36, 239-46
Sato Kojiro, 118-19
Sato Naotake, 204-206
schools, *see* education
Scott, Robert L., 217-19, 221-25, 227-28, 232, 236
Shanghai incident, 169-70
Shimazaki Toson, 4-5, 79-108, 252, 256, 262
Shimizu Ikutaro, 195
Shimonaka Yasaburo, 138, 140
Shirokita Yasushi, 118
Sholokoff, Mikhail, 107
Showa Study Group, 138, 140, 148-50
Sun Yat-sen, 139-40

Taiping rebellion, 18
Takagi Rikuro, 206
Takagi Yasaka, 196
Takaishi Shingoro, 189-90
Tamura Kosaku, 190
T'ao K'ang-te, 202
telegraph, 40-57
telephone, 40-57
Tokiwa Daijo, 206
Tokugawa Nariaki, 22, 26-27, 29, 31-32
Tokugawa Yoshinobu, 27, 29, 32
Tokutomi Soho, 189
Totten, George O., III, 39-42

Uchida Ryohei, 136, 257
Ugaki Kazushige, 153, 155
U.S., Japanese images of, 7-9, 157-83, 187-97, 207-208, 213-47; relations with Japan, 22-24, 26-28, 30-31; war with Japan, 115-29

Wang Chao, 75
war forecasts, 5, 115-29, 178-81
Wei Yuan, 12, 19, 34
World War II, 8-9, 154, 198; fighter pilots, 213-47; *see also* war forecasts
Wu Wen-chi, 204

Yano Jin'ichi, 137, 146
Yonai Mitsumasa, 143-44
Yonayama Tsuneo, 202-203